PTSD Heroes Odyssey

PTSD Heroes Odyssey

~ LOVE IS THE DOOR WAY INTO OUR MIND, BODY,
HEART, AND SOUL; AND INTO HEAVEN ~

James John Prattas

Copyright © 2015 James John Prattas
All rights reserved.

ISBN: 1508854653
ISBN 13: 9781508854654

CHAPTER 1
Love Is The Door Way In

Spiritual Love Is The Door Way Into Our Mind, Body, Heart, Soul and Into Heaven.

I learned this The Hard Way.

This good book is written first for my own healing. From my own personal Spiritual Odyssey as a Combat Soldier. With my own real hard life PTSD experience's to share with you today.

We are all living within a PTSD Global iCloud Today.

This is my true story about a small part of my personal life experiences that I Am sharing with you My Friend.

Ever since I read Homer, Plato and Socrates in an old early 1900 Harvard Classics I decided that they are right. I enjoyed how I had to figure out how to understand what they were saying to me. There is a spiritual code within this Odyssey. I hope these words do not appear to be dry but very juicy! It is a spiritual language. Thank You.

It Will Come as a Big Orgasm. It is Top Secret. The Holy Grail.

It may appear to be Invisible, Impossible, Wild and Crazy yet as you take each step forward you will see The Light Within each step you take into Enlightenment.

I pray my PTSD Heroes Odyssey does the same for you. Words have power. My Odyssey is All one liners of Light.

I know It Will Work for you too. Freedom!

It is a Looking Glass Mirror into Our Spiritual Soul Life.

First, I wanted to experience many things good and not so good in my life to prepare my self to accomplish this task.

Many of my personal experiences in life have been very much like going to Hades, Heaven and then returning again to Earth.

I want you to know that I am speaking from my mind, heart, body, soul and from my own personal life experiences.

I have waited, prayed, meditated. I have asked God for Divine Guidance, Inspiration and Divine Knowledge in writing this good book of Gods for us all.

It is my prayer that this good book gives you faith in God Father and God Mother. Inspiration in yourself a Child of God to CO-Create a Good life for you and others while you are here on Earth.

I only ask that you look into what I am speaking about with an Open Mind in Peace and in Harmony.

I would also ask you to please think about this story in a Peaceful Setting after you have read this good story. Remember to breath in and out The LIGHT and Truth.

I would like you to personally experience the goodness that comes to you in your own way which is the Truth for you.

I only ask you that you please read this material slowly in Methinketh.

Because, Methinketh is a very Timeless Scientific Art of Thinking.

Which is also Thinking Spiritual Love in an Enormous Hollow in the Earth in my Spiritual Metaphysical Philosopher drawings of my heart, mind, body and soul, that I have scratched upon this cave wall with my own souls blood.

It is my Prayer and Wishes that I have written this good work book so that anybody in the world who can read a little bit of American English will be able to understand this discourse about my life's majestical soul journey and possibly your souls life journey.

American English is not my first language.

There may be errors on my part, please forgive me. The story speaks for itself.

I grew up speaking Greek. Yasou Malaka! Very Funny!

Some things in this Odyssey are funny and others are very painful and ugly.

I would like us to Imagine, to Visualize and Realize that we are for a moment in time Resting on a very comfortable round Turquoise Velvet Spiritual Love Seat Floating in the Universal Ocean of Unconditional Love. Just like being a child floating on the ocean on an inner tube at Kealakekua Bay, Hawaii.

This magical story is a Drop of Luminous Crystal Clear Light Dew.

Resting upon a Magical Leaf of Gracious Green Grass. In an Illuminating Beautiful Meadow full of Majestical Spiritual Monarch Butterflies fluttering Angelic messages to us all.

As We Cross Over This Spiritual Golden Gate Bridge within our beautiful mind we begin our Odyssey.

This Poetic Love story will take a little time to unfold for you, as it has for me. As a Beautiful Lotus blossom unfolds.

Please be patient. We will be rewarded with its Beauty.

The Good Words in this good book, Will Reinforce and CO-Create within us, a good Healthy Self Esteem.

Simply and Effortlessly manifesting in our good life as we read and say the Words.

They are Majestically good and Magically CO-Creating Goodness in our life.

Our good story Love Is The Door Way In is now unfolding as a Beautiful Lotus Blossom in The Ocean of Unconditional Spiritual Love within us all.

I realize, I am me and I know nothing and I am nothing.

I am me, I am.

Homer, no-name is my Name, and no-name they call me, my father and my mother and my good friends.

I am sharing with you my good and my lovely Epic Soul Journey. We know you will enjoy the good tales as if you are Walking and Talking with Homer and Socrates and Jesus Christ and Buddha and Allah and Krishna and Lono and Pele and God and all of Gods God's and Goddesses.

My Life and your Life is a Majestical Spiritual Soul Journey, Whether we know this or not, or whether we like this, or not.

I have experienced much pain and suffering in my life to reach this place of self realization, understanding and spiritual enlightenment that, I am on a Majestical Spiritual Soul Journey.

Since I am on this Spiritual Soul Journey called LIFE, I am in agreement with myself, you and God, that I should share my good and this Soul Love Story with us all. To enjoy the Soul Journey.

We go on with the good flow as God wills this good.

For me I have Self Realized that my life is a Majestical Spiritual Soul Journey here on Earth as well as in Heaven.

I realize that I am a spiritual soul from Heaven. Born here onto Earth, and so are you.

We may not be aware of this knowledge or of our spiritual soul journey at this time in our life yet in time we will have a Recollection by the Grace of God.

Through our own pain and suffering in life we will come to our own spiritual soul enlightenment one way or another which is Good.

The Truth.

Our spiritual enlightenment becomes an anonymous anodyne in our life.

I did not understand this discourse and material when I was younger. Because, I was busy living my life. Not paying attention to God within me.

I am learning, as I am going forward, living my good life. I am still learning, and so are you, in thankfulness to God.

This beautiful love story is about my souls self realization and possibly yours.

I needed to experience and to feel my pain, my suffering in my life, before, I was ready to learn to Remember and to Recollect my life, from my beginning before my birth, to today.

This is the same spiritual process for you.

We, may think, it is impossible to Remember our life, before our birth.

We can recollect it within our mind, and it will come to us gracefully.

We will be in Awe and Surprised as to what Images and Spiritual Messages will come to us into our consciousness, within our mind, body, heart and soul, when we sit quietly in Meditation and Prayer with God and me, Methinking.

We will probably have to Give at least a minimum of 5 minutes a day in Meditation and Prayer for several days. Then suddenly our recollection will come to us love pedal by love pedal just as a Beautiful Rose unfolding into Beauty.

The Recollection of our good life, may also come to us, effortlessly, as we read this good book, and God wills it to us.

We may want to Re + Member what it was like in Heaven. When we all stood together looking at life here on Earth.

We all Looked, and Talked about the wonderful things we are going to experience and to do here on Earth for ourselves, and for others and for God.

For most of us, We have Forgotten our Beginning.

Our Sacred Agreement with Our Selves and with Other Souls. With God Father & God Mother, and Gods God's and Goddesses.

Life can have an Imperceptible Way of keeping us all Preoccupied and Unaware of our Own Self and Our True Soul Purpose if we allow It to do so.

We all have Sacred Spiritual Agreements.

Spiritually Willing and in favor of our Acceptance of our Karma.

The Task's to be performed and completed by us on Earth in our life in Spiritual Agreement with God, Before we Came Here onto Earth.

We Can and Will Remember what our Sacred Contract is with God if we chose to at this very moment, for our own goodness.

Please Rest Quietly and Remember to Breath The Light in and out peacefully.

Say a good Prayer to God father and God mother and Ask them in Sincerity and we Will Receive a Recollection about our own Life.

Be Cause.

God our Parents have the family Spiritual Photo Album from our Conception in Heaven to today. The Akashic Record.

We All Agreed to Live, to Learn, and to Fulfill our Karma. Our True Spiritual Purpose in Our Life.

Our Destiny while we are on our Spiritual Soul Journey to the Best of Our Abilities.

I am saying, this is a Spiritual Process. Living a Spiritual Life on Earth. This is what I am saying is The Good LIFE.

Today, we accept our Life, our Lot, in the Present. We are in the Being Here Now. Which Spiritually and Physically will move us along in our Life day by day. We fulfill our Karma, and our Sacred Agreements with ourselves, with others, and with God.

By doing so, we Will to Improve our life, our Lot, as we Choose the Right Good Opportunities.

They will Come to us from Heaven with our Good Thoughts and our Right Actions and Deeds.

They will come with the Good in our life, and with our True Good Soul Purpose, Intentions and our Good Destiny Will Unfold.

We must be willing to work Strongly in Spirit for our Own Good. In Spiritual Service to ourselves and to God.

Yes, We will be tested by our Own Good and Not good Thoughts. By our Own Good Actions and by our Own Good Faith. By our Own Good Belief's in our Own Souls Self in God Consciousness by our Real Life Experiences each day.

To God, It does not really matter if it appeared to us that we Succeeded or if we Failed in our life.

What is most Important to God and to our soul and to ourselves is our True Intentions, as we live our good life Purposely.

What I am meaning by our Intentions is What We did Consciously Think About and Do. What we tried to do in our life.

Did we Give our Life our Best Good Conscious Thoughts?

Our Best Right Choices of Goodness? Our Best Right Good Actions and Deeds?

Did we give our life, our Not so Good Thoughts and our Not so Good Choices and our Not so Good Actions and Deeds while we are living our life on Earth?

The Reasons WHY things happen to us.

What I am saying is, It really does not matter to God if we so called Succeeded or Failed in our mission here on Earth.

Did we do our Best no matter what good happened for us or others?

What really does matter to ourselves and God is living and doing our True Soul Purpose.

Our Sacred Agreement with God.

Example.

Because of ones karma, good or not so good, or what appears to be good or not so good, we may have to lay in the dirty streets of Calcutta, India, or New York City or our city streets, begging or dying in the street.

Homeless.

We the passers by looking at us laying here on the street as if we are looking at an evil curse thinking this poor soul has failed in their life and has done something not so good to be in this condition, yet we are full filing our karma with God on our street.

This humbly does not mean that we the passer by, as a Mother Teresa, will not have a Choice to Share our Good Deed or Spiritual Compassion and Give something of goodness as $1-$5 dollars for a cup of coffee and a little food. Even to help this poor soul in some humane Spiritual Compassionate Way.

We may want somebody to do for us a Compassionate Act and Forgive us, as if it is our soul laying in the streets of Calcutta or New York City or on our city streets. On your spiritual way back home, full filling our karma.

Even if it is a very Difficult and Painful Way to lay in the streets amongst so many wealthy intelligent people passing us by daily as they watch us dying in the name of God, Country and Karma.

I am also speaking about our personal Compassion for our self.

Some of our life's experiences and lessons on Earth are not very pleasant at all. Very difficult and very painful to endure, as they may be for you too.

These karmic learning experiences are what they are. They are no-thing more or less, than what they are. We are Learning by doing them and living them with God.

Usually Our Memory is Veiled before our birth of what our life will be like here on Earth.

Most of us do not Recollect our True Spiritual Soul Purpose in Life for one very Simple and Compassionate Good Reason.

The Reason is, I and you have to Pay our $200 dollar fine and Karmic Dues first to get out of this Cosmic Jail.

We are playing a cosmic Monopoly game called Our Life with God, Others and Nature.

We all owe dues from the past. We all are sinners of Ignorance of Innocence from our past life.

This is the real Soul Reason Why We are all here in Earth today on this Magical Mystery Soul Journey.

Some of our Karma is very Pleasant and Peaceful and Enjoyable and very Good. Our karma is not all ways terrible or horrible in any way. It just is what it is and this is Good.

We Honestly and Naturally all want our Good. We all want to fulfill our obligations, our good Karma, with God and others.

I am also calling Life, Living our Good Karma.

If at birth, I and you were to Remember Everything we are going to experience in our life, we would most likely go into Shock. We would be Terrified.

We would go Crazy if not go Insane from all this Spiritual Wisdom & Knowledge.

The Good Reason Being Is that life Thankfully unfolds pedal by pedal.

It would be very Horrifying for anyone to know all at once all the pain and suffering and all the fear and doubt and hell they are going to go through in their life, to Arrive here with me and God in the Be Here Now.

Most people would Not do any thing. Because We would be Mentally Psychologically in Shock. Physically Mortified.

Frozen in our Fear and Disbelief at such an Unbelievably difficult and painful personal task.

99.99% of WE the human race on the planet Earth would become as those in an Insane Asylum.

We would be Gobbling down many legal or illegal Drugs, and Booze to change our Reality of the Truth of what we see for ourselves. Most of us are afraid of the Reality of the Truth.

Because it would be overwhelming us. We would not be able to do anything difficult, painful or challenging as life requires from us all at certain times in our life. Especially without Gods help.

For most of us, our life is just going on and on as The Ever Ready Bunny. Being the same old thing. Doing the same old thing. Doing whatever one is doing, not being aware of, or Conscious of Real True Life.

Then all of a sudden our life changes for what appears to be not so good. It becomes really challenging to say the least.

Some evil god threw a Cosmic Monkey Wrench into our bicycle wheel of life. Everything suddenly stopped.

Suddenly, We went flying off our bicycle seat, into a Very Different direction than the one we had planned on.

As down on the ground, face first. We got all cut up, and we are bleeding on the painful concrete street of our Life called our Karma.

Then this part of our Life's Reality is paying the Big Ugly Horrifying Cosmic Bill Collector Who Mysteriously knocks on our door Unexpectedly in the middle of the night. He asking us for his Cosmic Karmic money Now.

The past due Karma bills that we failed to pay when we where so young and innocent and ignorant about Life.

We thought Life is FREE!

Many good souls do ask God in prayer for healing and forgiveness and well being by saying this very simple prayer.

Our Father and Mother whom Art in Heaven, Hallowed be thy name. Thy Kingdom Come.

Thy will be done on Earth as it is in Heaven.

Give us this day our daily bread.

Forgive us of Our debts. Lead us out of Temptation. Deliver us from our own evil and our own ignorance.

For Thine is the Kingdom, and the Power, and the Glory, for ever more. Amen.

This Forgiveness may also require from us and includes, us coming back here onto Earth. To those that need us for their good whom we may have injured in the past.

Or they owe us. We owe Karma dues to them for something good they did for us in the past. We must make good where we made not so good. We needed their support in the past and they chose to do a good deed for us.

Round and Round we go on the merry go round of our life with God.

We are thankful to have the Opportunity to do good. It is up to Us and God. Gods Chosen Administrators in Heaven make all the decisions concerning our Karma.

A part of our life is about the Past.

A part of our life is about the Present.

Anon a part of our life is about the Future.

Because of our Environmental Conditioning here on Earth and because of our Karma, We do not all at once Recollect our True Soul Purpose in our life until our dues are paid and fulfilled up to a certain moment in our life.

Until we have suffered enough pain to ask God for help. We are in a great pain. In a great suffering.

Which leads us to our immature ego wondering how did we get here? Anon to our Spiritual Soul Enlightenment which returns us to God.

Healing.

The gentle unfolding of our Lotus Blossom Soul is a Step by Step Spiritual Enlightenment Process.

A baby learning to walk for the very first time. Then and only then, do little bits of Spiritual Love Enlightenment come into our life as Flash Backs, Recollections, and Flash Forwards of our True Soul Purpose in our life.

Now our Majestical Soul Journey begins.

I am not judging myself nor anyone about the Truth. I can Recollect when I was Conceived in Heaven and into my mothers womb in Sparta, Greece, and when I was born into Indianapolis, Indiana.

Of course I can remember growing up within my family. Going to school. Having to learn with other children that were very different. Living in a neighborhood where the neighbors were different, if not strange.

When I was working at some job and the other employees appeared crazy or insane to me, or I to them.

In my Family Relationships, or in my Schooling, or in my Social Relationships, or in my Community, or in my Church, or in my City Environment and what all this knowledge means to me Spiritually today.

As we look backwards and forward upon our souls life we Methinketh.

There were many times that I realized that my life was as living in Hell.

I did not know then, Why I felt this way, yet I did.

I would Cry Out either Orally or Mentally or Spiritually to God.

God Help me.

God get me out of here.

God this is all insane!

Life on the planet Earth can be a living hell and is for most people in a physical body.

Being born into this type of environmental conditioning on Earth, compounded by an Inadequate Spiritual Education, creates unconscious living suffering humans, as I used to be.

We may find ourselves at some time in our life living in our own Family Nut House. Talking, Crying or Laughing Insanely at ourselves, and at Life. In Disbelief and in Denial of this Truth.

Many people who have become Residents of their own Crazy Country Club or in Mental Institutions or are residents in Long Term Care facilities, joining their Wonderful Crazy Friends, are a Classic Example of those who Totally Freaked Out.

Seeing how they and other people Really are Crazy, Insane or Possessed.

That Life can be a living hell on Earth; and they are afraid to Speak this Truth to anyone. They usually they see their life for being what it is. Living in Hell.

They do not know what to do with their life, or how to ask God for help. They think it is better to Keep Silent, and be Drugged, and Locked Up.

Feeling Safer, and Protected in an Institution with other Strange Peanuts not having to live in the outside world. Because they are Scared to Death of the Truth and God.

At the least they know the real world as most people know it is Crazy. Because most Human Societies on the planet Earth are out of Spiritual Harmony, and so are they.

They know for themselves that everyone else in Insane. Because the Insane do not know they are Crazy living in a world without Spiritual Love. This is why their LIFE is so Crazy and Insane without GOD.

Some people call being Crazy normal.

It may be true for them. Because they know their own State of Mind of Frenzy and Disharmony and Unhappiness and Dissatisfaction within their own life. They Truly are out of HARMONY with Themselves, God and Nature so they are Suffering. Misery Loves Company.

Today most of the Earth's population is Not Well and living out of HARMONY. This is the reason so many people around the world have Societal PTSD.

Combat Veterans PTSD started with societies PTSD that has been going on for thousands of years due to all the wars and injustice through out history. Read the Old Testament.

They abuse themselves, their loved ones, their family, alcohol, drugs, food, government, military, education, religion, sex, health, money, animals, pets, people, children, the environment or whatever, and even have Soul Wars to Numb the Reality of their denial of the Truth.

They are living in a Hellish Environment. Way Out of Harmony with God and Nature.

Why do we have Pain and Suffering and Sickness and Disease and Wars on the planet Earth?

Because, We as a Human Race Are out of Harmony with Ourselves and God. Even today most of our belief system's on our planet Earth are out of Harmony.

Almost everyone I have meet or know including myself on the planet Earth needs Spiritual Love, Compassion, Understanding, Forgiveness, Healing, Goodness, Abundance and Especially God in our lives because all good comes from God.

Some of us are very close to becoming Spiritually Gratefully Dead out of our Fear and Doubt of living a Successful Life in Harmony with God. There is a Higher Power other than ourselves.

We might even Go Crazy if we haven't already. Not knowing why?Because of our denial of the Spiritual Truth.

We are afraid to admit the Truth even to ourselves or to a friend or to a family member or to God as we look around at everybody else wondering, Are they also Going Crazy?

We wonder why us?

We look at all the beautiful people passing us by as we sip our Expresso cup of organic coffee or Chai tea on a busy city street corner at a Starbucks Café.

We wonder, are they also going crazy?

Most of us good people fear and doubt that we can have and Actually Live the Beautiful Good life we really Want and Deserve for our own Good.

Fear and Doubt are our Greatest Illusionary enemies in our life.

We have to have Faith in Ourselves and in God.

We have to Believe in Ourselves and in God.

What we think, we become.

I Think, Therefore, I am.

We can do Good for ourselves. The Good we Believe in within our minds-body. With our good Faith and our good Belief System. With our good Positive Actions as we Let Go of our Procrastination.

Not me nor God nor anybody is going to Give us our Goodness in life. Unless we Do what we are Supposed to Do.

This is called Spiritually Work for ourselves and for God in Spiritual Service to ourselves and for God.

I am also saying that, Work is also Service to ourselves and to God and to others. All this Work and Service is Good. We will be Surprised what Good Miracles will come to us all from Work and Service.

I would like to humbly suggest to you to please open a Webster's New Collegiate Dictionary and find the words Work & Service and read the definition of the words Work & Service.

I believe you will find Work & Service Very Interesting and Very Inspiring if you read them with a Positive Attitude. There is All Ways Hope, and Miracles. There is All Ways Salvation in our life Today.

This is why Homer, Socrates, Plato, Moses, Jesus Christ, Buddha, Krishna, Mohammed, James, Joan of Arc, Athena, Gaia, Abraham and many other good men and women have come to Earth throughout history in all continents doing Gods Good Work. We Send our Suns and Daughters to Earth.

They may be spiritual aliens.

What is an alien?

Beings from another world?

Where is Heaven?

Our Work and Our Service to and for ourselves and for God, Inspired with True Soul Intention and our Faith and Belief in Gods Goodness and Oneness Will CO-Create All of our Goodness that we need in our good life.

We will be CO-Creating our Good Positive Thoughts and Good Positive Actions and Good Deeds which is the CO-Creative Process for Spiritually Creating our Goodness for the Good Today on Earth.

If we are one of those people who believe there are Negative Influences Sabotaging and Undermining your Success in this world, then we can help you Realize that You Can and Will Overcome them by reading this good book.

FREEDOM IS WITHIN THIS STORY.

Many believe there is a Satan that is tempting, thwarting and even possibly possessing them and others and even possibly the USA government.

Stopping them of their Success in life yet this is not true.

It is our THOUGHTS.

Satan Has No Power over you.

We are the Children of God.

We live in The Light.

Nothing and nobody has power over God and HIS Children.

Fear and Doubt is an Illusion.

NOT good governments use Fear and Doubt to Control their Citizens.

It is true that Fear and Doubt have Stopped many good souls from Becoming a Winner. Fear NOT Being a Success.

Fear and Doubt has created a tremendous amount of pain and suffering in this world and in most of our lives.

We Can Overcome Fear and Doubt by our GOOD Knowledgable Positive Spiritual THINKING. Truly, peoples negative influences and the devil have no power over us.

This is stated many times in The Holly Bible and in many other Holly texts from all around this good world Remember God created the devil to tempt us all.

The devil works for God so We can find out what we are made out of.

What are our Weaknesses?

What do we tempt ourselves with in our own good life?

Nobody makes us do things that are not good. We do them to our self to find out the Truth.

The negative influences and the devil is an illusion disguised as fear and doubt. Which is an illusion to Scare The Hell Out Of Us and Teach us a good lesson about our fears and doubts and our faith and belief in God. God created All and God is in All.

God has Power over the Devil. We have power over the devil.

Just as God has Power over us all.

An example is the devils temptation of Jesus Christ, The Saints, Buddha, Mohammed, Krishna, Socrates, Lao Tzu, Homer, Plato, and Gods God's and Goddesses and their loved ones.

Anon the illusionary devils temptations as an evil emperor from Star Wars will Tempt all of God's Good Daughter's and all of Gods Good Son's' Soul's throughout this Earth. Throughout all Countries, and throughout all Governments, and continues throughout all of history for Gods good, and our own good too.

You and I are not the first nor the last ones to be Tempted and Tested by God. Everybody gets tested!

Fear and Doubt want to challenge us to See if WE Truly believe in God, ourselves, and our True Soul Purpose in Life and what we are doing in our life for your own good.

This is why Fear and Doubt is called a Devils Temptation.

I also want us all to realize that our Soul life on Earth is where we have had to come to, to learn all about Life and God at this time in our life.

Maybe we think we should have gone to some other planet or dimension in life and we really don't belong living in the Be Here Now with me and God on Earth.

We may think we would be better off some place else as maybe on Krypton with Superman, or Pleiades but this is not true, or we would be there.

The things I am going to talk about with us today I had to learn the Hard Way.

Some things have come Effortlessly to us like a child playing with sand in a sandbox. I Am sure life is the same for you.

I am only talking about the Spiritual TRUTH.

I am looking at our souls life on Earth.

This is a Discourse on my soul life journey as I am experiencing my life. It is the same for you.

This Good Spiritual Book is a Good Self Soul Realization Experience for us. This is Gods Good Spiritual Work Book in Spiritual Methinketh.

I did not learn nor know life's lessons by Revelation, Wisdom or Knowledge. I had to experience them for myself and you do to.

We realize that our life experiences in our Life, have lead us to a Self Realization about ourselves, about our soul, about others, about Nature, about LIFE and what GOOD GOD is for us.

I realize I know no-thing.

I am no-thing.

I am Spirit.

We are living in The Light This Good Soul Book is an expression of my souls life experiences to this day.

You will find yourself having Gentle Awakenings, Flash Backs, Flash Forwards and Dreams of your own life that may be very helpful to you. In life there are Many Points of View.

Many Invisible Spiritual Dimensions that we are all learning about, thank God. There are over 7 billion souls on our planet Earth today in the year 2015.

We realize that there are also over 7 billions ways to look at life. Very much like looking at life through a Kaleidoscope.

There are many ways to live life as history has taught us about the many civilizations that have come and gone on Earth. Many have failed the Test of time.

Our Soul, Gods Soul is a Majestical Spiritual Soul Road that we travel upon to Reach our Destination. Our Destiny, Our True Soul Purpose in Life. For most of us there is a High Road, a Middle Road and a Lower Road that we can travel upon.

Some roads of life are less traveled than others.

There are also other roads that you are unaware of at this time in your life and that is OK, Ola Kala. They are not important to you now. They will be later on in your Spiritual life.

The other roads will be revealed to you when the time is right.

These Other Roads lead to Gods many Hidden Kingdoms, Spiritual Dimensions and Spiritual Universes within Life. They are in and on the Earth and in Heaven. They will be experience by you when God Wills It. God Is a Great Mystery.

Being Here and Now with me is what is important for us all.

Some of the roads we travel upon in life are more Joyful and Scenic while others are more painful and Rocky.

It has been stated many times for millions upon millions of years that through our own Pain and Suffering we will come to our own Spiritual Souls Enlightenment and to Godhead.

It appears that some roads we have chosen to travel upon are Very Rocky and Deeply Pitted.

While other roads are as Smooth as a Putting Green. As Beautiful as a Meadow full of Wild Flowers with Luminescent Monarch Butterflies Fluttering all around us and we are in Spiritual LOVE.

The Acceptance of our life in the Spiritual Being Here Now and the Choices we make are Our Spiritual Teachers. Our God's and Goddesses of Spiritual Knowledge all along The Soul Way home to God Consciousness and God in Heaven.

We are the Him & Her God. The Holy Blessed Child. The Christ. The Captain of our own vessel in our own life, and in Gods LIFE.

One thing about life that we can count on is that we are all born, and we all will die at some place on or in Earth at some time on this Magical Spiritual Soul Journey. Most of us will not know when the time will come and that is OK, Ola Kala.

I Will It that our Life will now be to you More Gentle, Graceful, Merciful, Forgiving, Healing, Compassionate, Abundant and Kind to you as you read this Good Spiritual Love Work Book in CO-Creating your Good.

We are The Conscious Spiritual Lord's and Lady's of The Spiritual Light Force.

In between Birth and Death is called LIFE.

LIFE is not only black and white, nor right and wrong, nor good and bad, but a Rainbow of Infinite Majestical Colors, Expressions and Experiences of our Life.

Life is a Good Spiritual Mystery that will Unfold as we Live It, Read It, Walk It, Talk It, Eat It, Breath It in and out, Love in It and Die in It.

Life will explain itself to us in our due time.

Remember to Breath In Spiritual Love Light and Breath Spiritual Love Light Out Regularly in Harmony.

This life of ours is always Changing in LIFE as LIFE is ALWAYS Changing Constantly. We can count on this as a UNIVERSAL TRUTH. Nothing in life stands still. God Is Still. God Is Silent. God Is Eternal.

AUM is a Spiritual Vibration.

We are always changing cell by cell, moment by moment until death and beyond. Some of us Want life to Stand Still for us.

To be Safe, so We can Grasp It and Hold on to it.

To Savor it, and Manipulate it, and Control it. Instead of Living Life and Flowing Within Life.

As Being on a Magical Carpet Ride going where ever God wants us to go, on Gods Majestical Spiritual Soul Journey. It is a Magical Spiritual Merry-go-round.

Life is as our first breath that we were Given. It is very exciting!

We breath Spiritual LIFE into our body and into our life until our last breath in life as God wills It in all LIFE. God is our Invisible Spiritual Breath of Life.

God is our life in LIFE.

We cannot hold on to our life.

We can only Live our life Moment by Moment. Gods Spiritual Breath of Life is Within our life. God is our Life Force and Energy.

Breathing teaches us to let go of the past.

Move along in our Life in Spiritual Love with our next new spiritual love breath until the end of our life. Our Breath and Our Breathing, and Our Thoughts breathings are to be in Rhythm & Harmony. As the Ocean Waves of Unconditional Love Flowing from The Universal Sun of Love to us all on Earth in HARMONY.

Very much as the Sun is Shinning upon the Earth The Spiritual Light of Love, Health and COCreation, Wisdom and Knowledge.

Our True life experiences come to us Unexpectedly while we are busy doing something else.

We Can live our life to its Fullest every day. Or do nothing creative.

Anyone can become a couch potato if they chose to.

How do we become fat?

Most of us miss so many Good Opportunities in our life. We Think we will have time later on. Or that we do not Deserve the GOOD in our life because of our Poor Self Esteem.

GOOD Opportunities are available to us today in our life. They Rarely Return as the same opportunities later on if ever.

Who amongst us Can Relive our life that has just past us by today?

What good opportunities did we miss and we did not take in our life?'Probably many.

The Opportunities that I am speaking about are also Spiritual Opportunities of Our minds body, Heart and Soul.

These Opportunities have to do with our Love, Compassion, Forgiveness, Healing and Abundance for our soul self's Well Being and for Others and with God.

It is true that there are Opportunities in life that will come along for our Professional lives that have to do with a Healthy Abundance, Personal Empowerment, Self Satisfaction, Personal Accomplishments and all of Those Things that We think are Really Important.

The Other Spiritual Opportunities that I am speaking about Will also come our Way. They Will give us everything good in our life that has TRUE Value.

This is to Give ourselves, God and others Unconditional Spiritual Love, with our Own Personal Understanding, Compassion and Actions.

By Giving Love, we will receive Love and many other Wonderful Opportunities to Prosper with. We will be Majestically in Awe.

We must first Give LIFE what we Want in our life.

We cannot take our money, or our possessions, or our awards, or our decorations with us when we Pass On to the Other Side.

They are Worthless on the other side of the fence. Because they are Physical. The other side of the fence is Spiritual.

The Great Pyramids and the Egyptian Pharaohs are one of many good examples through out history that we cannot take the Golden Lyre with us. We might as well Play It Now while we still can Strum a string or two and laugh about it too.

The Pharaohs tried to take their Gold and Treasures and even their children's Toys with them that were hidden in the Great Pyramids to the Other Side of LIFE.

They hid their gold instead of doing GOOD with their gold money. The Pyramids were later covered up by GOD in the Great Sand Box of LIFE. They believed in their high priests.

They all failed. They are roaming the desert at night as ghosts trying to find their way back home. They cannot for what they did do to so many innocent people.

Karma. Their gold and treasures were left behind for others to rob their tombs for many years.

We can see what is left of their gold treasures in the museums and in private collections if we do not believe God.

When you pass on in LIFE to the Other Side and See The Face God, you can only take with you your good deeds if any. Your knowledge of your experiences from your life in your Souls Spirit.

If we worked Strongly in Spirit in our life, we will have our Spiritual Love, and our Good Deeds to take with us. This is Spiritual in Nature. This will have a Great Deal of Value for us on our Spiritual Soul Journey back to Heaven.

If we worked Weakly in our Spiritual life, we will have our weak love and weak deeds to take with us that is also spiritual in nature. This will not have a great deal of value to us on our spiritual journey. Not to Heaven. Back onto Earth or Hades. To try again of course. In a more polluted environment as time evolves.

WE can only imagine what dark evil psychic & mental & physical Chaos and the Pollution that will exist in Los Angeles, New York, Atlanta, Washington DC, Denver, Seattle, Chicago, Indianapolis, Trenton, Bronx, Houston, Katmandu, Dallas, Kansas City, Tokyo, London, Buenos Aires, Rome, Baghdad, St Moritz, Salzburg, Toronto, Shiraz, Frankfurt, Moscow, Mogadishu, Stockholm, Damascus, Tabriz, Amsterdam, Paris, Athens, Cairo, Mexico City, Jerusalem, Palestine, Istanbul, Madrid, Hong Kong, Singapore, Taipei, Osaka, Sidney, Riyadh, Bangkok, Bombay, Karachi, New Delhi, Hanoi, Sofia, Beijing, Honolulu and in any other city if this world still exists in two hundred years because we are heading for a collision course with DESTINY.

Again. I am Seeing Who Cares.

We can very easily See through Demographic Graphs and in these cities historical Growth Cycles What these cities will all look like in a 100 more years.

Especially more important for us to look at is the way these cities are all evolving out of Harmony with God. Because we will know what kind of Life or Hell or Hades anybody will be living in. Life will not be very easy.

Life will be much more challenging without freedom.

Anon we can imagine having to come back to live in one of those great polluted cities out of Harmony with God trying to live our life again. We will be saying, Oh My God.

I Pray to God for our Children's Children and that this world population now wakes up consciously today, to help make this a better world to live in.

There is a Whole lot of GOOD in this good world. If we will only look for the GOOD. We need Spiritual Work for the GOOD in our life, and in LIFE.

Not only our own well being, but for our children's, children's, children's well being and our future! DESTINY.

Of course the Weakly will not arrive in Heaven, but at some other appropriate destination for their own good as Gods Wills.

Some of us will decide to wait until We Retire, or have Enough Money, or what ever reason we give ourselves for not Living our True Soul Purpose. True Soul Purpose is what we Really want to do in our minds-body, heart and soul each and every day.

If we look back upon our missed good opportunities in life, we will most likely realize, that the good opportunities we missed really were not about a lack of money as we may think.

They are about our lack of a Good Self Esteem. Our missed good opportunities in life is about our fear and doubt of a Successful Life in our mind, heart, body and soul then in our life.

After allowing several wonderful good opportunities to pass us by we become Spiritually Lackadaisical.

Devoid of a living a good life we Entrench Ourselves in our own Self Made Dugout, Watching life Pass Us By.

While at the same time Praising all those other Souls on TV or in the movies who become Stars in their life.

They Did Follow their Hearts Desire.

If we could live our life again, what would we do differently?

How would we feel about it today if we live our dream life?Old age and Sickness can Stop us Dead from Realizing our Dreams in our life.

Most likely we will never know the Moment nor the time when we will pass on in our life. It could be now and it could be later today. It could be tonight. It could be in our sleep and Not Be Later as we may have thought to ourselves.

Be Cause we do not know what God has in store for us!

When GOOD opportunities do come again to us, they will never be the same opportunities that were available before to us. It will be a New GOOD opportunity.

Who knows, it could be a Better GOOD opportunity. It is True that Patience is a Virtue, yet not always true.

When a New Spiritual Opportunity comes to us, will we accept the opportunity?

Will we accept our Gift from God?Life is a Miracle.

A New Opportunity is an Unexpected Gift from Heaven and God because God is LOVE. God does know everyone and everything.

This Love, this GOODNESS, this Spiritual Opportunity, is also a Gift from ourselves to ourselves spiritually.

Because we have now chosen to live rightly GOOD. In our Goodness for our own Good.

We will Be Gracious and Lovingly Thankful.

We will have FUN and ENJOY our Good Gift from GOD. OK, Ola Kala is Greek for all is OK.

We Will live our True Soul Purpose Well & Good.

Will we let life pass us by again for another day which may never come? NO!

We never know when our time has arrived to leave the Earth.

Unless Angels from Heaven have announced our Arrival and pending Departure on Earth, most of us come into this world Unannounced and we will most likely leave this way.

I would laugh if anybody told you, you will receive an invitation of your Pending Departure and Reunion with God. Written on Fine Linen Paper and delivered by the postal clerk to your home with an ornate Year of the Ram stamp on the envelope.

Yes, Today it is better to Live and Love in our Life Truthfully than to let life pass us by.

There will be No Regrets for those of us who live Our True Soul Purpose in Our GOOD Life to its Fullest. Living all the love we can. Every day to the best of our ability.

Some of us are waiting to go on our next soul journey into the unknown called Death to this world and Birth into a New Unknown World with Regrets of our life Unfulfilled.

It is our own spiritual weaknesses and faults and nobody is to blame but ourselves.

Have we learned How to Pass On in our life Properly or will we fail at death too?

Ah yes my good friend, There is a Spiritual Stranger Spiritual Alien here on Earth from a Strange Spiritual land called Heaven.

Will we Grok this gift of goodness visit while there is still time?

Our life does not have to be sad, unhappy and unfulfilled.

Most of us will have to return to Earth or some other place and live our life again.

To fulfill our Sacred Agreements with ourselves, others and God. This is OK. Ola Kala. It's just The Way It Is.

Life is very Similar to Sports. We keep on trying until we get it right.

We fail our Way to Success!

The important part is to live our life Consciously and with our True Soul Purpose.

Life can be very depressing and worthless without Work, Service, Fun, Love, Abundance, Patience, Compassion, Healing and Forgiveness of ourselves and for others.

Today, even if we are bedridden and in a hospital we can Ask and Receive New Spiritual Opportunities within our mind-body, heart and soul from God to fulfill our life.

Life is a Spiritual Dream. Our Life is a Spiritual Dream. Oh My God.

OK, Ola Kala.

Anon Most of us Are Dreaming the Wrong Dream that is not even our own dream. It is a dream of our past conditioning.

What is this strange dream my friend that you are suffering in?

In pain in? In sorrow in? Living in out of Harmony with God. Out of Harmony with yourself?

This Wrong Other Person's Dream is an illusion to your true soul purpose dream.

Many of us have received and continue to pass on for generations the wrong dream because we did not know better. Our families did not know better. Ignorance.

Knowledge.

Most of us have never Learned how to Dream our Good Dream Life.

We Really Want to live our dream today and Every day. Most of us have never learned how to Think Right and Methinketh on God and The Light of Truth.

We have to use our Own Good Imagination and CO-Create our Own Good Dream Life with True Intention and Soul Purpose with our own good mind, body, heart and soul.

Once We Can See our own Good Dream Life, We Will It!God Wills it. The Rest of this good CO-Creation Process will become history.

Very much as True Lovers having a Majestical Orgasm Together while they are making good love.

Everything is evolving right before our eyes and most of us are unaware of it. OK, Ola Kala.

A false life without true soul purpose and intention, or without spiritual love can be an illusion and a diversion to us living our goodness in our life and us being happy and content.

It has been said that life on Earth is a Long and Winding Road back into Heaven. If we can live rightly our life, a good soul journey. In Heaven there is no long and winding road, nor timely anything. Heaven Is Timeless.

I believe that once we are spiritually enlightened about our life, we will chose the goodness in our life. The road becomes a Beautiful Straight Path on Earth.

Just as the Setting Sun that Shines upon the Unconditional Ocean of Love is Magically Illuminating a Golden Straight Path Way upon the Ocean, The Way, unto its Self, to the Golden Vessel of Love, The Holy Grail.

Some of us will at some time in our life experience the good, the not so good, the bad and the ugly things of life. How else will we learn life's lessons? This is OK. Ola Kala.

We will not be the first, nor the last, to experience God. Life is composed of no-thing and everything, and All is God.

We should be aware of, and have a spiritual understanding of, what good we are, is made out of Gods Good.

We come onto Earth to live and Grow Spiritually, mentally and physically by our personal experiences so that we can go forward on our Spiritual Soul Life Journey in Peace.

We are all manifesting God. We are a part of God. God is all there is.

Our life is Gods life.

Most of us do not understand this manifestation. Life is also known as Gods Infinite Spiritual Soul in Evolution on the Material Plane.

Life on our planet Earth can be as living in Hades or a little bit of Heaven by our choices that we make in our life. It is up to us. We are the Captain of our Spiritual Space Ship.

By living and doing good we will know for ourselves the TRUTH. The Truth is Self Evident. We will then have Real Life Experiences that will give us True personal experiential Wisdom and Knowledge about the Life we Live In, Nature and God.

There is Much to Learn. Wisdom and Knowledge are Truthfully Good and are God. Wisdom & Knowledge are a God and a Goddess of God. Wisdom and Knowledge are Eternal Beings.

Wisdom & Knowledge are Spiritual Universal Teachers.

Wisdom and Knowledge come from God yet we have to live our life Spiritually to know them in our mind, heart body and soul.

We have to personally experience Knowledge and Wisdom in LIFE to know Wisdom and Knowledge as Spiritual TEACHERS in our good life.

True Spiritual Wisdom & Knowledge is in The Light. In The Air we breath. True Wisdom and Knowledge is not in books. We men & women write books from our life experiences. These books over time are all rewritten. Some translations are accurate. Others are a mess.

We humans share our learned experiences of Wisdom and Knowledge in Books, Craft, Tools, Art, Music, Song and Dance.

We can learn Technological Information from books and the THINGS we SEE in LIFE.

It is my prayer that some things in life do not need to be experienced by all of us. Some life experiences can be horrifying and very ugly and evil.

God forbid them and keep us safe, guided and protected being a good son or daughter of God that we are.

I know this truth because there are many ugly evil horrifying things I have experienced that I wouldn't want anyone to live through in their life unless it is there calling to find out the SPIRITUAL TRUTH as I did.

Life is Good when we look for the Good.

Without Life, or our life, Gods LIFE, We would Know Nothing.

Without Gods Life nothing would exist. Not some-thing. Nothing!

Without our life we would not Grow Personally, Spiritually, Mentally or Physically. With our life we will learn about Ourselves and Gods Good Creation.

This is good because it is a part of us that we live within everyday. It can take a moment or it will take a lifetime. Possibly many lives to learn all about our soul self, God.

Life is Eternal and Infinite, Thank God for Being Thankful, Gracious and very Creative.

Life on this planet Earth is a Microcosm of the Macrocosm in a Beautiful Miraculous Living Organism in Spiritual Evolution.

One day Take the Time and Look Up into the Sky on a Clear Night.

You will Notice there are many Beautiful Radiant Twinkling Stars in the Universal Sky.

The Beautiful Soul Stars are all Interconnected Together In Our Unknown Universe, Gods Universe.

There is Not One Beautiful Radiating Soul Star Out of Harmony within Gods Eternal Universe.

Everything is Going Around and Around within God in Harmony and in Universal Peace.

As we Look Up into Life into Gods Universe We can Breath into ourselves STAR Inspiration.

We See and Experience Universal Unconditional Spiritual Peace, Love, Light, Harmony, Enlightenment for All of us to Share in our Being Here Now.

Yes, There Really is a Twinkling Star Up Above in the Great Sky in this Milky Way of Life that we can identify within ourselves. Oh My God It Is Us.

I know we can Self Soul Realize that We Are also a Beautiful Twinkling Radiant Soul Star among this Amazing Universal Sky Above us in Harmony.

I would like you to Self Realize that we are all a part of Gods Universe. This Universal Peace, Unconditional Spiritual Love, Spiritual Enlightenment is All around us and within us 24 hours a day forever.

We come and go.

Please, a few good questions to ask our self.

Are we in Peace and do we have Peace of Mind?

Are we at War with ourselves and others?

Where are we in our life today?

How do you Feel Today?

What is our life about?

What is our life's True Soul Purpose?

What is your Intention?

What Can we Bless you with That is Missing in your life that will give you Peace of Mind?

How Would you like to CO-Create Today your Goodness in your own life Peacefully, Lovingly, Graciously and Thankfully?

My Good Soul Star, How do you Radiate your Spiritual Love daily?

How do You share Your Good Loving Life?

First with yourself?

Then with others in your life while you are on this Majestical, Spiritual, Soul Journey here on Earth?

What other Twinkling Stars in this Amazing Wonderful Universe here on Earth can you be in a Harmonious Constellation with for Your and Their Well Being, Support, and Personal Spiritual Growth?

Spiritually, Mentally and Physically.

Is your Relationship with yourself in Harmony with Gods Universal Peace, Spiritual Love and Enlightenment?How is your Personal Relationship with your loved ones, family, friends, work, environment and God?

The Time to Let Go of anything or anyone not in Spiritual Harmony with your wellbeing is NOW.

Love is Letting Go of Fear and Doubt.

What Is Best For YOU?

We Do Know Deep Within our Mind, Body, Heart and Soul what is good. Daily We Take Positive Action Living our true soul purpose, our dream life, our spiritual life.

Today We Can Chose Rightly GOOD to Improve our Life.

We want to share this good story Love Is The Door Way Into our Heart, Mind, Body, Soul and into Heaven is all about us on Earth.

We are Unfolding as a Beautiful Amazing Lotus Blossom into a Bright and Shining Soul Star within Great Spirits Universal Oneness.

We Allow the Spiritual Love Light Flowing In and Out from Within our Beautiful Warm Spiritual Heart as We Breath In and Out The Light of our True Love.

We Will Recollect all of this Spiritual Wisdom & Knowledge at this time in our life.

Our good friends Patience and Virtue and The Mentors will share with us Graciously that We Really are on a Majestical Spiritual Soul Journey with God.

We do not have to be lost in the darkness of the night or in the day!

We do have a Desire to Chose Our Good. What will it be? GOOD.

Are you presently happy or are you sad about your past choices in life?It is never too late to make new good choices.

You can start anew this very moment in your life.

Remember this.

YOU are very important to God!

This Spiritual Knowledge Will Help YOU Self Soul Realize You Are Good. Your Love Is The Door Way In and It Will Set You Free. FREEDOM.

Here is a very simple humble beginning.

Look into your mirror on your wall and say to yourself, I love You.

I love You God.

Today you have chosen that you will live your own Good Dream of our own good life.

Our God Mother and Our God Father and Gods God's and Goddesses and Gods Angels Will Assist us.

We Ask and Pray for Gods Assistance.

Many Good Souls have Succeeded in Life and they have become Winners in Their Life with Gods Good help.

You are a Winner.

You Can Do It!

CHAPTER 2
The Great Soul War

This story is about King James Odysseus I am.

As a young man I went off to fight in a Great War called the Great Soul War with my fellow men and women.

As we know there are many other soul wars throughout our history on planet Earth.

We may also be kind to think that this Great Soul Journey of ours is also a Beautiful Love Story and a Great Epic Poem, which it is.

We may even think more kindly that this soul journey of ours is a Great Soul Movie that we spiritually Methinketh we have seen before some place in time.

A famous Hollywood movie Producer and Director CO-Created this great epic movie for us. Hollywood's Best Actors and Performers are acting the role's of King James, Odysseus, our Queen Penelope, U Telemachus, Zeus, The Mentors, The Goddess Athena, The Holy Shepherds, The Nurse, The Maidens, the God's and Goddesses, the Evil Emperor Evelyn George Bill Hussein O Antonious and his evil wooers.

Yet to us this Good Story is a Tale of a True Soul Story about our life's Soul Journey on Earth.

I King James was once in a past life a King in Greece and in England.

Today King James became by Destiny a Spiritual Warrior King from Heaven as God Willed in The USA of Ithaca. The King James I am in Great Spirit.

I am writhing and I am crying my heart and soul out to us all.

I am in a great sorrow and pain being a hapless wretched soul.

To me this Poetic Love Story is as finding something of Great Spiritual Value.

A Priceless Misplaced Heirloom which is my heart, my soul, my mind, and my body, that I have just recovered by the moss covered rocks by this great majestical pool in this magical forest by a great awesome spiritual waterfall 5,000 miles high.

I look up into the stars and it is thundering and it is rushing millions and millions of gallons of mystical thoughts of spiritual mist.

It is talking in Gods Language and I Am happy and I AM crying for joy.

There is a time in my life when I had difficulty believing in God and in the Spiritual Truth because of my ignorance of what God is and what the Spiritual Truth is.

Please follow me along on this majestical spiritual odyssey we are now embarking upon until the end.

There you will be Rewarded. We will find our Pot of Gold in the Great Hall of Spiritual Love.

Here we will be blessed, and we will receive our spiritual goodness.

Here in this Beautiful and Luminous Rainbow, we will find our True Soul Purpose in our life.

Our Soul, our Wealth, Health, our Abundance, our Goodness, our Spiritual Love and Peace of Mind in Harmony.

At night, in our good restful sleep, Gods Angels, sight unseen will come to us in a spiritual dream, and in a spiritual vision, with a blessing for us from God Father and God Mother and Gods God's & Goddesses from Heaven.

We will be Guided and Protected by God and Gods Angels all the days of our life.

Once upon a time in a land of Magical Dragons and Beasts so far and away I thought that dying young was the last thing in the world I would want to do.

I wanted to live my life just like everybody else does in the wonderful fairy tale.

I wanted all the goodness in my life just like we all do. I did not realize that the life that I was living in out of Harmony, was really an illusionary life.

As a shadow following me around!

Living in a strange embryo of life that I call living my life.

That my dying is really living into another part of this strange embryo. I call death being born into our spiritual soul life again in the Truth of The Light.

Around and around my good soul life goes.

I Am on a Magical Merry-go-round. Wonderful exciting animals to ride upon going up and down and all around in my life as I hold on to this Illuminating Magical Brass Pole until the end of the ride.

As God wills it to be so with many Musical Chimes Playing Happy Music. I Am laughing and giggling and excited and I Am crying with joy to ride again. I Am laughing, and I Am happy that I Am so fortunate to ride this Spiritual Merry-go-round.

Yes, it is all true. Time will tell me all the good things in life in my own time as this Smiling Happy Royal Blue Transparent Dragon of Tale Unfolds page by page.

I See so many Wonderful Exotic Spiritual Butterflies and the most Beautiful Tropical Birds flying all around me.

Many Magical African, Amazon and Asian Animals Pop right Out of the Pages moving around us in living 9D color as if we were on an African Safari.

They are Racing off Into our Minds Garden as I Am reading this good book wondering how did all this happened?

What is this all about?

On March 5 1970 I died and traveled through The Sun and into Heaven and visited with God, our God Father & God Mother, Jesus, my earth father who had passed away and my relatives and Gods God's and Goddesses the Children of God and our animal and plant friends.

I was a Team Leader walking as Point Man for my own ARP-LRRP team while on patrol in the Great Trojan War.

At this time in my life, dying was the last thing and the best thing that could have ever happened to me.

Homer, It took me twenty years to come back home to Ithaca.

Our United States of America by the Grace of God.

Actually, it has now been 45 years and I have just arrived home to you and Hawaii. Aloha!

The night before on March 4 I received a message from our God.

My Guardian Angel Michael said to me. King James It is your time to give up your life.

Your time King James has come!

You are going to die tomorrow.

How will it to be?

What did you say Michael?I went into soul shock and disbelief.

My knees were loosened and my heart melted within me.

I became very nervous and uncomfortable as you might well imagine if this is happening to you.

It was like seeing an Ugly Black Dragon all of a sudden in my bed with his feet upon my chest breathing Hot Fames in my face.

I could not fall sleep this night. I broke out in a sweat laying on my Python Green Army cot thinking about this awe inspiring message.

I thought to myself, Oh God where Art Thou?

Why do you do this evil deed to me?

A Holy Ghost Spoke. King James greetings!

May your happiness be thine in time to come. As for now, You are fast holden in many Sorrows and Pains and Tribulations coming to you.

Father God, no other God is more baneful than you!

What kind of God are you?

Do you remember your Everlasting Covenant with me?

Tin god!

Your bargain is Tin.

What good is your bargain?

It crumples in my hand! God you have no compassion on men that are of thine own begetting. You make them to have fellowship with evil and with bitter pains and sorrows just to know you.

Where is your faith now god? Yours and mine?

All night long I tossed and I turned and I wrestled with wretched fear from my Angel Michael's message.

I could not believe it was true. I could hear my own inner voice crying out aloud.

My guts were all knotted up and wrenching. I was shaking in fear, saying the same thing to myself. Why now?

Why Destiny knocks upon my door.

The Holy Sheepherder Said: The sweat broke out upon me and all about me when I beheld Him.

Mine eyes stand full of tears for memory of King James. He too, Methinketh, is clad in such vile raiment as this and is wandering among men in the Great PTSD Soul War.

If happily he yet lives and Sees the Sunlight again.

As he thought to himself. If He is dead already and in the house of Hades then woe is for me and all on Earth.

The Noble King James, who set me over his Great Buffalo while I was but a lad in the land of Spiritual Love in America.

At another time now these Mystical beautiful curly hair Spirit Buffalo grow numberless. In no better wise way could bread of Broad-Browed Buffalo of any mortal increase, even as the ears of purple rye and golden corn and red wheat.

My friend, Evil Wooers Command Me to be ever driving these for themselves to devour in their own greed and selfishness in Ithaka USA.

The evil wooers care nothing for their Heir in the house.

Nor do they tremble at the vengeance of God and the Gods & Goddesses that will be their doom.

For the evil wooers are Eager to Divide among themselves the Possessions of our Lord who is long and far away in the land of dragons and beasts at the Great Soul War. Conspiracy!

I was almost asleep on my Green Bamboo Viper Army Cot back at Black Horse base camp at Quan Loi.

We Spiritual Warriors slept, if you can call what we did sleeping. One eye open and a finger on the trigger of our weapon. A stinking hot humid mosquito, cockroach, spider, bug infested army green canvas duffel bag.

Our Muggy Maggot Hutch always Stunk with burning mosquito coil smoke. Camel & Marlboro Cigarettes. Mary Jane Dragon Smoke.

Hot stinking beer and Whiskey. The worst is a Hodgepodge of Foul Wooers Air from Washington, DC.

Our cots were mounted on wooded Lincoln Log Pallets usually stacked 2-3 feet high. The dirty floors were usually muddy Pigs Pens during the monsoon rains.

We also had the privilege to live a with Ricky the Rat. A North Vietnam Tunnel Rat who dinned on everyone's Care package from back home.

Ah So. Ricky was a very cleaver Stinky Evil Wooers Rat. He would even eat our Mary Jane at night for a Night Cap thinking about that cute little Vietnamese Woman Rat he saw the other night as he was running through the tunnel into the Land of Cambodia where all the other communist rats and hedgehogs live.

Late at night as an Evil Wooer NewYorkLondonMoscowBeijing politician, Ricky would even jump from a Soldiers Chest on to an another soldiers back while he made his getaway while we were sleeping.

Ricky The Wooers Rat was like an evil ghost bandit shocking the hell out of us in the middle of the night with FEAR while we were sleeping, as if the Trojan War was not bad enough. He was getting away with our mothers, spouses and girl friends chocolate chip booty in his mouth.

Ricky is as Big and Fat as a mall Ugly Scraggly Wooers dog. Stinks Afoul and Possessed by a devil wooer dragon like a tunnel rat is. Out of frustration a few of the men in the hutch have even tried to Shoot Him with their AR-15 bows and Silver Arrows. Ricky was as fast as an Ugly Vulture. As a Wooers Vampire on the run with Death in his mouth dripping out.

There are thousands of Magical Sand Bags stacked all around Black Horse Base Camp as you might imagine our base camp in the middle of hell while Rockets Rained upon us at night.

All the bucking new Black Horse's have to fill Sand Bags their first two weeks in country. I did too. We all filled magical sand bags. It is a Humid Humble Sweaty Dirty job.

Bagging our fairy Mother Earth for our Command & Control bunkers, perimeter lookouts and sleeping quarters.

I thank God and all those Who Filled the magical sand bags around our sleeping quarters. Miracles do happen with sand bags which very easily have been filled with fairy dust if you did not know this.

The Gods fairy dust protected us, when we dozed off from exhaustion called One Eye sleep.

Dreams from rockets and mortar shrapnel that went flying through the air in the middle of the black night. The fire works of the evil wooers dragon.

Our ARP-LRRP Team hutch is very close to the air strip where the Black Winged Cobra and Black Winged Huey Hawk ships of the gods are parked. We were always on a 5 minute Standby alert for Emergencies.

Rescuing downed US Angel pilots, and any reconnaissance work for Zeus's G-2 military intelligence.

We always tried to beat the enemy to our downed black winged warrior pilots and ships and those who needed our support.

A downed black winged pilot and aircraft is a heart wrenching experience to witness.

Usually upon our arrival the pilots were passed on to other Angels from the crash. A few pilots have survived a crash without a scratch. They were the Lucky Ones by the Grace of God Zeus's will to fight another day in Hades.

A Black winged Eagle Jet Fighter plane or black winged King Cobra helicopter would most likely be demolished on impact buried several feet into the mothers jungle of joy with the commander pilot her holy son.

Those Angels of God who crashed are a Warrior Prince's or King's buried with his Horse and Golden Chariot, a son of the Great King.

To the 11th Armored Cavalry Regiment, The Black Horse Regiment, and Our ARP-LRRP team's, it did not matter which Service of God the pilots were flying with as in the Air Force, Navy or Army of Zeus.

They were our warrior brothers, the men of The Great King and Queen and we were there for them.

All for one, and one for all, for from Heaven we really are One. We stand Tall in spirit, and in might, and what a holy sight. A bright light is this stranger Black Horse.

The Pilots provided us the air support of Zeus lighting bolts when we need them and we provide them their ground support of the Goddess Athena, the Great Mentor in Disguise, when they needed us. It is amazing what One Minute in time can mean between life and death.

Think of God and goodness more often than you breathe air. ~ Epictetus.

My Guardian Angel Michael said: King James, it is true, your time has come.

I thought to myself, No! It is not possible God, why now?

I am short in days of my departure of this Great Vietnam Soul War.

I only have 15 days to go to Return to my Good Queen Penelope who is Weaving her Good Cosmic Web in the day and unweaving the web at night.

The Holy Spirit spake: Sun of John of the seeds of Zeus. King James Odysseus of many devices.

Ah you Wretched one you are!

Hapless too I see.

Do you too lead such a life of Evil Doom, as I endured beneath the Rays of the Great Sun?

I was the Sun of Cronion.

I had trouble beyond measure.

I was subdued unto a man far worse than evil.

King James is in Spiritual Disguise as a Sergeant E-5 and a Team Leader of a Aero Rifle Platoon in the 11th Armored Cavalry Regiment, Air Cavalry Troop.

I have been Warring in this horrible Vietnam War for eleven and a half months.

I am exhausted yet still alive and in one piece. Give or take a few Pieces of Grenade Shrapnel in my back. The Arrows Tips of my Evil Enemy Chewing away at my life.

My friend, I have passed through so many Bewildering Trials of Physical Torment I have been destroyed spiritually.

Inescapable Tribulations of Mortal Mental Pains. Horrifying Spiritual Sorrows.

That if I have survived, I have only survived by the Grace of God through by My Prayers to my Lord Jesus.

My own self talk, and even Luck if you believe in such a thing.

I kept reminding myself in my prayers and in my belief that I only have 15 days left to serve in the Vietnam Soul War. I am out of here to return to my Kingdom in the United States of America.

I can go home to my Queen Penelope by the Grace of God Be it Your and My Will Oh Lord.

I should have been out of this Wooers Camels Wretched Evil Feld when I was 30 days Short of Breath.

There was not anyone to replace me at this time in my life who had the Will of God. A Spiritual Warrior Prince or even a Spiritual King like me to step forward in my place.

I though to myself, no way God. I am out of here and Hermes the Messenger of Zeus and my guardian Angel Michael of God must be in error!

Maybe it was the Purple Libation of the Elders Wine that I drunk and the Pot that night that dizzied my mind and my thoughts and feelings.

I was talking to myself in Denial of my True Instinctive Inner Feelings as if I was fighting a giant black Boa King Snake with a Diamond on his forehead.

He has me trapped within his Buddha Belly feeling content with my Destiny within him.

Deep down inside of myself I knew the Truth. Hermes is never wrong nor is the Arc Angel Michael.

The God's are always right, they Speak the Truth for God.

The Holy Ghost spoke: You King James are on a Soul Journey to Olympia to See the Work of the Great Phidias.

Gods holds a misfortune for you to live.

Behold These Things, before you die again to See the Clear Light within me and All. You may Methink my friend, there is No Need even to take this Bitter Soul Journey Love Is The door Way In.

You are On The Spot now my child.

This Majestical Soul Journey to Mount Olympia has begun already, with These Works Before You on The Path. Have you No Care to Contemplate and Study These Things?

The Holy Ghost spake this way.

Will you my friend not then perceive either Who You are My Soul I am.

To what end you were born unto that I am.

What Purpose the Power of Contemplation has been Bestowed Upon You now that I am Within You and you Methinketh me?

The Holy Spirit spoke again.

Well, good now my friend King James, but in life there are Some Things Disagreeable and Hard to Bear are they not?

Are their none Others at Olympia King James?

Are you not King James Scorched by the Heat of Life?

Are you King James not Cramped for Room to Breath of Life?

Have you King James not to Bathe in the Discomfort of Life?

Are you not my Lord King James Drenched in the Rains of Life?

Have you not King James to also to Endure the Clamors and Shouting's and all the Other Annoyances of Life my Lord?

Well, and good my friend King James.

I suppose you Set all this over against the Splendor of the Spectacle of Life.

You bear it Patiently.

What Virtue is in this?

What then and What Devices will you do my good friend King James?

Have you King James not Received your Greatness of Heart?

Your Brave Heart? Your Good Will? Have you not Received your Lions Courage?

Have you not Received your Fortitude from the Lord God?

What care Am I, if I am Great of Heart, the Lion King?

Whatever good will that can Come to Pass, Will Pass Will it not my friend King James?

What Evil shall Cast Me Down or disturb me if any in this Great Soul War my Lord God of I am?

What shall Seem Painful and Evil to you and me?

Will you Suffer also as Others do?

Shall I, King James a Spiritual Warrior King in Service to God not use my Good Power to the Good End for which I received it? Instead of me Moaning, Groaning and Wailing over Whatever Will Comes to happen of my good life?

After being in the Great Soul War as a LRRP & ARP and Seeing so Much Bloody Death, Horror, Pain and Sorrow, I and others Know from Real War Experience that Our Inner Gorilla Feelings, our Swan's Intuition, the Chatter of the Gods, the I am Within us All, is all Knowing Omniscient and Present.

When it is our time It Is Our Time. One should Accept it with Honor and Gratitude in Thankfulness.

It is a good day to die!

It doesn't matter whether its a Good Time or Not so good Time my Lord and my Lady, its just your time and this is The Way Life is by the Will and Grace of God.

I call this Time also Destiny.

When I first arrived in The Great Trojan Vietnam Soul War I was assigned to the 11th Armored Cavalry Regiment, Black Horse.

I really didn't like the name Black Horse when I was first assigned to the 11th Armored Cavalry Regiment because I was still very innocently young man from Indianapolis, Indiana and very naive.

This Black Horse sounded so Deep and Dark and scary to me, when I heard Black Horse the very first time. Then when I saw him with my eyes as he was so Justly Prancing Upon Evil Wooers into the ground. A Horrifying Black Spirited Horse he is.

The Warrior Spirit Black Horse. A God that he is in His Own Name. He Tramples all evil wooer people Into Doom in the Middle of the Night as they sleep.

Even in the day light when the wooer Blinks an Eye, or tries to sleep. Zeus Rides his Spiritual Transparent Black Horse with Justice Upon All he Chooses to. Zeus is to be Feared and to be Respected as He Wills it.

In my innocent young mind, I liked Zeus's White Horse better. Methinking, it was bringing Good Blessings from God yet I was wrong. I found the Truth. Black is Beautiful. I Grew into a

Spiritual Warrior of Maturity. To Respect the Power of Zeus's Majestical Black Winged Horse as time went on.

My first assignment is being an Office Personnel Specialist (SP-E5), in Head Quarters, Military Intelligence (S-2) department. S-2 had me Planning Zeus B-52 Lighting Bolt missions. The ARC Light Thunderbolt Missions that shook the Hell out of Vietnam and Cambodia and even Laos. I am handling Confidential, Secret and Top Secret documents as a spiritual Warrior King in disguise as a personnel specialist. I am Seeing What Our military is doing in this Black Trojan Horse Soul War.

I learned how to gather the Intelligence Information on enemy activity in our area from these Top Secret reports. Then I would determine what Coordinates to use from the Double Agent Intelligence Reports.

I would then plot the coordinates on to a large wall map in the War Room. I would then type a report for my commanding officer who would then Sign the Orders for the Arc Light missions, the B-52 bombing raids, and I would send the documents to the Air Force to be executed.

As a (E-5) Personnel Specialist at this time I thought it Personally and Morally Alarming for Me and others to have such power planning the B-52 missions Without Real on the Ground Intelligence Experience over so many peoples lives, as a good warrior King would require of his Staff.

I thought to myself, maybe The Gods have Gone Crazy? I discovered it was the Washington, DC evil wooers who are crazy.

My thoughts were: Who, What, When, Why and Where are these bombs falling upon?

At this time in my life I am a 20 year old young man that Incarnated into Indianapolis, Indiana. Innocent as Golden Corn growing in a corn.

A Popcorn Delicacy for the Gods to Devour as They Watched and Laughed at the Movie of our Life on Earth.

We all are the Actors in Performance for the Gods.

My friend, there is a Great Soul Watching a Greek Tragedy being Performed at the Acropolis Amphitheater. The Odeon of Herodes. This is a Great Poetic American Tragedy and Love Story.

I Am sorry there were not More Spiritual Women in the Play to Love the Warriors with their Healing Love Balm. So many of the spiritual warriors in such a great need to be healed by the goddesses love balm.

I was totally in Amazement, and Morally and Spiritually Quizzing myself to Discover that this is The Unconscious Way of Ithacas USA Military intelligence Programs of G-2 & S-2. The Pentagon, and The State Department. This is how they planned ALL the B-52 missions. The Arc Light missions for most of the Army Infantry Divisions, Air Force and The Navy.

What was the most Interesting and Bewildering to me was with this so called Top Secret Intelligence reports provided by an Anonymous Mr. Nueyen a so called Double Agent?

To my amazement, My Ithaca White House Government, the State Department, the Pentagon, and our Military leaders, and our Commander in Chief's and their Subordinates all Paid for this Information.

Even the North Vietnamese Army also paid Mr. Nueyen to provide to us and them with bogus Top Secret intelligence.

You are probably wondering Who is Mr. Nueyen?

Ah yes. Strange Evil Wooer's in Disguise in The USA Ithaca.

I was Astounded and Overwhelmed with this Brilliant Intelligence the Department of Defense, the Pentagon, and Our Military used to fight the Great Trojan Vietnam Soul War with to No Victory in Sight.

A Great Loss of Americas Heart, Mind, Body and Soul. Our Soldiers lives destroyed.

Creating PTSD.

This so called Mr. Nueyen is where Most of the Intelligence Information came from to Provide the Air Support for our soldiers on the ground Sacrificing their Lives for God, Country and The Evil Wooers. Wow Methinketh.

I realized the State Department and the Department of Defense was a Blind Evil Duffer.

What has happened to my Ithaca my USA back home while I have been Warring in this Great Soul War?

What more Evil have all these wooers done in my Ithaca and in my Kingdom Methinketh?

I couldn't Stand Myself Anymore. Or to listen to Hermes's Chattering's Waking me up. He was Driving Me Crazily to the This Buds for You and the Purple Wine of the Elders.

Methinketh I should ask my commanding officer, obviously somebody more intelligent than me a Very Important Question. Sir, Who are these bombs really landing on?

Is it upon Innocent Villagers? Even our own Innocent Troops? Just into the Dense Innocent Vietnam Jungle making Billionaires of Those Who own the Bow and Arrow factories? Possibly Filling the Purses of the Evil Wooers of my USA and my Sacred and Holy America and Europe?

Sgt. James, the only people who know the truth are the ARP's & LRRP's, The Black Berets Kind Sir, Who and What is a Black Winged Beret pray tell me sir. Kind Sir, I have heard of the Gods Army Green Berets and Marine Forest Reconnaissance soldiers and Navy Seals but what is an Army Black Beret sir?My Arc Light Specialist of Zeus's Thunder bolt's. Our Brave Hearted One.

The Great King in disguise.

Black Berets are Brave black Winged Volunteers as in the Green Berets, the Navy Seals, the Marine Forest Reconnaissance soldiers who have security clearances.

They are from many different infantry units in the military of Zeus. They also my good man have prior combat experience and are Warrior Prince's of the Great King and Queen.

Ah yes my good friend Sgt. James, they do all the Special black winged Operations and the Missions Impossible of the Gods that nobody else will do or wants to do or even Can Do by the Grace of Zeus.

Black winged Berets do the Missions Impossible for the US Army and any other intelligence agency for the good of Ithacas government.

These Brave Hearted Soldiers have pledged their life for God & Country. They have a Life Expectancy of 3-6 months at best, by Gods Grace.

Black Berets, ARP and LRRP, and Marine Forest Reconnaissance, Green Berets, Navy Seals, Special Operations, are the only Brave Hearted soldiers who go Behind Enemy lines in 5 to 6 man teams to See what's really going on in Evil Lands to Gather Intelligence Information or Execute Stealth Missions and Fire Bolts of Lightening by the Gods will.

The Holy spirit spake. Son of John, seeds of Zeus, King James of Many Devices. Lion Heart man. Overbold my Black winged young Beret. What New Deed and Hardier than this Wilt you Devise in Thy Heart?

By Zeus's Grace they will make it Back to Tell all from the Evil Darkness from within this Trojan Black Horse. They will give us their Evil Tale of the Battle. What they Witnessed. Good or not so good for Them and Us to see Between the Light Rays of Truth. These Winged One's lived another day to go out in Hades again for God & Country by the Gods will.

These men are the very Brave Heart One's. They Sail Upon their black winged Vessel's On the Razors Edge of the Waves of life upon Poseidon's Great Sea of The Unknown.

Their Adrenaline and Death is their Drinking Wine. Whiskey and Drugs of the Elders. The Goddess Aphrodite's Loving Goddess's is there healing balm.

Being very young and innocent back then it seemed to me like a Great Waste of good Human Life to know that we are sending these Heroes, these Warrior Prince's and King's out into a Trojan Vietnam Soul War that has No Real Leadership from the White House at this time in Ithaca's history of evil wooers. The Evil Wooers did Receive their evil Invisible Curse.

My good friend any Special Operations soldier from a CIA Civilian Clothed Private in Political Camouflage to a 2nd Lieutenant Knew more of what is really going on in the Great Trojan Vietnam War than any General in Ithacas Army, or Marines or Navy, or the Secretary of Defense, or the President, or the Congress or the Senate of Ithaca. Unless the evil wooers back then in the government Exaggerated the Truth in Ithacas USA and throughout the world.

The Holy Sheepherder Said: Now God be My Witness before any god. This hospitable Holy Board. This Hearth of the Noble King James, where upon I am come.

That King James is even now a Surety in his Own Country. Resting and Fairing. Learning of these evil wooers deeds. He Sowing the Seeds of Evil for All the Wooers of Washington, DC. Because the time has Now Come Methinketh. King James rides a Black Spirited Horse named Oh my God.

Then Out of the Royal Blue Sky the Great Queen Penelope appeared before this Black Beret Stranger.

I will first boldly ask you this. Who Art Thou of the Sons of Men and Gods? Where is Thy City? Where are They that Birthed you My Stranger of The Light who wants to see Gods Truth and Justice manifest today?

King James of Many Counsels answered the Queen and said: My Lady, No one of mortal men in the whole wide world could find fault with thee. Because, your Fame Goes Up to the Whole Wide Heaven. As does the Fame of a Blameless King I am King James.

The One that Fears God and Reigns among many men and women. I Am maintaining Right.

While the golden brown Earth Bears Wheat and Barley Rye. The trees are Laden Full with Good Fruit.

The Goats, Sheep and Buffalo bring Forth. They Fail not being Waxless in Number. The Great Sea gives a Warehouse full of fish.

All of this Good my dear Queen is God I am. Out of this Good Guidance I am and You are. The Good People Prosper from under Him & Her Our God of The Holy Light.

Then the Forever Wise and Beautiful Queen answered King James saying: Your Golden Good Words be now accomplished.

Now King James you will be aware of my Good Kindness.

The Many Wonderful Gifts from my Sweet Holy Golden Lips.

My Holy Golden Hands,

My Holy Golden Heart,

My Holy Golden Soul Upon You.

So that who so ever will Meet with You will call you Blessed Forever More. You shall live in your Castle The Grand Chateau St. Moritz and in the House of the Lord forever more.

Suddenly the Birds magically sang beautiful songs. Thank you my dear Queen and yet inquire not about my race and mine own country because if I think about them I will fill my heart with more pain and sorrows for I am a King with many.

The evil wooers meanwhile on Earth were before the Great Palace of King James.

Taking their Greedy Pleasure in Casting Weights and of Spears in their Egotistical place of Insolence and Ignorance of King James of many devices.

This Greatly Angered the Strange Angel Beggar in disguise as James the I Am, Methinketh.

The Holy Swineherd Eumaeus said to the Spiritual Stranger James of The I Am. Easily for You Knowest It. For indeed you Never Lacked Great Understanding. This stranger, the beggar man they call James said to Eumaeus.

Do Thou Go Before Me with the Angels and the Goddess Athena and with The Mentors.

I Will Mark and I Will Heed all this you Speakest to Me to One with Great Understanding.

Well, I know What it is To Be Smitten and Hurled at in life. My heart is Full of Hardiness for much evil I have suffered in the Perils and Sorrows in The Waves of The Wooers Soul War and Life.

As the Spiritual Stranger James went Forward. I Stepped over the Great Threshold of Life.

There lay his beloved Sunny.

Now an old dog of Argos. Full of Vermin. Happy to See his Wise Master.

The stranger King James I am looked Aside and Wiped away his Tears as he Continued Forward into the Great Banquet Hall of the evil wooers. Their doom is approaching.

There with the many God's invisible, King James Passed within the Fair-Lying House. Went Stealth Straight into the Great Hall on Earth to the Company of the Proud arrogant evil wooers. Yet upon Sunny Argos came the fate of Black Death. Even in the hour that he beheld King James. God Bless his Sunny Soul.

Close Behind him King James Odysseus, The Lion Hearted King, the Waster of Wooer Cities, entered the house in the Disguise as a Beggar man. Who appeared as a Hapless Wretched Soul of a man. Very old looking, and leaning on his Koa Staff and clothed with Pitiful Raiment. You Telemachus, his son called the Holy Swineherd to Him.

Took a Whole Loaf of Purple Rye Bread out of the Goodness Basket. He gathered Plenty of Holy Meat. Much as his hands could hold in their grasp and said to him.

Take and Give this to the Spiritual Stranger Named King James Odysseus to eat. Then Bid him to go Beg Himself of all the evil wooers in their turn. Humiliation is an ill mate of a needy man.

The Holy Swineherd said to the Stranger King James Odysseus.

Telemachus gives you these Holy Sacraments. He bids you go about and beg of All the wooers on Earth and in their turn. Then King James Odysseus of many councils and devices answered him and said.

King Zeus grant me that my god son and my goddess daughter may be Very Happy among men and women. They may have all of their Good Hearts Desire.

The beggar James in disguise accepted the Holy Sacramental Gifts in both hands. Ate his Holy purple bread and Holy meat washed down with the Holy wine of the Elders with the minstrel singing in the Great Halls of King James Odysseus. Anon magical things went in the Great Palace Hall of King James.

The evil Wooers Raised Aloud Clamor through the Great Halls of Earth.

The Goddess Athena and The Mentors stood by King James in His Invisible spiritual disguise as the beggar man. Sun of John, seeds of Zeus moved him to Gathering Morsels of bread among the wooers.

To Learn Which were Righteous and Which were Unjust So that They May Receive their karma from God.

Yet not even so was the Great Goddess Athena fated to Redeem Anyone Man or Woman of Them from an evil doom. Their destiny.

So the stranger James set out beginning on the right to ask every man.

Stretching out his hand on every side. Though he were a beggar man. The evil wooers were amazed and overwhelmed by the beggar man James. Asking each other who he was? Whence he came from?

Why Now?

The Holy Eumaeus Said: Listen to me You Evil Wooers of the USA and from around the world.

Concerning this Stranger Beggar man James who is called I am. Verily I have seen him before again in Time. The Holy Swineherd Truly was His Guide here. But of Him, I have no certain knowledge. Whence He The I Am Avows to be born of The Holy Grail and of The Light.

No Great Wonder so many Holy Swan are Correct in Saying there is No Intelligence In the Wooers Government's of Earth during the Great Soul War. Now an Ugly Black Evil Fate will Become Them.

So Spoke He the Holy Swineherd.

Yet the evil King Evelyn George Hussein O Antinous, the Head of All the Evil Wooers Rebuked the Holy Swineherd with a Foul Stinking Political Wooers Breath, Saying thus:

Oh Notorious Holy Swineherd, Why I pray thee?

Why did you bring this spiritual man with No Name to Washington, DC?

Have We not Enough Beggars Besides this Strange Beggar you call James?

What have you brought Upon Us all as a Killjoy of the Wooers Feast on Earth?

Do you Holy Swineherd Count it a Light Thing that the wooers assemble here devour the living of thy Lord, but thou call in this beggar James also?

I was now a 20 year old young man Reincarnated from Ithaca to Indianapolis, Indiana.

I grew up believing that there were NO Evil Political Wooers in our Ithacas Congress, Senate, White House, Presidency, State Department and Department of Defense or Supreme Courts.

The Evil Wooers Rightly Knew within themselves what they are doing.

Controlling The News Media World Wide and Manipulating the Computer Voting Machines and Polling Stations throughout The USA and the world.

Being foolishly elected by Television brain washed citizens as The New World Order leaders for Our United States of Ithaca.

The Democracy of the Great Spirit. The American Way in Freedom on our Earth. So Thy Will Be Done my evil wooers. Thy Good has Come to you Now as your good doom blessing from Zeus.

Wow was I full of the Nectar of the False Gods to Believe our Governments Evil Political Religious Wooers during the Great Soul War.

Methinketh, How could our Own government of evil wooers be Supporting this Slaughter of Human Souls?

On both sides of the War? For which god? Who's Country?

They Fear not Zeus?

Is Ithaca Now really a Government and Country of Evil Political Wooers Full of Greed, Hate and Evil for Ill Gained Money that is not good for them but a Curse now, methinketh. I pondered.

I am wondering. What and how Zeus is really doing all his good deeds. Knowing, Seeing, and Testing all the evil wooers.

Waiting for them all Along The Road Way to the Great Feast. To Drink of their good wine. His Good Wine methinketh.

The Gods and Goddesses are Laughing Upon the Fools on the Hill Knowing the Black evil doom that awaits the evil wooers as they drink Zeus's Holy Wine for their good doom.

I am thinking to myself. Is this Great Soul War some Political Opera of the Gods & Goddesses? Some evil Insanity?

A Cosmic evil Joke for the Jokers, and the evil wooers of life?

The Sacrificing of Our good Sons and good Daughters Lives.

That we all Impassioned God that he would Bless us with?Oh My God.

I had to Research the Universe. So very deep to Recollect this Truth for myself in the Trojan Vietnam Soul War. As in most wars.

What is Our government in Ithaca is Really Doing while We Are away at the Soul War.

Now I Am Being a Spiritual Warrior King from The USA and Sparta, Greece and England from the seeds of Zeus in disguise.

Now I was Willing to Give Up My Life. Gods Life.

That he gave me, to Find Out the Holy Truth and the Spiritual Holy Grail. Because I wanted to know Truth and I found this TRUTH as a Spiritual Warrior King from Earth and Heaven, What True Soul Purpose and Justice I must now do.

Thy Good Will Be Done Oh Lord.

Now this is a True Good Tale of The Holy Grail.

My faith in Myself and in My father & My mother God. The Gods God's and Goddesses, and in James & in Christ, in My Country Is of Thee. The United States of America of Ithaca and my fellow good citizens of our planet Earth. Our USA!

After a few months of planning B-52 missions and Arc Light thunder bolt missions I was morally and Spiritually Quizzical. In Spiritual Shock by the Great Soul War. What Our Government and Other Governments throughout Mother Earth are doing from their Evil dishonest wooers mind set mentality. While, WE are Away at the Great Soul War.

One Strange Day my friend I walked out of the Headquarters of the 11th Armored Cavalry Regiment's S-2 Underground Intelligence bunker complex. My friend, this S-2 Intelligence Bunker Complex is a Dark Stinking Chamber of No Oxygen. A Cigarette and Cigar smoke filled hell hole. The bunker is constantly Humming Aloud from all the Radio Equipment.

Listening to Commanders Screaming Orders During Battle. The Horrible Sounds of Company Commanders over the radio's Crying of their Slaughtered Men and Companies.

I would not be Surprised if any a good Soldier and even one Who's military Occupation Skill is a Radio Operator, Who did not loose Half his Spiritual Hearing Mind's Ears.

Everyone else half their Stinking Breath and Heart and Soul. This is the underground bunker complex that I worked in planing Arc Light Missions on Who knows Who's Spiritual Head I really did not know.

My friend, I walked out of this stinking intelligence bunker complex to go Smoke a Stinking Cigarette. That would never help me feel good about what I was doing in My Stinking Life my friend.

Across the way from the bunker complex is a small Dirt Road lined with Bananas and Holy Armor Tank Dust.

I decided to take a Walk Along the road and Smoke a Cigarette of Spiritual Pain and Prayer.

As I lit my cigarette I Noticed the Silhouette of a Woman Walking Towards me.

Methinketh. I thought to myself. How unusual.

A woman.

A Stranger I see. Walking towards me.

I must be Seeing Things from all this wooers evil foul air I Am breathing. My friend I looked Again. Rubbed my Eyes. This time I noticed the Silhouette Is not Only a Silhouette of a Woman yet of an American Ithaca Woman.

Ah, Even Spiritually Stranger Wethinketh.

This American Woman is Walking Towards me.

Along this banana lined dusty dirt road outside of this stinking military intelligence bunker complex With The Sun behind Her as She Is Walking along The Road making all this a good mystery. Destiny. Oh My God. My good friend.

She looked like an Angel walking towards me. Yet all I could See of Her was a Dark Shadow walking towards me as an Angel or some Goddess in disguise.

As I watched Her walking towards Us in Shadow Form, as I am watching photographic film being developed second by second. She Changed from a Shadow Form into a Real Alive Woman in Living Spiritual Color my friend. My friend.

I rubbed my Eyes in Disbelief.

Because I knew or I thought I knew that there are No USA American Women Running Around as Spiritual Soldiers in the Deep Jungles of the Trojan Vietnam Soul War.

I also know there were no USO Shows going on at Black Horse Base Camp because we were very close to the Cambodian border that did not exist. Ah yes my friend the stranger, She was Smoking a stinking Cigarette too. Methinketh.

I Decided to slowly walk towards her and Say Hello.

My friend, I thought to my self, Why not?

Now WE never know Who we will meet in the Jungles of the Great Soul War. My Friend, as we got Closer to Each Other It was Obvious that She Is an American Woman!I can tell just from the way She Walked. How She Looked. By her Holy Eagle Features.

My friend I started a Conversation with Her.

I said, Hello.

She said: Hello back to me. Wow, I talked to a Real American Woman I thought to myself. I asked her, where did You Come From?

She said. I was captured in the jungle by the 11th Armored Cavalry Regiment. Wow we methinketh.

I said, Excuse me. What did You Say?

My friend, In my Mind I thought to myself, I Am Spiritually Flabbergasted!She said, I was captured in the jungle by the 11th Armored Cavalry Regiment.

I asked her, Where are you from in the USA?She said: I am from Berkley, California. She said, I am a Spiritual Antiwar Protester.

She said to me, I sneaked into Vietnam from Thailand.

Walking Through The Jungle Country Side. Methinketh.

My friend, She said to me again: I was living in the jungle with the North Vietnamese Army soldiers Protesting the Wooers Governments involvement in the Great Soul War. My friend, I thought to myself.

Oh Shit.

This Is Really Happening.

My good friend, as I looked and listened to her on this Sunny lit Banana Lined Dirt Road out side of the 11th Armored Cavalry Regiments military intelligence bunker complex I got Goose bumps all over my body.

I felt as I am talking to a very Unusual Stranger. A Woman Spiritual Warrior. Possibly an Angel or a Goddess in spiritual disguised as an antiwar protester we methinketh.

I asked her, What are you doing walking down this dirt road?

She said to us, I am being Interrogated by the Army. They let me out of the bunker to smoke a cigarette. I Am on a cigarette break from being interrogated. Well, now my friend, I looked around my shoulder and there were two soldiers watching her movements and mine too.

She was a Harmless Weak Soul.

There was No Place for Her to Run To or Hide. She knew that Her Soul Mission in the Vietnam Soul War was Over for Her.

She said to me, You should get out of Vietnam and the Vietnam Soul War now. She said to me, It is Spiritually Wrong what the USA Wooers government and all the other wooer governments are doing in Vietnam. She said, All this killing is Wrong!

Ah my friend I told her: I agree with you but I can't leave Vietnam. I am a soldier Seeing the Truth in spiritual disguise. Witnessing.

My friend I told her, Where would I go? Into the jungle and be killed by the North Vietnamese Army?

As a soldier I have a duty to God and our country. We are also living in this unjust war just like the Vietnamese people are whether we like it or not by Gods Will.

My friend, This woman has Very high Spiritual Spooky kind of Spiritual Energy. She is obviously Very Committed to her political and spiritual beliefs, You may know Her. You may have heard about her journey in Berkley, California.

My friend Do You know her?

She has Gray Eyes and Brown Hair. She is about 5'7'Inches in height. I can tell she was an Attractive Woman when she lived in Berkley, California.

Now Her appearance is Frightful and Spooky from Exhaustion. Now She looks Very Skinny my friend. She had Lost a considerable amount of Weight.

She was Malnourished from living in the jungle with the North Vietnamese soldiers. The last thing she said to me was, If You want to, You can get out Here and Go Home.

I said to her: Good Luck American Woman. I hope the Army sends you back Home to California soon and well. The Army guards came for her and took her back into the intelligence bunker where she is being interrogated. I never saw her again.

By the way my friend the last thing she said to me is. There are other antiwar protesters out in the jungle with the North Vietnamese soldiers. I Methinketh a Really Big Wow.

My good friend, I was Literally Blown Away Meeting Her.

I had Goose Bumps All Over me as they took her away. What about you?

We have to Honor Her in her Faith in God.

In Her True Soul Purpose as an antiwar protester. Even as a Woman Spiritual Warrior Monk of Peace.

It must have been Very Difficult for her to live with the North Vietnamese Army soldiers in the Deep Spiritual Jungles of the Great Soul War. She Miraculously Amazed me in Methinketh. How about you my friend?

I went right back into my intelligence bunker with these spiritual spooky goose bumps all over my hapless wretched soul. I asked my commanding officer who She was. If it is True that the 11th Armored Cavalry Troopers picked her up in the jungle after a fire-fight with the North Vietnamese Army Regulars. My Commanding officer who was in charge of military intelligence for the 11th Armored Cavalry Regiment S-2 said it is true. The good officer said.

Please James, don't tell anybody outside of this intelligence bunker complex about this incident with this American Woman antiwar protester being in The Vietnam Soul War. This good soldier said.

The good soldiers Would Flip Mentally and Spiritually Out if they knew there were Innocent antiwar protesters in the Jungles of Vietnam being Foolishly used as Human Shields by the North Vietnamese soldiers.

I knew when I Raised my Right Hand and Swore my Allegiance to God and Country at the Induction Center in downtown Indianapolis, Indiana on March 28th 1968 I knew I was going on a soul journey that was somehow going to change my entire life.

At the time of my induction, I had a very strange feeling within me. I cannot explain it in words. It was a Soul feeling.

All of my friends warned me not to go into the Army.

They said: the Vietnam War was all Wrong.

The Great Vietnam Soul War was all about Money for the Military Industrial Complex Owners. It had nothing to do with True Justice or the American Way. They said: Even our past President of

Ithaca President Dwight Eisenhower Warned us all, of the Dangers of the military industrial complex in Ithaca. That the International Bankers of the Evil Wooers have taken over the country after the Second Great War.

My friends All warned me: Don't go into the Army.

Go to Canada. Go to Europe.

Escape and Hide from the evil wooer government.

As a 19 year old I was Bewildered in methinketh.

I did not know Who or What to Believe in anymore.

I didn't even Trust my own Intuition.

I wanted to believe what my friends said about the Great Soul War is True. Because they were my friends. We all grew up together. We went to high school together. We partied together. I did not believe them nor did I know God within me. Or the Truth then.

I needed to discover The One we call God and His Truth for myself.

I believed in Jesus Christ, my Country and Government.

I am Innocent as the corn growing in Indiana.

I was Raised to Believe Blindly in our Elected Leaders and in our Country, in our Government.

They would Never Ever Lie to us or use Us Unjustly as Lambs for War Slaughter.

These Noble politicians definitely would Never become Knowingly Evil Wooers in Disguise for a Secret foreign elite world government.

A Secret Government and Secret Court the New World Order. Becoming by their Design Traitors and Conspirators to our America, Our USA.

Methinketh. An Evil Wooers life is an Ignoble Position in Life. Because they had a stolen honor.

They had noble and comfortable positions among themselves in their wooers thieves life.

They knew King Agamemnon, and God knew their fathers.

I believed that Our Government leaders Would Never Do Anything Ignominious or Unjust.

Because it is not the American Way.

Nor Gods Way. In God We Trust.

Who's god the wooers asked?

As they Raised their Hand upon the Holly Bible.

I believe Our Government is the Best in the World. I still do believe this. Our USA Government stands for The Truth, Freedom and Justice for All.

What Happened to Our United States of America?

We were taken over by them a long time ago! Officially after President John Kennedy, Bobby Kennedy and Martin Luther King Jr were assassinated. Invisible Transition by Tragedy.

Today how will we Free Ourselves in America of these Evil Wooers?

Back then I believed we were all Fighting this Evil Empire from the Land of The Wooers. The Communism Dragon. This Communist Evil Emperor in this Strange Star Wars Soul Battle. This Terrible Evil Dragon Beast Is Devouring the Earth's good people.

The wooer King will soon die by my Spiritual Lighting Bolt Upon his evil head.

I Pray tell you now my friend. I could not then even Tell you the Difference between the Evil Wooers in Ithaca Compared to You. Disguised as Religious Political Wolf's in Aunt Macy's Finest Gourmet Sheep's clothing from the Babbling Brooks Brothers. They look as Clean Proper Looking Lady's & Gentleman. The wooer Political Twins in disguise. Looking Sharply as fine Upright Religious Citizens of who's god and who's country?

My friend these evil wooers are in Conspiratorial Traitors Disguise.

They really did not believe in Our God.

Nor in The Light.

Nor in our Good Country and Government. The believed only in their own evil wooers empire of The New World Order.

My friend they all look Squeaky Clean. They know WE Would expect the Good to look as Professionals.

Compared to Geo Engineered and Camouflaged to look even like the good citizens of Ithaca and from other Ithaca's around the world.

They Look as the Royals of the British, French, Germans, Spaniards, Russian and Chinese Wooers.

I am a veiled 19 years old from Indianapolis, Indiana. I knew Nothing.

I am Innocent as Pop Corn, a Halloween Pumpkin, a Toad Frog in a Holy Fairy Tale, as The Lone Ranger and Red Apples being grown in Indianapolis, Indiana in my Ithaca on Earth.

After the Completion of the Swearing in Ceremony at the induction center, I Could Feel my Soul Shaking within my body.

Oh my God what is happening to me?

My friend, I could feel Fear and Doubt.

I was now beginning a Strange Sacred Spiritual Ceremony of Initiation by the Gods and Goddesses at Zeus's request.

Better is it that thou shouldest not vow, than that thou shouldest vow and not pay. ~ Ecclesiastes 5.5 ~

Within my Soul Self I realized in a peculiar way I have Sold My Soul into a Bondage for this Great Vietnam Soul War Homer. I had to Recollect this Truth I am seeking Socrates. How Will I Get my soul Back?

I could Hear Gods Voice, the I am Soul Within me Spake. By living Your Destiny my good son.

Here is Thy Twin Edged Sword of Dragons Breath Tempered Steel.

Thy Holy Koa Staff. I am With You from Your Beginnings to Your End my son. Through your Pain and your Suffering you will Come Home to Me. To Your Spiritual Souls Enlightenment.

I was Going Crazy being in The War as so many of my fellow Prince and King Warriors.

My friend, everybody back home in Ithaca was having a Wonderful Time going to the Exhibitionist of the Antiwar Movement. Endless Bucking's in the Park.

Protesting within Musical Rock Festivals of their Mind. Following the Minstrels of the Other Wooers. Smoking their Governments Jamaican, Colombian, and Mexican Mary Jane's Dragon

Smoke. Happily Ingesting their Psychedelic Mushrooms and the Wooer Governments LSD. Going No Place.

Discovering Nothing but a Transparent Illusion of Saran Wrap Raped around their simple innocent minds.

My friend everybody was Desperately Trying to Climb Over Heavens Walls. Trying to Get Into Heaven without the Keys of Life to Gods Eternal Kingdom. Without Gods Permission.

Thinking they are Righteous and Religious. Being devoured by the Gods and Goddesses. Thunder bolt's that do Protect Heaven.

Believing in their actions of PEACE and Justice. So Methinketh upon these things my friends.

My good friend, All along Their Own Holy Way with Holly, they are making their Baneful Love All Night long in the name of a Pandora's Peace Park. It does not Really Exist for them either. In their Mind as they too Sold Their Soul into a Bondage.

They Gave a Vow for a Sacred Majestical Odyssey to a Trojan Horses Soul War.

In their Own Holy Face on their Earth. Fellow Spiritual Actors in the Great Opera of The USA Tragedy. Methinketh Peace.

There were times during the Great War I wished I was there with them being Tempted by the Sirens and Minstrels of the other wooers. Having a so called good time Yet.

What is a Good Time? What is the Value of a good Name? A good Soul? What is our True Soul Purpose any Wise Way? What is The Good? I must Recollect this God. This Truth for myself my good friend Socrates.

It is obviously My Karma to be a Spiritual Warrior King from Ithaca at this Time in my life. To Serve My God and Country.

I Am a self soul realized that Responsibility comes in Many Forms. In many Ways to every one of us.

We should want to Listen to God Father and God Mother within us. The Great Spirit I am within us all. We have to Live our Karma to its Fullest.

This is Our Cup that Runneth Over. Life for me is a Spiritual Warriors life for God and Good. Spiritual King James I am of Many Devices. The Lion Hearted. The Brave Heart. A hero of a Thousand Faces of God I am.

For others life is a Protesters Life of the Great Protest for God and Good. As the life of Jesus and James and Paul and Mary Christ and Socrates and Homer too.

You Never Know what you are really Going to Do Until its your Time in the Be Here Now and to Do It Well.

One thing I do know my friend is that many brave and honorable men and women and even children from many countries, and moreover in the American Revolution defended and died for us all. As the great Spartans of Life for Freedom and for God.

NOT for the evil wooers of Ithaca in Greece or in the USA or in England or in Scotland or in France or in Germany or in Russia or in China or in Israel or in Palestine or South America or in Africa or in India or in Australia or in Japan or in Afghanistan and in any other country place on Earth. For the Spiritual Truth and Justice of Our Good Spirit Soul, God.

Their Honorable Sacrifice made it Possible so that we All Can have Freedom and Liberty in America. Even to Protest the Truth. While these The Brave Good Hearted Ones, these Lion Hearted Ones Worked and Served their Country and God for all of our Good. What have most of us done for God and Country?Nothing.

Life is a Great Majestical Magical Spiritual Soul Journey whether we know it or not.

Whether we Like It or Not.

To me, Deep Within my Soul Self I Secretly Understood everybody.

We are all One. Because God is One Great Spiritual Opera with many Actors and Performers. God is Seeing Who is Good and Not so good. As Food for the Gods as God wills it good. My friend, of course many Good Souls were Rightly Protesting the War in Peace and in Love. Meditating and Following their Oracles.

They were Paying their good Tax Dollars all along The Way to the wooers NWO government. Peacefully and Humbly in Love of course. Helping the wooers to buy the Bow and Arrows that they Picked the Mango Tofu from out of their Teeth while they Smiled Namaste.

Chanting Om Mani Pade Me Om.

Crucifying their own children soldiers. How Holy and Chosen they must Feel being wooer gods Chosen people Suffering even today in methinketh our truth.

If my Recollection is Correct Homer, The good Citizens in Israel and in Greece and through out this world paid Caesar their Tax good Dollars as Caesar's good Citizens are Demanded and Expected to Pay unto him. Unless they also want to be Crucified for Being as Good as Jesus Christ and Socrates.

It is my Recollection Socrates, that the Roman Soldiers that Crucified the Good Jesus Christ, One of Gods own good Sons, were paid with those good Tax Dollars collected from the same good wooer citizens of Israel. Just As in the Great Vietnam Soul War that are financed by our own good wooer citizens USA tax dollars.

The evil wooers Understand and Know how to Use Economics methinketh.

Do you my good friend?Socrates I thinketh this must be the same historical good tax Dollar Process Used even to this day that the Ithaca government, the North Vietnamese government, the Chinese government, the Russian government and the European Union and All governments who participate in War Collect to Pay their wooer soldiers. Also Pay the owners of the bow & arrow factories for the Trojan Vietnam War and All other Wars as Wooer Caesar wills it.

It is very interesting to me my good friend that with our good citizens tax dollars I am and others can be imprisoned, Sacrificed, Crucified and Slaughtered in Honor for a Wooer God and Country and for a Stable and Profitable Economy for the wooers well being.

Thank You, your Wooer Highness's. Food for the evil gods ye be.

Oh My God what a Great Opera we all live in.

God decided it is Time now for me to move on in Life and to Recollect this Haughtiness of Spirit. This truth of God and his Spiritual Story.

One of my most Cherished Psalms in the Holy Bible is Psalms 23.

I have read this Psalm at least a thousand times during the Great Trojan Soul War.

The Lord is my Shepard; I shall Not Want. God Maketh me to lie down in Green Pastures. God Leadeth me Beside the Still Waters. God Restoreth My Soul. God Leadeth me in the Paths of Righteousness for His & Her name's sake. Yea, Thou I Walk Through the Valley of the Shadow of Death, I Will Fear NO evil: for Thou Art with me; Thy Sword and Thy Staff Comfort me. Thou Preparest a Table before me in the Presence of mine Enemies. Thou Anointest my Head with Olive oil. My Cup Runneth Over. Surely Goodness and Mercy Shall Follow me All the days of My life: and I will Dwell in the House of the Lord for Ever. Amen.

Now We Go and See what on Earth is Really going on here in our USA my good friends.

One day while working in the intelligence bunker I heard that the Black Berets Lost some men and needed a Sergeant E-5 who could become a Team Leader. A Squad Leader. Somebody who would have to Volunteer for the ARP's and who had a Top Secret Security Clearance. After Hearing this News I volunteered to join the ARP's, the Aero Rifle Platoon. I became a Squad Leader which is also called a Team Leader as a Black Beret in the Black Horse Air Cavalry Troop.

I am probably One of Few if not the only Spiritual Warrior Sovereign in Disguise as an office personnel specialist SP-5 a desk jockey to become a Black Beret to See the Truth for Himself.

My friend, I left my military intelligence position in Headquarters S-2 a Safe Position in military life to discover the truth and the Holy Grail in the Trojan Vietnam Soul War.

Obviously my good friend, Most people would say I did not have Any Intelligence as in the military.

I did have a Tremendous amount of Spiritual Courage and Curiosity to find out the Truth of God and Country and to Seek out the evil wooers of my Ithaca. Now my friend, One Moment I am the office clerk turned into an Infantry Soldier, as Clark Kent becoming Superman. I had to Learn Every Infantry Position by On the Job Training. I learned every man's good position by doing his job in the field. I walked as Point Man which is Very Scary.

We can get our Face or Leg or Arm Blown Off and be the First to Die with Honor. I carried the Radio which is a Pain in the Back and the Okole. I carried the M60 Machine gun. I carried the M60 machine gun ammunition, which is Heavy and a Great pain in the ass. I walked tail which is very Scary.

We can get Shot in the Back or our Ass without honor. I carried the LAW'S. I carried an M-79 that I blew his evil head off with in the middle of the night. I carried C4 so all could See the Bright Light with a Great Bang. I went into the underground bunker complex's. I became a Tunnel Rat which scares the hell out of anybody including me.

I learned to Repel from a Hovering Black Winged Black Hawk Helicopter unto a Hot Landing Zone with the enemy shooting from below and this is Not Fun Either. We can get our Balls Blown off.

My friend, I did everything the Hard Way by Living and Walking the Talk. Just as everyone else in the ARP'S and LRRP'S.

This is my On the Job training of Becoming a Black Beret in Black Horse.

I started out in the Vietnam War in disguise as a personnel specialist in S-2. I ended up as an ARP and a Black Beret. A Brave Lion Hearted One as all my Fellow Spiritual Brothers in the ARP's. Becoming and being a ARP or a LRRP is Not Easy my friend. I don't believe you would like it at all.

Being in Special Operations is a Very Difficult life Laced with Pain and Sorrow the Hard Way that Truth can be in Time. Our Training is nothing compared to Live Contact.

I wanted to find out the Intelligence G2 TRUTH about the Vietnam Soul War. What our government and the evil wooers in Ithaca are Really doing. The Only Way I knew that was Truthful, Honest and Sincere. This Is The Hard Way.

Put my Life On The Line.

Do It Myself. Live the life of a Spiritual Warrior. I had to put my life on the line as all real men & women spiritual warriors always do. Ask the President of Our Ithaca of my great Faith in God and Country. He would never go to war being a coward.

Personally my good friend, I would not in any way call myself anything other than a good soldier. Definitely Not a Hero as others are or as some would like to be called. I was only doing my duty to God and Country. My good Commanding Officer friend tried to Persuade me Not to go into the ARP's and God bless his soul.

He said, James you could get Shot and Die for Nothing.

He recommended that I stay in Headquarters and in S-2 where I would be Safe Throwing Arc Lightning bolt's upon the enemy.

My good friend said, Black Berets are all Crazy and Wise. Their life is a Hell of a Life being turned into a Frankenstein for the wooers wars.

Don't risk your life James for a War that nobody really cares about in America.

The Evil Washington, DC Wooers have all gone Crazy with Treason and Corruption of their Soul with Greed. My dear friend, in the End my Commanding Officer and My Indianapolis Friends were Really Right about the Vietnam Soul War.

Yet they did Not Know the Whole Truth so help them God. They definitely never found The Holy Grail Within themselves. I am this Truth I am.

For me my good friends Homer and Socrates I found God, Jesus Christ, My Soul and the Truth in the middle of Hell in this Great Wooers Soul War.

Time has Passed on Now.

You may not Recognize Me Anymore my friend.

I am a Very Ugly and Painful and Hapless and Wretched.

I am all Scarred Up all about My Face and Around my Heart and Soul and Body too.

There are these Wooers Tattoo Scars Everywhere about me.

There is Holy Blood Dripping from my Heart and my Minds Body.

I may frighten you. I do not want to. I may Scare You Off.

I do not want to.

If you Look At Me Now I will Understand if you Run Away in Denial, I would.

I used to be So Innocent. Handsome I was. Spiritually Whole and Noble. So good.

Now my good friend, I am a Frankenstein.

I am Hiding Under this Black Veil of Sorrow.

I can See You through this Very Tiny Hole.

Right Here where my Bloody Finger is Sticking out at you.

I do not want You to See Me.

I am in Writhe and in Mortal Soul Pain.

My friend, You May Cry Tears from Witnessing my Wooers Tattoo Scars in my Minds body.

In your mind and heart and soul too.

You may Even Scream in Horror and Run Away from my Emotional Spiritual Disillusionment and Pain.

I would not blame you One Iota my good friend.

I am not the same innocent child from Heaven, from my Sparta, Greece and from Indianapolis, Indiana, or England and from my beloved America.

I am not a Gump in the Forest anymore.

I was Crucified the other day by an Evil Wooers Dragon. I died upon a Bleeding Cross as Jesus did.

They Placed me into a Dark Cavern of Doom. They Moved a Great Stone in Front of the Entrance to Protect my good soul as I now Rest in Spiritual Peace with my Father and Mother God in Heaven. My good friend, I have become a wooers frankenstein. A Monster of Pain, as all the Special Forces of the Special Operations of good soldiers become Unknowingly, Unconsciously, Unwittingly from the Wooers Horrors of a Great Soul War.

In the name of their God and a Country that they may Not Know or Recognize anymore.

My good friend, you are probably Wondering what do I mean by becoming a Frankenstein. Frankenstein is a German word. A wooers war monster? This will scare you.

In Time All Things go Around and Around. Things Change from Not so Good to Good, or what Appears to be not so good or good.

Time is This Way and so is Life on Earth. My friend, In Time and in History there are Good governments. There are Not so good governments. They and their leadership Can Change Depending on their Leadership, and of their Own Citizens Will of What goodness is.

Governments are as Automobiles. Governments are a Political Man Made Machine that Governs Men and Women on Earth. As an Automobile is Man Made of Composites Man Created through Methinking.

They Governments do not have a Thinking Mind. They do not have a Heart and a Soul. They do not Feel. My friend, Most Governments are a Headless Heartless Monster.

Governments that are not good are an Unconscious Cyclops.

Cyclops, Here Take and Drink my good Purple Wine after thy Feast of Man's Meat that you may Know what good Manner of Drink this is that my Sun Star Ship Beholds for you.

The Cyclops Spake, Give It to Me. Thy good Grace and Tell me Thy Good Name Straight Away. I may give you a good Stranger's Gift where in you may be Glad.

Yes, my good friend for the Golden Earth, the grain Giver of Purple Rye Bears for the Cyclopes the Clusters of The Spiritual Juice of the Ruby Grape of Wine. The Rain of God Gives Increase, yet this is a Doom Nectar of the Gods.

The Cyclops Spake Repeatedly Three Times in his great Folly. Cyclops drank my good Purple Wine of Wooers Doom and Lost His Wits.

Then King James Secretly and Quietly Spoke to him Whispering.

Cyclops, You asked me my Renowned name. I will now Tale It unto you.

You Cyclops do Grant me a Strangers good Gift as you have Promised me.

No-man I am is my name and no man I am they call me, my father and my mother and all of my good friends too.

Out of his Pitiless Heart the Cyclops Spake. No-man, I will Eat You Last in Number of your good fellows and the others before you. This is my Wooers Gift to you my Spiritual Stranger.

Do you Grok?

Now the Cyclops drank all the Great Goddess Athena's Purple Potion Wine and a Deep Seep overcame him as Her Wine Potion Conquers all wooer men and women as She Wills it Good.

My good friend, I Quietly Spoke to my Companions Comfortable Words of Encouragement Lest they should Hang Back from Fear and Doubt.

When the Post of Olive Wood was Aflame We Drew It from the Hot Coals as my fellows Gathered about me.

God breathed a Great Spirit into us all.

We Thrust the Blazing Holy Olive Staff into his Wooer Eye.

We Whirled it all around in his Eye.

The Cyclops eyelids and eye brows are aflame.

His eye ball Burnt Away and Popped into a Thousand Pieces.

The Cyclops Crackled in the Fame as a Sparkler on the 4th of July. Cyclops died a horrible death.

What has distressed you my good Polyphemus his good wooer friends asked him?

No-man is Slaying me by Spiritual Craftiness and His Spiritual Art. Again his wooer friends spoke Winged Words of knowledge to Polyphemus The Wooer Cyclops.

Then Polyphemus if the I Am is Violently Handling You in your solitude. It Can in No Wise Way be that Thou Should Escape the Sickness and Evil sent by Mighty God.

This is the Wise and Noble Knowledge the wooers all spoke in fear. The wooers departed. My heart within me Laughed to See how my name and my Cunning Counsel of Many Devices had Beguiled the Evil Cyclops.

Cyclops Governments go were the wooer driver drives them into destruction.

Design Obsoleteness in Machines, Autos and the tools of our life that we use and in OUR Governments by the wooers hidden Communist World Wide agendas.

These type of governments have no real heart, or soul or mind other than the evil wooers drivers political mind if he has one. Methinketh.

In time and in history through out civilization for thousands of years, their have been Gods good wise Spiritual Warrior Prince, King and Queen leaders, and good wise citizens in Gods good governments.

There have also been not so wise nor good, non spiritual, non-warrior wooer leaders. Not so wise citizens, the followers of wooers, in not so good governments. Driving the Golden Chariot.

It time and in history God and Gods God's & Goddesses have Clearly Shown the Good Way and the goodness to be received for those of us who follow God and Who Live with God. God has also shown The Way for those who do not follow God and do not live with God. They also receive their Karma from God as wooers all pay for their evil deeds. God is Justice. God is a Jealous God. God is to be feared. Not man nor Cyclops Governments.

God is Omnipresent, Omniscient, Omnipotent and All Powerful of all Good & Vengeance which is Gods good Justice. Vengeance is His alone. God works in Ways that are Invisible to the Naked Eye of those who are Vain and do Not Believe God, nor hear God, nor see God, nor do the best we can as God Wills.

God is at Work with His Legions of The Light & The Dark Angels that do Gods work even while we are asleep.

God is even at a Banquet of Wooers protected by their secret armed guards. Drinking Gods wine and eating Gods good abundance as evil wooer political and global banking thieves do.

Wooers Mocking God even in places that are Holy to God in their vanity lost in their drunken illusion, that wooers have the power to do as they will. Planing to kill Gods Sons and Daughters and Spiritual Leaders. Only to Find Themselves and Theirs Cursed.

Removed by the Dark Angels of Doom. On to their way to a Living Hell Worse than Death. Time and History has Shown and Proved many times over the thousands of years of life on Earth.

There are Fates Worse than Death for those who do not believe God is Great.

Just look at what happened to all the wooer Pharaoh's of Egypt.

Look what Happened to The Roman Elite Senator's and what they received.

The English King's & Queen's and their Fates. The French King and Queen's and what happened to theirs. The Spaniards King's & Queen's and what they received. The Muslim's and what they received. The Israelis and what they received. The Athenians who put Socrates to death and what they received.

The Japanese and what they received. The Chinese Emperor's and what they received. The American President's and Senator's and Members of Congress, and what they received.

Non of us are above God and Gods Justice which is Gods Truth.

The good curse Follows the Evil Wooers where ever They Go. From Underground Caves to Mountain Tops. Through the Valleys and into the Plains. Turning their lives into a Scorching Hot Desert. God will not be mocked.

Everyone who chooses to become an evil wooer, becomes a slave to an evil emperor who works in disguise for God watching over Gods Hell as God wills the wooers into the Deep Doom of a Sea of No Hope. There is no spiritual air to breath, nor Spiritual Light, nor a good life to speak about. They all are joining the other Spiritually Blind Evil Wooer Political Religious Sharks as they Chew Upon Each other for Meat in a living Hades.

In the United States of America We have Seen all of evil wooers. The so called good, and the Ugly Ones.

The men and women in Red Outfits.

The rest of the world has witnessed them in all countries on Earth.

My friends, a Frankenstein government is administered by evil wooers who know Gods right way to live. They chose not to do good in vain.

They choose to live Out of Harmony in their own Ignorant Gluttonous Ways Corrupting themselves and their citizens with God and Nature watching every one of their choices. Knowing they Will all Receive their Justice and their own good deeds as they have now willed them for themselves by their deeds. Have no fear, God is Here.

A very simple example is in The Brothers Grimm Tale of The Fisher man and His Willful Spouse Ilsebill.

Being greedy the Fisher man's spouse did not want the fisher man's way of a peaceful content life. She wanted to be King, then the Pope, then the Emperor.

Finally she wanted to be God and so God returned them both to their vinegar jar.

Frankenstein wants to be your God, but he is not God Father & God Mother. Frankenstein chose to do evil for his hidden political agendas because of his Lust for Power and Greed because he Received Not from God. Frankenstein tries to imitate God with his Meaningless Political Religious Rhetoric.

Using Gods words, laws, religions and everything he can find to Woo the good people. By turning them around in an Opposite Direction from Good. While wearing his fine Brook Brothers and Macy's attire trying to look noble and clean. Hiding the Stains of their Victims Blood. Our Blood. Our Children's Blood. Our Veterans Blood. Innocent Peoples Blood. Even Natures blood.

Because if you meet a wooer You Will Right Away Know he or she is a wooer in disguise by Looking them straight In their evil eyes. By speaking with him or her the wooer. As meeting Polyphemus the Cyclops. Because their breath Stinks Afoul with Words of Dishonesty.

Wooers eyes will shift from Side to Side and all around instead of looking us Straight in our Honest eyes.

Because we will see the Truth is NOT in them. This is all very simple and clear. We are Protected by God. We Good are Ola Kala.

Frankenstein uses Gods Good children when they are Ignorant of Gods good ways to do evil.

Disguising evil as good deeds. For their god and their country.

Amazingly, most of the good people Do Not Know what they are really doing in life.

We are Under a Televised Hypnotic Witches Spell in a not good fairy tale.

Thinking we are doing good. When we may be doing Not good.

A government, a Vehicle, a Chariot, if you will Allow Me to call a government a vehicle, is as an automobile.

It has No Real Power of its Own other than the power of the spirit of its people. The Peoples Soul Horse Power which is a Governments Fuel.

This Government Vehicle can be driven as a driver drives an automobile wherever he chooses and wills it.

As to the political right or to the political left or the Conservative Straight ahead.

The driver as a Presidential driver can chose to be a good honest safe Presidential driver, driving a Good safe Government straight ahead by OUR CONSTITUTION and be in Harmony with God and Nature.

A government wooer Presidential driver, and the wooer Senators can drive the Vehicle of the Will of the People and chose to become a frankenstein evil wooer driver.

Driving Crazily on the Political Highway of Life.

Destroying our country on a wooers purpose. Communism. NOT being a good government Presidential driver. Being totally Out of Harmony with God and Nature.

At a Great Expense of itself, Its own citizens.

Racing to a Political Self Destruction by its own conscious destructive wooer will power.

Design Obsolescence by the wooers hidden political NWO agendas.

God gave All men and All women Free Will. A Good Soul to choose their Own Path. Their own destiny. Their own Karma.

In any Great Soul War for Justice and Freedom, it is full of Pain, Suffering and Sorrow and very little Joy. The Sacrifice of our good citizens lives and souls, is sometimes called the Acts of Noble Work, Duty.

Service to God and Country. These Acts of Spiritual Nobility and Justice Truly depend on OUR Intentions.

The True Soul Purpose.

Why We go to a Great Soul War and Whether they are in fact Noble?

Can We Win this Soul War?Yes. If NOT. We Do Not Go To War if possible. Whether it is a Just War or Just Another War. Whether the pain and suffering is Noble or ignoble.

Gods will or evil wooers will. This is the real question to ask our self about any Great Soul War. Even in a meaningless war.

My example is The American Revolution.

During the American Revolution, The good citizens of America wanted to Declare Our Independence from England and their evil Royal wooers.

We in America desired our Souls Spiritual Freedom.

We wanted our Bill of Rights.

Our Constitution. We earned them the hard way with our blood. By our spiritual will power in battle for FREEDOM.

This Great Soul War called the American Revolution was Victoriously Won with our Good Citizens Blood. With Our Good Citizens Lives and Souls in Service to Ourselves, God, and Our Country. Americans fought a War by Faith in God for these Freedoms and Rights. Many good souls gave their lives for you and me called The United States of America.

This brilliant torch of Freedom symbolized in the Statue of Liberty from France holds Graciously UP into the Great Sky These Bill of Rights, Constitution and this Declaration of Independence, this Free Soul and the Freedom we know today.

This Brilliant Souls Freedom Torch of Democracy is the gift of God and Gods God's and Goddesses of Ancient Greece and from The Sun. It came through France.

Vive La France.

This Brilliant Spiritual Torch of Clear Light, as in the Ancient Greek Olympics that Starts the Great Games of Spiritual Freedom travels around Greece and ALL around this Good Earth through a Good Spiritual Soul.

The great souls journey writings of Homer in the Iliad, in the Odyssey and in Plato's The Apology of Socrates, Phaedo, Crito is self explanatory.

All this good knowledge from Mt. Olympus that Inspired many good souls from around the world to come to the United States of America for Spiritual, Mental and Physical Freedom started in Ancient Greece.

Many Others from many Faiths and Beliefs and Countries have contributed to The United States of America's majestical spiritual soul journey for our Freedoms and the many Modern Interpreters of the Holy Bible.

An Atlantis Good Note of Ancient Greek History Unknown.

If we read Homer who is Gods Voice, Gods Oracle, and self realize that He lived in a Great Spiritual Enlightenment called Atlantis. We read HIS story The Odyssey. We will realized that the Interpreters of the Holy Bible and all the other spiritual writers of Holy Books of Time have all borrowed from Homer and The Odyssey. They also borrowed from Socrates and Plato. The Ways of God.

Back then in Time to really Understand, Grasp and to Grok what Homer, Socrates & Other Greek writers said and did do was travel to Ancient Greece. Many tourist from all over this Earth do this today.

All the Pilgrim spiritual good souls, Disciples & Writers did do this.

They came to Ancient Greece to Bathe in Gods Olive Oil of Divine Wisdom and Divine Knowledge and to have their First and Last Supper with God and Gods God's and Goddesses of Greece.

They all made their Great Odyssey Step by Step on Foot, by Donkey, by Horse, by Jackass, by Wagon and by Ship. They came from many countries from all over the Mediterranean coastal areas. From India they came and back again on the Old Trade Routes. Spiritual Monks from all over the world.

They came to Atlantis in Ancient Greece to meet with HOMER, SOCRATES, Plato and the Other Mentors.

Many good souls did visit them. They Watched, Studied and Learned how to understand and read these Authors in Ancient Greek. They Learned how to Live the life style of Faith in God. How to Pray and Meditate.

How to Methinketh. They Learned How to CO-Create Goodness in their lives and in others. These Good words and Good stories and tales of life and of God are the Simplest Way that anyone can say to us the Truth about God and Gods Goodness and how to live in HARMONY.

Very much like how to Use, Tune and Play a Golden Lyre.

A musical instrument which is symbolic of us. The Sound of Harmony in a soul living in a body. Learning about Life while we are on this Soul Odyssey called our life on the planet Earth.

As We read on my good friend, we will realize that Gods Atlantis and the Ancient Greeks where before the Holy Bible. We the Students of Life all received our Wisdom and Knowledge and Enlightenment from The Universal Light.

The Ancient Ones. Noman is my name, and Noman they call me, my father and my mother, and all my fellows in Ancient Greece.

We will realize my good friend that the Ancient Greeks really did live in a True Age of Spiritual Enlightenment. Whatever GOOD they Thought Of is CO-Created through Gods Universal Mind. Thinking In Methinketh.

Methinketh is a Scientific Mind Thinking Process. Holy Spiritual Thinking. This Methinketh. It is The Highest and Most Noble Science of the Art of Spiritual Thought on the planet Earth. On any other Earth in this Universe that God created.

What we Think about, We CO-Create. Spiritual Mind Into Matter. The Word and the name GREECE is the Olive Oil of God. Ancient Olive Oil Lamps in Clay Vessels. The Light. The Squeaky Wheel gets the Universal Spiritual Greece in our Life. It is Symbolic of The Universal Light Information that Gives Us the Knowledge to The Light Up the Whole World with our CO-Creations of Goodness.

We do not have to be Rocket Scientist or Einstein to SEE, READ and HEAR the Truth.

All we have to do is Have Desire to know the TRUTH in Life for our Good.

We are a CO-Creation with God. This Truth is all about us.

We can give ourselves a good education in any good library. Find ourselves a good old Harvard Classics book. Even go to Harvard University.

Turn On The Light and read Homer's The Odyssey slowly. Consciously with an Open Mind Being with Him. We will READ, HEAR and SEE God in Action. The Son of GOD, the seeds of Zeus, and the Odyssey of our Souls Life Journey here on Earth.

This Spiritual Atlantis is the place of the Age of Spiritual Enlightenment on Earth. This Atlantis is the Place within us where we as a Human Race have fallen out of HARMONY. We have fallen out of the GRACE of GOD.

This Atlantis, this Eden is also within Us.

It is Humanities Wooers Vain Ignorance of God, that History has recorded for thousands of years, even recorded All the Wars Pain's and Suffering's of our human soul's that are out of Harmony with God.

History has shown and proven to all of us humans beings that most of us humans are ignorant of GOD and NATURE and HARMONY. Because we are Egotistically Greedy and Vainly Foolish. Ignorant about God who created us. We chose to you live in Pain instead of the TRUTH. I am waiting for us to come to our souls true Home. Our Spiritual Home is within us all.

God Lives within us and Within All.

If we read all of this Good Truth in the Holy Bible and in other Holy writings we will See, Read, Hear, Feel and Know the TRUTH of God.

If we would like to know the Truth and we cannot read, then Sit Quietly in Prayer and in Meditate on The Light from the Universal Sun Of All Truth. Breath in and out the light.

By Praying God Father and God Mother and their Children Gods God's and Goddesses and Angels will visit with us from within our mind, body, heart and soul and we will Receive the TRUTH. In Truth we really do not need a teacher, a Guru nor anybody to show us the Truth in life because God is our true Guru. God is all within us and all around us in Life. God lives within Us.

God is not outside. God is inside everyone. Including Atoms and Molecules.

Do we live in Gods Consciousness is the real question to ask ourselves? This Consciousness, this Spiritual Atlantis is within us and within everything including our plants and animal friends. God is everything. We Can find God Him & Her within in us. We Learn to Listen. We can get in touch with God within us. Just Call within us God. Be Still.

Be patient. Listen for the inner voice conversation. It will be positive. God will answer, I am here. Spiritual Love, Divine Wisdom and Knowledge is within us all. Miracles are within Us.

The Whole Story of God is within Us. In The Sun Light. It is All Light Energy. Imagine if we have no Sun Light in our universe. We will have NO life. Consider we are all Light and Spirit is Light. We Are Created in Gods Image. Within Gods Image is everything GOOD.

All of Gods Good Wisdom and Knowledge is right within our Body, Mind and Soul. In our body's RNA and DNA Code. As God is within every Atom and Molecule in LIFE. God is in Our Breath What did we do with our goodness my friend?

All we have to do to restore our soul is nothing other than Self Realize that God and all Good and all Creation is Within Us and not OUT there in Outer Space.

We can effortlessly say the Lords Prayer and this is a good step forward in the right direction if we need help.

There are many good Prayers my friend that we can also say to our self that are also a step in the right direction.

We do not have to be a rocket scientist or Einstein to do this simple Compassionate Deed for ourselves.

God Mother and God Father have placed themselves right inside and within us.

If God were to hide from Man, where would he hide? Inside Man. Because God knows most of us are looking for God outside of us. Oh My God.

If we See God Father and God Mother within us my friend, we will see God right in front of us everywhere and in everyplace and within every-thing and in every-body. When we come to this Place of Spiritual Soul Enlightenment, this Spiritual Atlantis, We will SEE us.

We will see the Bright Clear Light of GOD that all the great Spiritual Teachers of God have spoken to us all about. Methinketh my good friend we will Truly become a Living Breathing Child of God doing all of Gods Good Purpose.

Which is to Enjoy and live our good life in Harmony, in Thankfulness, in Love, in Health, in Abundance, in Compassion, in Forgiveness, in Grace, in Peace, in Work, in Service and in All The Goodness. God intended us a Child of God to Live Wellness. Because God is all Good. God Mother and God Father Loves their good children us. God is Very Rich & Very Wealthy in All Goodness. They have blessed us with Unique Gifts and Talents right within us, to use for our own goodness.

Why are some of us Rich and Others Poor?

Because we who are Rich USE our Unique Gifts and Talents for our good. My friend, If we use our God Given Silver and Gold Unique Talents Wisely, Knowledgeably and Honestly, WE will be guided in our life to CO-Create Good in our Life. We will be protected by Gods Guardian Angels all the days of our life all the way into Heaven.

God has given each and every one of Us, Gods Unique sons and daughters all of our good in our Be Here Now Today from our beginnings in Heaven.

Methinks most of us do not even know all of our Spiritual and Physical Treasure is waiting for us now. To Discover it right here and now.

In this Sacred Cave that we are in while we are reading this good soul book called: Love Is The Door Way In to our Good Gods Treasure Chest right within our heart, mind, body and soul. We are Very Rich & Abundant in All.

Most of us do not even know this while we are starving to death thinking poorly. A little bit of Spiritual Knowledge is Worth a Fortune.

All of our Abundance in our Life all depends on US. What WE do with our good blessings! It is our Treasure Chest of Spiritual Love.

If we only know what to do with this Lucky Penny I am giving us. As this good Soul Book. We will share our good luck with somebody we love. Good love will come rushing back to us.

My friend when we read Socrates, Gods Oracle, and we read Plato, Gods Oracle, and we read The Apology of Socrates, Gods Oracle with an Open Mind, we realize that what we are reading is Gods words and Gods Thoughts from the Ancient Ones.

The Greek God's and Goddesses of God from Mount Olympus. Good things will Unfold for us. My good friends I would like us to realize that those Ancient Greek Epic Poetic Words have been Translated a Thousand times repeatedly from Ancient Greek into many world languages of what we have today.

Even what we call the English and American English language.

I hope my friend we do realize within ourselves that to translate Gods Ancient Greek Methinketh's into American English or whatever language we Read and Speak is very difficult.

No easier to grasp than looking at this Holy Petroglyph that I scratched upon this cave wall with my own blood in the hollows of this planet Earth then good for us.

Because WE Will See the Bright Clear Light of God in our life.

We will READ, HEAR and SEE Socrates as a Son of God, Saying and Giving the Sermon on the Ancient Greek Mount. The Last Ancient Greek Supper.

The Last Days of the Ancient One called Socrates.

As Jesus Christ did, after the Death of Socrates in Ancient Greece, which is Gods Story of our Life.

My friends today, Homer & Socrates & the Others are Walking and Talking and Doing good deeds just like Jesus & Mary Christ are Doing. They are Walking, and Talking in Good Soul Spirit to us. My friend as a matter of Socratic historical fact.

If we will read an old Harvard Classics volume of Socrates Apology then we will read and hear a Sermon of the Mount first spoken by Socrates before Jesus or Buddha was even born.

My good friend If we read an old Harvard Classics Volume with Plato's and Socrates Crito & Phaedo we will Recollect ourselves.

We become More Enlightened about our life and life in general from the Beginning to the End of our life.

It has all been said before. Socrates even told of the Coming of Christ before his death in Greece. The Greek Athenians in Greece, as the Ancient Jews of old Israel, Paid a Horrible Price, The Destruction of their Homeland, which cannot ever be rebuilt in this time period in Peace for crucifying a Child of God. Socrates and Jesus.

Socrates Himself Proclaimed to the Whole World before his death, GOD is sending someone. Ah this Stranger, This Christ, another son of God. Who Will Do Greater Deeds than Socrates ever did do?

There really is Karma in our life. Not only personally but Even Nations have Karma. Their people have Karma too.

Let us all Look at any government or nation or anybody who thought they were a Somebody. Important. Great and Mighty. Royal. A King or Queen. A Pharaoh, A Royal Sheik, a President, A Chairman or greater than God. Let us all Look at what happened to them all. Holy Yikes.

Go right ahead my friend and ask any nation, and ask its people, in any place on Earth, and they will tell us all, There is Karma.

This is the reason things are The Way they are in all our country's throughout Earth. Methinketh this is a very good reason to give good attention to God.

Fear not man, nor woman, nor government, nor nothing, but God. Because my friend God does not like to be mocked.

Look at all the disasters happening almost daily world wide. Look at all the political upheaval going on around the world. God is talking to us all. History Proves God to be REAL JUSTICE. GOD can be and is very VENGEFUL and Evil if he is mocked by any body or any nation or any people. Ask The Pharaohs of Egypt.

Flee out of the mist of Babylon, and deliver every man his soul: Be not Cut Off In Her Iniquity for This is the Time of the Lords VENGEANCE; God Will Render her a Recompence. " ~ Jeremiah 51.6

My good friends Everybody Spiritual and Wise has received their Knowledge from God and Gods God's and Goddesses and Gods Angels from the beginning of time. Call them Adam and Eve or Enoch or Homer or Socrates or Plato or Michael or Issac or Jacob. Abraham or Sarah or Noah or Moses or Joseph or Jesus Christ or James or all of the other good souls of this Good Earth. Call them Buddha, or Vishnu or the Lao-Tsu and their loved ones who also lived upon this Earth at one time or another. Walking and Talking and Doing Gods good deeds because they learned from God the Truth. Because my friends they are Gods Good Children and when they came to the Earth to Spiritually Enlighten everybody who wanted the Truth and the Light, They gave us and humanity their Goodness and their Spiritual Inspiration. As we will also receive our good if we ask God.

Simple.

My friend, we will Find God, if we Seek God. We will find God, if we look within us and all around us in Nature too.

The World that God Created in the beginning was dark and cold. He is Methinking. God has Compassion for the Earth and All His Relations. The Power of The Word. The Great God Spirit Spake the Word, Let their Be Light. There is LIGHT. The LIGHT is GOOD.

GOOD is in LIGHT. GOD is in the LIGHT. GOD is in LOVE.

GOD is GOOD. O.

The Great Spirit God Spake the GOOD WORD'S. GOD CREATED EVERYTHING IN GOODNESS ON EARTH. IN HEAVEN IS GODS GOOD. THE GOOD THOUGHTS & GOOD WORD'S & DEED'S CREATED BY GOD FATHER & GOD MOTHER. THEIR CREATION & THEIR GOOD CHILDREN Us, All in Spirit.

Another modern example is the Great Trojan Soul War called World War II.

The True Purpose is for Justice and Freedom for Europe.

Because THEY had Lost THEIR way with God because of their evil wooers. The world was under attack from the evil wooers of Germanys Elite Third Force supporters. Hitler as their leader.

All the other Hitler evil wooers from around the world tried to help Hitler take over the Kingdom of the Good, the Halls of Odysseus in Ithaca Europe.

Obviously World War II had its Just and Noble political agendas yet Freedom is the True Purpose at this time in history.

Everybody who had Faith in The Truth, God and Gods Good Supported the Cause of Freedom. They were Focused and Determined to Win the War at all costs, by their good will and desire.

Give me Liberty or Give me Death.

Ultimately from a Faith and Belief in God, many good souls Sacrificed their lives. The European Nations came in Spirit to Victory in World War II with the help of The USA.

Without the USA there is no Europe.

Not only was Europe and the World Freed from the Hitler evil wooers Mentality and Evil Consciousness but so were the Jews FREED who had become Frankensteins Sacrificial Experimental Lambs to do as Hitler and The Nazi wished.

Killing Jews by the millions.

Hitler was defeated at a Great Cost of human souls, lives and resources.

Of course my friends Europe Today could be the Land of Evil Wooers too. They are back again in full Third Force Energy.

The death of lives and soul of Millions would never have ended, if the United States of America with her good Christian, Native American, African American, Japanese, Chinese, Russian, and Jewish American citizens and their military resources did not come to her rescue as a Black Horse with the Lightening Bolts of Zeus and give the Europeans the needed help of The Goddess Athena and God.

My good friends, I pray and hope for their sake that there are a few Europeans left including the Good Queen of England and Her Children who think of us in America in their prayers to God and give thanks to God for the Good USA.

My good friends, we never Know If Today there are any evil wooers left in Europe who woo her good people.

Are there any Your Highness Queen Elizabeth and Prince Phillip?

During the Great Trojan Vietnam Soul War, The Political Agendas were obviously NOT supported by the majority of the people, nor even those in our USA Government.

The wooers ran the war. The wooers started the war.

The Government was NOT focused on Gods Truth. Nor Determined to Win the Trojan Vietnam War earnestly.

It obviously was a War for the evil wooers to Make Money and Kill our Son's and Innocent Vietnamese People.

If the Ithaca USA Government was Truly Focused and Determined to Win the Trojan Vietnam Soul War, The Department of Defense, The Pentagon, Would have Dropped an Atomic Bomb on Hanoi, as we did on Japan during WWII.

This would have been the end of this Trojan Soul War in Vietnam.

The Government of Ithaca could have Saved many of Thousands of its Own Sons lives who died in the Vietnam War.

Many of our soldiers were Wounded for life. Many of the 58,000+ Veterans who Committed suicide from PTSD after the Trojan Vietnam Soul War could have been avoided.

My own brother, A Marine, Committed Suicide several years after he returned from the Vietnam War.

Yet the evil wooers loved the damage done to our sons and daughters.

Their children did not fight in the Vietnam Soul War.

We should all ask our selves WHY NOT if it was an Honorable War that they the wooers created?

Obviously my friend, many evil wooer's made a handsome profit. As International Banker Vampires Sucking Life Blood Effortlessly from our babies heart who is born on the 4th of July.

It is my Understanding my good friend that more veterans have died from PTSD and suicide after the Vietnam War than those who died during the Vietnam Soul War in Combat.

Millions of Vietnamese died. Hundreds of Thousands Suffered from Agent Orange. Did the evil wooers of America and Europe who made billions suffer?No. Did their children suffer?NO.

Why did they all get away with Crimes Against Humanity? They are evil and they control the world. They will all live in a Mental Psychological Hades. It is called a Curse has befallen them all.

The Veterans Administration of Ithaca has Amazing Suicide and PTSD Statistics. Their Studies are available to anybody who wants to understand the True Damage from the Frankensteinian Evil Wooers Mentality and Consciousness of The Wooers Soul War.

They USE US!

They Kill us.

We are their Lambs to be Sacrificed in Their Evil Wars.

The good people of earth.

When we read PTSD material we may even Think that we have PTSD just from living our life. Not being Aware of the Generations of Damage to us all from WAR throughout our history on our planet Earth. It does Pass On. The wooers use FEAR to Control, US.

Fear Not. I am here with you.

The Government of The USA did not Declare War on Vietnam.

Because the evil wooers knew that if they did they would have to use all of their weapons including the Atomic Bomb to win the war.

They decided to use us instead. The Odysseus I am.

Our Countries Good Sons and Daughters as Sacrificial Animals to Vainly, Weakly, to Disguise their Hidden Agenda, Not to Win the War.

There weakly evil wooers political agendas are for a Handsome Profit to the Owners of the Bow and Arrow Factories. They want to kill us. To hell with the wooers knowing they have received their good from God.

Obviously our USA evil wooer government back then and even their Leadership Today ARE NOT Committed to the Spiritual Truth. Nor to True Soul Purpose or True Intention in Truth during the Trojan Vietnam War, Iraq, Kuwait, Afghanistan Wars.

The question today for us my friends is, Are their evil wooers in our USA today? Mr. President, you are a wooer too.

Time Will Tell All to us my friends. WE will See the Truth. WE will Smell the Truth. We will Taste the Truth, so help us God.

Obviously our USA Wooer Government is Satisfied to Look like the truth. Marvel and Cry at The Vietnam War Memorial Wall. Tearfully Remorseful with their hidden Political Agendas.

The wooers acknowledged their errors with our Veterans at their side. We read the names of those loved ones who were Sacrificial Lambs during Wooers Vietnam War.

Our Government said it has learned a lesson in Intention. Not being in Truthful. Not being in Gods True Purpose. Not being Determined to win. Not being Focused in Wisdom and Knowledge. When We as a Nation go to any more Trojan Wars.

Today my friends, We methinketh.

WE question whether we are Truly Focused in the Spiritual Truth, and in Our Good Purpose as a Nation under God and in God Consciousness.

My friends, Of course there are evil wooers in our government who want the USA to fall down to the ground Below its Knees. All the other nations are Conquered.

The wooers want us to believe that our true government and its true soul purpose has nothing to do with God. Nor that We in America do believe In God We Trust.

The wooers are not honest people. Nor to be believed.

Because evil political wooers will tell endless political lies.

The Truth my friend is in our face. Will we have the courage to look into the mirror of life in the Vietnam War Memorial Wall mirror and See the Truth? Today?

I am not judging Ithacas Government nor any government nor anybody.

This is a discourse in Spiritual Love. This Recollection is of my souls life on the planet Earth.

My friend It is our duty as Citizens of God, on this planet Earth. As Citizens of Ithaca and the USA. As Citizens of All Good Nations. To stand UP for the Truth. To live a Good True soul Purpose.

The Truth Will set US All Free by our good will with Gods Goods Grace.

The truth I am referring to about Frankenstein, and Frankenstein's monster's is whether Frankenstein's Wooers Evil Virtues are of being good or not so good?

All the while as all this good is going on around this world, Frankenstein's wooers are creating not good karma for our own country. Nor for any country on Earth. What good we give is what good we will receive. This is Gods Good will. God is Good and God is also Justice. My good friends.

Do we know what the difference is between Good and God?

The difference my friend between God and Good is the letter O. O our good thoughts or our not so good thoughts. This good O is our life and our good that we will create with. We will have to live with our good karma O. Oh My God.

Oh my good thoughts we Methinketh. My good friends. If We as a Nation give Pain and Suffering to other Nations. Then we as a Nation will receive Pain and Suffering for any Wooers Evil Soul War. Even to this day. My friend this truth. What we give is what we get.

What we Give and Receive is a Revolving spiritual cycle. What we give Life is a circle of energy going around and around. Anon anon and around and around it goes this good gift and where it stops nobody knows.

Spiritually my friends we take a good look at what is still going on in Middle East of our planet Earth and elsewhere. These wooers war's have been going on for thousands of years! We all live in a PTSD ICloud.

Why do we think there is no peace on Earth? Wethinketh upon this thought. Why do the evil wooers do this Homer? Let us Methinketh. My friends.

All of This good giving to The Vietnamese is our Not Good Will as a good country and as good citizens of our good country of wooers during the Vietnam War.

Are we being paid back? I believe Yes.

Do we See the Natural Disasters, Financial Corruptions, Political Gangs and Murders going on in our country?

What is the goodwill of America to foreign countries today?

What do other countries think of us today?

Shall we my friends have Peace on Earth? Shall we have another Trojan Soul War?

Shall we all keep on Suffering and Wasting our most precious resource? Our good innocent souls and our hard earned money?

The Earth being polluted with Mansanto Agent Orange, Land Mines, Nuclear Radiation, FEAR. When we can be CO-creating GOODNESS!

We cried then, and I am still CryingThinking how Miserable of a Lot and Wretched souls we humans are when we are out of Harmony with God and Nature.

This is how I and many other soldiers unconsciously became a wooers Frankenstein Monster not only in the Vietnam Soul War but in most of the Insane, Ridiculous and Unjust wars throughout our planet Earth.

We my friend may Come to Realize as I have that we don't have to be in a War to become a Frankenstein monster living in pain. Suffering daily in our Own cities.

Are you suffering? And You Do not know why?

Most of our cities are gang war zones because the wooers wanted to destroy your home town with criminals. Most of the poor live in these war zones.

The Real Illusionary Frankenstein is a Country, a Nation, a Cyclops Government with its hidden political and religious agendas out of harmony with God by its wooers will.

Frankensteins government is not Gods good government. It is an evil government. An evil Empire run by an evil men & women.

Little emperor wooers as in the movie Star Wars or in the movie the Avatar.

Frankenstein's government citizens will Genetically Generate More Monsters to do its evil Bidding.

Life is mimicking the movies today.

Subconsciously.

Subliminally. What we see in the movies from Industrial Light & Magic or Spielberg films. Or even from DOD.

Wooers will CO-Create millions of geo engineered genetically created monsters.

Human machines that do not think.

Even millions of military machines. Drones to be used by the evil wooers on innocent humans who do not even think for themselves. Because The Wooers only Do as They have Been Programmed by the evil Emperor.

Who commands all the wooers through their Television Programmings. What is Genetic Research really all about?

Trying to CO-create Children of a Lesser God. A New Hot Dog in frankensteins image. Frankensteins that have No Soul of God. No heart to Feel with. No mind to Freely think!Yes, Sir!

Frankenstein Wooers will Generate and Use our Innocent Son's and Daughter's life, mind, body and soul.

That you prayed to God to bless you with, to do his evil harm?

To betray you?

I am not speaking of Good Governments as our own government. Nor your government Am I?

You evil ugly wooer's, You Frankenstein's.

You sent innocent children to the Great Trojan Vietnam War, Iraq, Afghanistan, Kuwait, Kosovo to do our killing for a God and a Country that I question if we truly know. Methinketh.

While our Holy Son is in the jungles of fighting our war, he lived worse off than our dog, horse, cat, bird, cattle, sheep or pet pig who safely lives with us. My friend our Holy Son ate food if we could call it that. Shit that is worse than Old Dog Food out of a c-ration can. As the Giant 30 foot long Boa's wiggle with our human souls in their bellies. Because WE left them in the jungle to rot in Hades by The State Department. The POW's we left behind at the State Departments request.

My friend our holy son Drank Dirty water tainted with Mansanto Agent Orange Dew with Cool Aid in it. To Disguise it as Palatable water that became Undetectable Cancer Poison. To wash down his Malaria pills that made him Sicker. WE wonder where his Desert Storm sickness came from?Our Own USA evil wooers.

My friend our holy Son lived in Hades. In Hellish Situations that we will Fain into a Dark Hell if we saw how our son Lived. We did not rescue him by the Grace of The Wooer God. We failed to be all we can be. My friend our holy son and daughter owned only 2 sets of tattered fatigues from Brooks Brothers and his uncle Zack's store. They were usually Muggy Wet. Dirty our Son's they were. Our holy Son has Crotch Rot as his Lover. While We back home made our Baneful love with Macy & Bill, George & HusseinO & Evelyn holding on to The War Memorial in Washington, DC crying out oh my god.

My friend our holy Son's Feet, had Jungle Rot because he only had 2 or 3 pairs of wet socks. One pair of Wet Boots while we where Fishing with Eddie's fine Fly Fishing boots in the Russian River celebrating our NWO. Fly Fishing for our Lost Soul that WE cannot find.

My good friend as our the holy son is Tormented by the Warring at His Soul War in the jungles of Hades. Those little brainless general's and colonel's The Washington, DC Paper pushers of needless paper clips needing their time in a Command of No Honor causing more damage.

No real Personal Combat War experience. Just as THE USA Presidents of today. Unqualified in Saigon procuring from their Supply Sergeant Fine Silk stockings and French Perfume. Johnny Walkered Ngoc good. His Vietnamese Concubine girl. Ngoc's lips around his head that their spouses back home always wondered about yet afraid to ask. Who's lip stick is on your collar?

My friend our holy son Smoked the Pharaohs brown Camels Hump of Cigarettes. Because he Walked at least a mile in hell a day for us. WE will walk for ever more miles in Hades. It is a very long dark and painful walk. My friend our holy son smoked the Luckiest Strikes from Hades. Because he needed some Luck being in the Vietnam Soul War. Where we left him to die. WE wooers will die a thousand deaths of doom for this.

My friend our holy son lived upon Gods White Crosses in his Crucified Pain. Watching US for days on end. Because our son could Not Sleep Upon the Jesus Cross in the jungle at night. The enemy would kill him. My friend our holy son could not trust even his own men. Not to falling asleep on guard duty. Because they would be high on the enemies evil of Heroin and Opium and his Siren Mary Jane.

With our booze, gone crazy and hallucinating he is in Hades. Just plain Exhausted from our wooer warring War.

My friend our holy son would be Chased by his Evil Enemy through the jungles at 2 a.m. in the morning. Breaking trees branches with his Adrenaline White Cross body in fear of being Hung Upside down upon a Vietnamese Christmas jungle tree. To be Dressed as an Evil Pig as he is Flying Through the jungle. Faster than a Speeding Bullet. Faster than Superman. Our Holy Sons fatigues are torn off his body by the evil Bushes Brier Witches and Vietnamese Sirens. The Witches and Sirens look as a bad as Washington, DC wooers dream we are now having yet his is real and so is ours.

My friend our holy son would have his position and his Base Camp Over Run by thousands of enemy soldiers at midnight. While we safely sleep in our comfortable Lambs Wool Comforter with Indigestion of a Black Dogma Death. Our holy son Marveled in the morning after at his enemies dead bodies. 400+ scattered all about.

He noticed the Holy Vietnamese Christmas tree out side his base camp. Hundreds of Heroin Needles hanging as holiday Christmas ornaments. In Thankfulness of a god of No Pain.

As the bullets passed through his body at midnight as the clock struck 12:01 a.m. My friend our holy son would Live in Fear and Terror throughout the night. Praying to God to See the Sun Rise just one more time. If he would please be allowed to live again Jesus. To witness this Majestical Spiritual Wonder he called the Holy Sun.

My friend our holy son had to watch his Every Step in Horror. Because of the Bamboo Booby traps we left behind him at his mothers home. The land mines of his evil enemies mind that had Stabbed his Hardened Heart. Blew his or his friends Favorite Leg or Arm or Face off his holy body.

For all the World to Witness the Truth of the Wooers Great Soul War back home. It has become our favorite leg and arm and ugly wooers face lost in Ithaca as we look into the mirror of our life.

Scream of our own horrible wretched life you wooer Prince and Princes, Queen and King and President's and senators too. There is no wooer escaping Zeus.

My friend our holy Son's Spirit and Moral is almost totally destroyed from his own wooer people in the United States of Ithaca America. Most of us have become Hypocrites and Gluttonous wooers Prospering from Gods sons and daughters being Slaughtered at the Slaughter House in the Great Soul War.

My friend our holy son would maybe return. You hoped not. A Wretchedly Torn Holy Soul, Jesus on The Cross, to his muddy base camp under water. Laying in the Mud of Sorrow for days on end.

Without a Rain Poncho to protect him as he Froze his Ass Off at night. Walking Pneumonia from the Rains of no Compassion from Ithaca full of Pendelton raincoat's.

His bodies skin Wrinkled like Pigs Feet. So will our heart rot too from what we did do as a people and a nation of wooers.

There are many good Vietnamese people. They are as we are. They are a people who have fought many wars. They have never lost. All at a great expense of human souls and nature destroyed. What for?Wooers.

My friend our holy son, was Covered with Mosquito Bites. Snake bites. Spider bites the size of Sand Dollars. Poison Wooer Welts covered with Filth. Leaches from Head to Toe. In his crotch.

Green bamboo viper snakes around his toes of all colors of green. Sizing up his life for them looking as someone from hell. You wooers are on our way to Hades now.

My friend our holy son's Mind and Body is Wretchedly Twisted. Stretched to the Maximum like a Catapult of an Atomic Bomb ready to Explode from the PTSD Despair. From the White Crosses.

He is stretched upon the jungle wall while we dined on the Turkeys we are for Thanksgiving and Christmas dinner as he reads his Dear James letter. The good news of the day from back home.

The evil Senators, the wooers have taken over his kingdom The USA. They wanted to marry his wife and kill his son. The holy son Odysseus I Am saw a great evil in his eyes for the wooers back home. He knew of his return in a Vision from Hermes. My friend our holy son, Odysseus I am, gets off the Black Hawk winged helicopter alive today and returns to his Black Horse base camp. Everybody will get Out of his Way. He looks so evil, so wretched and so ugly from the warring as a monster should look like and he is in our face now devouring us as a hungry Lion King is doing now.

My friend our son, Odysseus I am, just might even kill them wooers all. Without thinking about it. For just being in His Sovereign way rightly so methinketh. Even so Odysseus Spoke.

The Goddess Athena opened the doors of the fair-lying halls of the Great Hall. She came forth. Telemachus led the way before her.

The Goddess Athena found Odysseus I am among the bodies of the dead wooers. Stained with blood of the Toil of Battle. Lion King of The Sun Heart that has eaten of a Buffalo on the homestead and goes on his way. All of his Chest and his Cheeks and face on either side are Splattered with blood. He is so terrible to behold. Odysseus I Am.

My friend our holy sons breath stinks with the blood, sweat and tears of a Great Soul War and Hell. He will return in Zeus Shinning Armor to See the Coming of the Lord and so will we.

My friend the Holy son Odysseus I am will go rest his soul in the Holy Hollow of Penelope's Peace Park Heart, Body and Soul. Replenish.

In the Great Trojan War our son's and his fellow warrior Comrades of Horror will grasp a really big Hookah of the gods and put a hand full of the Siren Mary Janes incense from Cambodian in their bowl. A big ball of Chinese Mud Opium incense in the center my friend. We said it was all illegal. What is killing Innocent people? A prayer of incense to our wooers gods senselessness. Knock Out. No Pain?

Here in Vietnam some of his holy good fellows Warrior Prince and Kings of an evil sorrow and pain in the Great War. May even Stab Themselves in a small little Dark corner of Disbelief. On one of their Veins Roads of Adrenaline. Let the blood run out with a black evil needle called The Horse-of-Pain No-More. Just to see if our holy son is alive or dead or in Hades my fiend.

My friend there in The Great Holy Soul War our holy warrior son's, our Prince and Kings will inhale all their evil pain and sorrow. Their Fellow Sacrificial Lambs Bah-ing from the White Cross's Adrenaline. Rushing through their veins of the Great Soul War. While filling their Hollow Palace with their Holy Myrrh and Frankincense from the enemy of insanity.

My friend our Holy son Vainly attempts one more time to Wash his Pain away with Johnny Walkers son's holy water. Hoping, Praying he could become Normal Again. He knows he is only fooling himself and in denial of Gods Spiritual Truth.

My friend our holy son looks around this warriors Trojan battle field in a Bloody Stupor. He realizes that what he has consumed is only Hawaiian Pupus of the gods and goddesses. There is more to come.

Aloha.

My friend our holy son, will then Guzzle down Hot Beers. This Bud is for you. Silently Deeply within himself Crying his silent tears of Angry Hateful Whiskey. To try to hide the Memory of his own Hapless wretched Soul. Possibly a miserable death. God Bless his soul to fight another day in wooers hell for us again tomorrow.

My friend our Holy son, Odysseus I am, Witnesses the Great Trojan Wars Vietnamese Children Crying and Eating Cow Dung for food.

While their parents lay wasted and their villages Burning to the ground. Thinking it was us. Our homes in America Crying oh my God. What have we done.

My friend our holy son Odysseus I am, Killed the other blessed sons on the Other side of the Fence. Such as him at such a young age. Knowing nobody would understand his Implacable Position or Soul Pain. Nor did we really care back home in The USA. Our Holy son killed his own evil wooer brothers in the Back out of Frustration in their denial of this truth.

My friend for the Healing Love that our holy son, Odysseus I am, The King so desperately needed from his Healing Queen Penelope. Our holy son is Offered Femme De Chambre poor village whores. Their families Sold into Slavery to the evil wooers Military High Command for our evil wooers blood money that he wants nothing to do with them all. My friend our holy Sons Love, is Consecrated with the Delicacy of an Insalubrious Gonorrhea and Syphilis with the Approbation of the High Martyrdom Command of wooers in Ithaca while they buck each other in their ass and Pass on this Blessing to our women at home knowing we may never return to Kick their ass's for what they have done to us all, yet Odysseus IAm has returned.

Do you enjoy King Evelyn George David O Antinous Bill HusseinO my Silver Arrow through your wretched little neck?

Today, Evil Wooers all live in Non-Spiritual Holographic Political Hades. With their families and friends for their evil deeds. We can meet any of them in their Walking Living Hell as they walk around the many capitals of New York or Washington, DC or Texas or Kansas or Chicago or London, Frankfurt, Paris, or Beijing or Saudi Arabia. All around the globe you will know why God is All True Justice. They have all been cursed by God. They have to live in their evil Karma.

My friend our holy good son's, and the Odysseus I am, became an evil Hells Angels. Unknowingly, unconsciously, unwittingly, innocently I swear. The wooers created this evil environment. Global Community TV Brainwashing.

My friend our holy son, lives in a Hell and Sleeps in a hell of Hades as the good GI Dog that our son was trained to be. As we wished him to be. To Obey his Martyrdom Wooer masters. For our god and our country that I question if we know them at all. Only for me to Chew Thy Head Off now with the Razor sharp teeth of an evil black tiger dog that I am. You Methinketh now?

My friend our holy son, has No Place to Turn to in his Hardened Heart. No Place to Cry to in his Painful Heart. No place to Scream out to in his Heart of Steel Armor. In his mortal anguish that we gave to him. Because Real Warrior Men Do Not Feel. Nor do they Cry. They have a Heart of Gold.

My friend WHO would care any Wise in Ithaca that has fallen to the evil wooers. Is no more but a name. No more good or with honor throughout this world. That the one you asked God to bless you with is Suffering. In pain 24 hours a day. Possibly even to this day.

Possibly even if he is Still a Wounded Soul. YET alive. Maybe there is Hope in us in Him.

Maybe through our Prayers His Spirit will come back to him. Back to us.

Maybe if we love him he will come back home to us and save our wretched soul and country the USA.

My friend our Holy Son, Odysseus I am, is as the Rolling Stones of Time. Can't Get No Satisfaction. Nor peace of mind. Nor rest. Nor real spiritual Love. Until he comes home to his Holy Goddess's Healing Love Shack.

Now my friend when the Holy Nurse of Queen Penelope saw all the bodies of the dead and the Great River Gore of Blood. She made ready to Cry Aloud for joy beholding so great an adventure.

My friend our Holy Son's, and Odysseus I am, is like a Dylan's Stone that Gathers No Moss in Hades. He does not want to Stop there and gather Hades Moss. Thank you but no thank you.

My friend Odysseus I am, Spake Winged Words of Wisdom and Knowledge. Within thine own heart Rejoice my wise holy beautiful nurse. Be still. Cry not to Aloud. It is an Unholy thing to boast over slain men we know.

My friend our holy son's, and Odysseus I am, is as the Beetles who are on a Magical Mystery Soul Tour. I want to Hold Your Hand. Who among us knows its a majestical spiritual tour? Do we too Methinketh so? Now my friend, these evil wooers have their own destiny of the gods to overcome. Their own cruel deeds they will suffer. My friend

Come and Tell me the Many Tales of the Women in my Halls. Which of them have Dishonored me? Which are Guiltless women?

Anon my friend our son, Odysseus I am, has no more Heart to Love but for his Beautiful Good Queen.

Now my friend Odysseus will tell us all the truth.

Thou have Fifty Women Servants in Thy Halls that we have taught the ways of good house wifely.

Of these Twelve all have gone the way of Wooers Shame and Dishonor of thy Queen I must tell you.

My friend our son, Odysseus I am, has No More Compassion for his Own Wretched soul, but for the Soul of God is his to become, The I am.

Anon my friend Odysseus I am of Many Counsels answered the good Holy Nurse to bid the women to Come Here Who in time past Behaved themselves Unseemly as wooers.

My friend our holy son Telemachus U, has no more Forgiveness for Frankensteins evil monsters. As the wooers do not understand themselves Crying Aloud.

Why have you forsaken us oh god?

My friend Odysseus I am of Many Devices Spoke to Holy U Telemachus.

Begin you now to Carry Out these Dead Wooers. Tell these Wooer Women to help You now. Have them Cleanse the fair High Seats of the Senate and The Nobles tables with Holy Water and Sponges.

When you have set all of the House in Order, Lead the Maidens Outside the Established Hall. Slay them with your Long Sliver Blades till they have Given Up the Many wooers Ghost's. Forgotten the love they had at the Bidding of the evil wooers in their secret political alliance together against me their King.

My friend our holy son U Telemachus has no more Faith or Beliefs in the wooers or as benefits to draw upon but Fear and Doubt. My friend U Telemachus our Holy Son spoke to his followers. God Forbid that I should take these women's lives by a Clean Death that have dishonored my Queen mother Penelope and laid with the evil wooers. So.

My friend our Holy Son U Telemachus Tied a Cable to the Great Pillar. Non may Touch the Floor with Her Feet. Thrushes of doves falling into a net as they seek their roosting. Even so the Twelve Women held their Heads in a Row.

All about their Necks the Nooses are Cast Tight that they may die a Pitiful Death. They Writhed with their Feet and Arms and Hands for Space in Time. Air no longer while we methinketh upon their death.

My friend even today our sons and our daughters suffer because they have lost their heart and soul. Even their Soul Mates. They do not know how to even find their heart and soul to heal themselves with Gods love that they do not understand, do we?

My friend, We Politically blind wooers sent our OWN son's and daughter's to the Wooers Slaughter House. To be Slaughtered in war as Sacrificial Lambs to a Wooers God & Country that we really do not know. Methinketh. Why would we do this because we are sickly in spirit?

My friend, Frankenstein is a Headless Evil Monster Running their selfish political hidden agendas. Drunk on the best of the god's Wines of 1966 ChateauLa Fite Rothschild. Appetizers of Alaskan Salmon Lox and Russian Beluga Caviar. Dinner on corn feed Texas Bush Filet Mignon. The Dinner Course is our Soldiers human souls and blood.

All around the world the evil wooers profited from the Great Soul War. The sacrificial slaughter house in Vietnam. Smoking Havana cigars on the Wall Street's of life Congratulating each other on a job well done. They are now done in by Zeus.

From Heaven, A Holy Lotus Blossom Martyr Son Rodney Yanoson. He looks down into the evil wooers Fine Golden Purse to See where they put all of His Abundant Black Horse life blood. My friend from Heaven Holy Rodney Sees the Wooers Bank account is full of his precious blood.

My friend Holy Rodney notices the wooers bank account is with the Bank of Blood in New York and London of course. All Lascivious Vampire Bloodsuckers have their account with these fine institution he methinketh. Now my friend another Martyr son Holy Larry Johnson. Our son from Harlem will look around from Heaven into Earth.

See Who Loves These Wooers. Dressed in Macy Sheep's clothing. Who kiss's their wooers hand, their feet and their ass before they go to bed each night. Which wooers they pray to. Because they have no truth, nor honor, your Honor. Larry Steps upon their shriveled wooers Face at night while they sleep with his Black Soul Foot for what they did to him and his brothers and sisters.

My friend another martyr son Holy Doug who is Rich. Will look around again from Heaven. See possibly his own kind. Unconsciously, unwittingly cherishing the wooers. Adoring the Wooers fine linen clothes.

Diamond trinkets dripping veterans blood. His parents, upon his return, as he lays in his bed of sorrow wet with blood of his lost men in combat, tell him for his own good. Be as the wooers when he returns from Hades. Doug Vomits in their Face's in Disbelief of a Fools Paradise in bitter disappointment.

Another son Garland from Heaven will Look around again. See that the wooers are Really International Banking Vampires who have Sucked all the blood out of the People's Rainbows of Life. Out of all Who Love Them. While our son and daughter is off to a Great Soul War. All in a great Odyssey of Oddity. As the Sacrificial Hero who might not return. Yet he does not as you once knew him while we lived in denial of the truth in America.

My friend another martyr son Holy John Jack. He will Look Around. Think that God is Dead in The United States of Ithaca America. Their are no more beautiful rainbows in his Ithaca country home. Our son will Cry the Tears that he would rather be a Grateful Dead Head. Than be as the evil wooers that WE have invited for dinner at The White House in Washington, DC and in New York and Kensington Palace.

My friend now our Holy Warrior son has been Driven Insane. His Soul has left him rightly so.

Our son is spiritually Empty and the Hollow inside of him. Demoralized and Trashed by Frankenstein's Evil Vanities and their morals we do knowingly. When in Rome, Do as the Romans?

My friend our Holy son is with his Holy Fear of God. His Lord and Savior Jesus Christ. He cannot look into Heaven now. He looks Down to Hades out of Fear of Judgment. He knows not Gods true will. He is spiritually wounded Nor does he our holy son Willfully want to Look Upon the Blood. Upon his Hands in Shame. Because WE raised him. Thou Shall Not Kill. WE have killed. Because he has killed. Frankenstein has lied to us all in The USA. Methinketh.

My friend our Holy son makes a Warriors Wooer Necklace of his evil Enemies Fingers. Ears and Scalps that he has killed for the evil Blood Thirsty Vampire Wooers. A good souvenir of our Frankensteinian insanity at the Metropolitan Museum of Art. Funded by the Smithsonian Institute.

The Ancient Ones Lead out the Wooer Melanthius Evelyn George David Hussein through the Door Way. Through the Court Doors of Justice. They Cut Off His Nostrils. His Ears. A Pitiless Sword.

Then they Drew Forth his Vitals for the wooers to devour raw. Afterwards they Cut off his Hands and Feet for the wooers to eat. Cruel anger that is justly Plainly so in the spiritual truth. Now my friend our Holy son Cures them Evil Ears and Fingers Properly English. In the face of Sunny God. In a Strange Spiritual Way, His own fingers. His own ears. His own Scalp too. Methinketh. My good friend he makes himself a fine Wooers Bloody Necklace of Sorrow and Pain for our twisted worthless wrenched wooers necks. To show us all our truths in Farce. Wooers gods which are none. Because he lived Gods Truth the hard way in Hades and the wooers will too.

My friend how much our Holy son and daughter loves us. Yet we do not love him or her. Nor truly know them in America. Do we? I doubt it.

Now my friend, For all of OUR Holy Sons Noble Sacrifice and Valor our son gives himself The PTSD Medal of Honor.

The final Coup De Grace to our sons own good Tormented Soul. For a God and a Country that has no truth, no value, no morals, no honor to our son and daughters anymore. He Kills Himself as a Sacrificial Lamb. Should not do to himself this Dishonor. Methinketh.

Now the wooers evil devil of ignorance loves this and has taken our Holy sons and daughters Soul. The Wooers too in the name of a God and Country. While we Prance Proudly to Hades on a Jackson Moon Walk dance in Denial of this Truth. Even that our son's and daughters served God and Country well. Even in our denial of the truth.

Oh what hapless wretched conscious unconscious souls we humans have become. Even till today. If not unconsciously wretched, then to Hades for sure we will go. I ask you my friend. Is there an Inherited Understanding. Compassion. Most of all, Forgiveness.

While we are Fiddling with 30 pieces of Silver Received for Jesus Christ, a good Sacrificial Lamb as our veterans?Denial.

Now my friend the Odysseus I am of Many Counsels Stripped himself of his Warrior Rags.

I Leaped on the Great Threshold with my Godly Bow and Quiver full of Zeus's silver wooer vampire arrows. I Poured forth all the Swift shafts there before my holy feet. Suddenly I spoke among the evil wooers.

This terrible trial has ended at last. Now I will know of Another Spiritual Mark. Which never yet man has smitten. I have hit it. Apollo, Athena and Zeus do grant me renown. Odysseus I am I pointed the Bitter Arrow at the evil King Antinous Evelyn George David Bill Hussein of all the wooers on earth. Now my friend, The King of all the wooers, King Antinous Evelyn, was about Raise to His lips a Gold Two-Winged Chalice of Zeus. He was handling it to drink of the wine of the gods.

Death was Far from his thoughts. Who would among you evil wooer men and women at this Great Feast in a Great Hall would deem that One Man amongst so many. How hardy soever he is. Would bring him a Foul Death. Black fate to all the wooers on Earth.

Odysseus I am, aimed.

I Smote him with the Silver Vampire wooer arrow in the Throat.

The Silver pointed Arrow Head Passed Clean out Through his wretched neck.

Antonious fell Gasping. Writhing. Sidelong. The Golden winged cup Dropped from his Wretched Hand as he was Smitten Violently.

All at once through his Nostrils there came up a Thick Jet of a slain man's evil blood.

Quickly the Evil Emperor of the Wooers Spurned the Table from him with his feet and his hands. He spilled all the food on the ground.

The bread and the Roasted wooers flesh were all defiled for all the wooers to eat forever. Fear struck them all. Anon then my friend.

Odysseus I am of Many Spiritual Counsels Looked Fiercely upon them wooers all. Odysseus I Am Spake so to them.

You dogs. You said in your hearts that I should never more come home from the land of the Great Vietnam Soul War. In that you Wasted my Home and Country. Laid with my Maidservants by Force. Traitorously Conspired and wooed my wife while I was yet alive.

You had no fear of God and Gods God's and Goddesses, that hold the Wide World Heaven. Nor of the Indignation of Men hereafter more?Now the Hands of time of death have been made fast upon your wretched wooers necks one and all.

Even so as Odysseus I am spoke. A Black Evil Fear Begot hold upon the wretched wooers limbs of all. Each man looked about Shaking and Writhing Where he might Shun Utter Doom they Methink. My friend, the Evil Wooer Eurymachus George David Evelyn Hussein O alone answered him, and spoke.

If that Art indeed Odysseus I am of Ithaca America, Come home Again. Right Wisdom you speakest thus of all that the Wooers have wrought upon America. The many Infatuate Deeds in thy White House, Senate and Holy Halls.

Many in the fields of our Life. Here now Lies the Evil Emperor King Antinous of All the wooers dead.

It is Antonious who brought all these things upon you. Another greedy soul with a hidden purpose that the Lord Cronion has not fulfilled for him. Namely, that He might Himself Be King Over all the Land of the Established Universal Ithaca.

He was to have Lain in Wait for thy Holy son U Telemachus and kill him.

King Antonious is slain after his just deserving this good. King Odysseus, Do you spare thy people, even thy own?Odysseus Spoke.

NO! Will we from now on go about the township and yield us amends for all that has been Eaten and Drunken in thy halls by all evil wooers.

Each wooer for himself bringing atonement of Twenty Buffalo Spiritual Worth. Requiting in all their gold and bronze and silver and diamonds. All their Estates. All their Lands. Till then none may blame you Odysseus that thou are angry with wooers. Then Odysseus I am of Many Spiritual Counsels looked fiercely upon him, and said.

Eurymachus George David Evelyn Bill Hussein O, Not even if You give me All your Estate and lands and Banks. Or All that you have. Whatsoever else you might in any wise add thereto.

So that I would henceforth hold my hands from slaying thee all.

All the wooers will pay for all their transgressions world wide.

Their will be none that shall escape from utter doom. The wooers Knees were Straightway Loosened. Their Hearts Melted within themselves with the Smell of Doom.

My friend later in time I hated myself for being in the Great Trojan Vietnam Soul War.

I hated from my own ignorance.

I had to learn to forgive myself and others. Ah Stranger. I rejoiced in finding God and the Gods and Goddesses. Good and Goodness in the Vietnam War. Majestically even my Good Soul. My friend in the Truth.

I recollected my friends Jesus, James, Socrates and Homer.

My friend I Consciously Unconsciously allowed myself to be turned into a wooers Frankenstein's monster to learn Truth in War.

My good friend I wanted to discover the whole truth so help me God. I did Re+Collect the truth the Hard Way.

My friend It is very difficult to go to Hades. Heaven and back again. To live through this majestical spiritual soul journey. Even for you too methinketh.

I Odysseus I am gave myself the permission to Discover and to Re+Collect the Spiritual Truth. In the Beginning of this Great Soul Odyssey.

I did not Realize the Price I was to pay for Truth, Wisdom, Knowledge, and God. He Restoreth My Soul. Personal Experience in Divine Wisdom and Knowledge can be very expensive.

Yet to me my friend many of us are Little Frankensteins. Consciously. Unwittingly. Unknowingly. Unconsciously creating genetically a lesser god. An unaware mutant named him and her. Giving wooers the power in their own image and in life.

Yes, my friend it is true. I and you will possibly go to Hades or to Heaven for our good deeds. Unless I and you confess our sins to ourselves and others, our Gods and Goddesses. Our Father & Mother God and fear NOT what is Thy Will Oh God.

My friend we cannot save our soul. Nor will we save others souls by being out of Harmony with God and Nature. There is No Political Power that can save a soul. Methinketh, Only God can do this miracle called Forgiveness and Healing.

We can forgive ourselves this is true. We also need LOVE a Higher Power. God. It is called Humility in Harmony. I knew back then in the Great Trojan Soul War that I could Never Return to a Normal Civilian life after my War experiences. I have been Changed for Life as All my fellow spiritual warriors who fought in the Great Vietnam war, or in any War for that matter on Earth.

Deep down inside of me I truly wanted to die. I could not stand myself anymore. I became a wooers sinner for God and Country. I wanted to give up this hellish life I was living in the wooers War. I was not afraid to die and face God. I was methinking often. When is death ever going to come to Free my soul?

I prayed often to God and Jesus Christ for Understanding, Mercy, Compassion, Forgiveness and Healing.

I did my best. I conducted myself as honorably as any good honorable Soldier is required to by the Code of Ethics. The Honor of a Spiritual Warrior.

I never in my Wildest Dreams ever Imagined that what I witnessed in the Great Soul War is how life really is in Hells wars on Earth. I did not know. I have never experienced war before. I am Positive others have seen more Ignoble Acts than I have. I thank God for that innocence. I did my best with what I had to work with in Hades.

I am a Spiritual Warrior. I Served my Country well and good. I Served My God. I Failed my Way into Success. I Live my karma and continue to do so by Gods Grace and will. I Smitten in the Line of Duty.

These are the Choice's I made. I have no excuses.

This Killing position, is the position all wooer governments put our young innocent men and women in a war. The War Cry. Kill or be killed!

Wooer Governments know that if you are faced with death we will kill to survive.

What Would You Do?

My friend this is Common Knowledge is it not? As Socrates spake. Re+Collection is in our Memory Within us all.

As Odysseus I am spake. I Re + Member. Do You Re+ Member?

I remember my spiritual be here now. Thou Shall Not Kill.

Is this true? In What Situation is this applicable?

We must all decide this for ourselves.

Unless my friend we are a spiritual warrior. We have to defend ourselves for Our God and Our Country, this is true.

Is there an Honorable War? What was WWII?

My friend I ask you this question. Are we not even today, unconsciously consciously politically religiously killing? What is Crime against Humanity? Most of humanity is living out of Harmony. Methinketh.

This Smitten is What I would call an Ancient Tragedy.

To defend our selves from an evil Third Force.

The Politics of Ecstasy. The insanely invisible hidden political and religious wooers agendas. My friend, I nor any of my men in my squad ever abused any enemy soldiers.

Others may have done crimes against humanity. You can ask them. They can tell you the truth if you have the courage to ask them.

Ask The President of The USA. Ask The Senators of our Wooers Senate. They may answer you honestly. If they have freed themselves of their political and religious emotional pain and bondage and conditioning.

They did Swear an Oath in Secret to the Evil Wooers who run the world and Ithaca to Keep Silent? Yes.

To Act Stupid. Yes.

Know and Acknowledge Nothing of their Secret Wooer hidden Conspiracy in America. A Secret Conspiracy all around the world. They and their Family members Die by their wooers oath.

My friend, I have never taken Gods finger, nor Gods ear, nor Gods scalp as wooers do. It is not Honorable to me. If war was not enough violence nor a crime against humanity. Wethinketh.

In truth it is our Wooer President and Senators who authorized and took the fingers of our enemy to be used as a fear and doubt to all who challenge them. They are the evil wooers.

Around my neck I wore my Cross and Dog tags. God/Dog tags of a warrior that Guided and Protected me through the Valley of the Shadow of Death in my mind as a Holy Cross if it was not my karma's cross methinketh. It made me sick to my stomach to see warriors who had taken body parts out of their insanity from their killing experiences in the Great War.

Thinking it was a Sign of Honor as many other warriors have done from many cultures from around the world. Even torturing prisoners of war as the North Vietnamese soldiers did at the Hanoi Hilton. I am sure the US Government and South Vietnamese Governments did too. Throwing enemy soldiers out of helicopters if they did not talk.

Water Boarding? Electrical shock treatment. Drug treatment. Presidential truth serum.

I am sorry for everyone.

It is all ridiculous. What a waste of human resource. Of Nature. Of good tax dollars war. WE methinketh. Odysseus Iam of Many Devices Methinketh Good thoughts. I am methinketh. We can CO-Create Goodness now that we know God.

In my squad my friend we saved Vietnamese children, Villagers and even Enemy soldiers lives that were wounded. I had them air evacuated to a US Army hospital in Saigon or Bien Hoa. We chose to do this as an Act of Compassion. We would want compassion given to us. It is only natural. My friend we realized in our squad that on both sides of the war we are our own enemy. Our Own savior. Our own god clothed as a warrior for God and Country. Some of us Realized that God lives in both of us. We are both Gods children. Methinketh.

We Invaded Vietnam. We had no business in Vietnam. It was about the Oil in the Gulf of Tonkin. The Chinese Golden Triangle Heroin.

Guns and Gold being traded with the enemy for Guns and Heroin. The Chinese and Russians obviously funded the North Vietnamese.

See All. See the whole picture. The wooers use us all.

The evil world wide wooers make money slaughtering the innocent on both sides of the fence.

They are never in the war. Nor are their children. They run the banks world wide. We did the best we could in the middle of hell. How would you do my friend?

I hope well when it is your turn. They way things are going in Ithaca, You may have an opportunity to show us all what you will do to defend your home or neighborhood or city or even your country that has been taken over by the evil wooers.

Life is mimicking the movies today. It used to be the opposite. If this is true, It will not be long for shit to hit the fan. Shit happens when we least suspect it. What is 9/11. America taken over by the NWO.

Somebody knew it was going to happen. You were not privileged as the White House and certain Senators who knew it was in the works.

Most of the time in war, it is hard to see Heaven from hells perspective. Because we are on the bottom looking up. Yet my friend once every so often in any moment of Hades.

In a Flash of Explosive Light or an act of compassion or in a Prayer to Christ. God would show Himself & Herself that They Are Here with me and you. Even with us right now. Angel Michael's message. James, the Time has come for you to give up your life. I was going around and around in my head methinketh, oh my God.

I was beginning to wonder, is it really true? If it is, what can I do?

Is there anything I could do to avoid my black fate?Maybe this Destiny is a Blessing in Disguise. I will go home to Heaven if God wills it. If it is true, I will gladly die tomorrow and go to Heaven. I will see the Light of my Ancestors and God too.

Who would not want to visit with Orpheus and Rhadamanthus. Christ and Homer and Palamedes and Plato.

You know my friend I could possibly Stay here as my Knees Loosen. I go on living in Hades with all my good warrior friends methinketh.

Tomorrow March 5th is my Squads turn to lead in a Reconnaissance Mission. My friend I could have made an excuse. Say I am Sick. Chicken Out. Run from Destiny and Life. Yet Why?I wondered my friend. Am I really going out on a mission tomorrow?

It could get cancelled. I really don't know what I will do tomorrow. I will see tomorrow.

Am I really going to Die methinketh repeatedly?

I am wondering. I thought about everything for a very long time.

It is amazing my friend how long a night can be. Ten Thousand years or more. This so called death is good I believe.

I didn't know what to do. I am a Buck Sergeant and the Squad Leader of our ARP team. I am supposed to be Brave Hearted. I am supposed to not have fear. Yet my friend I do have Fear and I am afraid.

Yet I will to go forward in life. I will not tell a lie.

This night I was even thinking of my New Men in my squad who are Inexperienced in combat. Our mission is to look for a North Vietnamese Guerrilla base camp. The NVA are smart and tuff.

I was wondering who will I ask to walk as Point Man tomorrow?

I don't like to ask anybody inexperienced to walk point just to save my life. It isn't right or Noble. It happens every day in war. What Am I going to do Oh Lord?

My friend after thinking about God and my guardian angels message all night and into the early morning I was exhausted.

I decided to walk Point Man myself.

You know my friend. I worked it all out in my head. It is better for me to walk as point man for my own squad. If God has willed it that I will be Smitten with a Golden Arrow and Die so be it. Better me than some young man who is inexperienced. He could live another day in Hades too. I seriously considered. I did receive a message from God Hermes and my Guardian Angel Michael concerning my fate.

Destiny. I thought to myself and God, that it was the safest thing I could do even if I did not want to die or get wounded tomorrow, Thy will be done Oh My Lord. My friend I decided I was Ready to give my life up for another life in Heaven.

To give our life is to receive our life. Reincarnation. Reborn.

I thought to God and to myself Silently. Oh God please take my soul to Heaven and don't stop anyplace in between!

FREEDOM.

I shared with my good friend John who I asked to walk back up for me, that I had this message from God and this Inner Gut Feeling that I was going to die or get shot. John told me he had the same feeling.

Ah Stranger, how strange is this? We had gone through so much together in Trojan Vietnam Soul War that sometimes we Think we are Invincible. We can Laugh at ourselves in Denial. Yet we knew deep down inside of us, John and I knew that today is our day.

We should remember to breath in and out The Light.

March 5th We ate our Powdered Eggs Breakfast and put our gear on and loaded into our Black Hawk winged helicopters. My friend I didn't tell anybody else but John about God and what my guardian angel Michael said to me that was going to happen to me. Because I didn't what anybody else to get Paranoid and Think Something Awful and a black fate is going to happen to them too. Four Black Hawk winged helicopters with four Long Range Reconnaissance Patrol teams. 6 men per tcam, were loaded and ready to go. We took off very quietly. We flew Gracefully up into the morning sky as Zeus's black winged ships with no identification can do. We always flew with the passenger side doors open as warriors do. I sat cross legged on the black winged eagle right up to the edge of the helicopter door with my winged golden bow AR-15 rifle in my lap looking down on the world below me as we flew over jungle on our mission. Once we were airborne gravity always held me in place like a Great Bald Eagle holding Zeus's mighty arrows in his powerful godly claw.

My friend It really is Very Beautiful up above in the sky. The gods and goddesses. The Angels. The birds, the pilots, the flight attendant's of God are so fortunate to have such marvelous views in life in a war zone. My friend Life is very Peaceful from up above and Inspiring.

All is Well. Ola Kala. Sun Rise and Sun Sets are a real wow.

We flew for about an hour and a half. We landed someplace close to the Cambodian border that does not exist. We arrived just before sunrise. We got out of the black winged ships and got our leather maps out and started on this mission to find this North Vietnamese Guerrilla base camp. My friend I lead the way walking as point man. John was behind me by 20 yards. The rest of the black winged men were spread out 50 to 100 yards behind us.

I had this feeling that it is going to be a very long, hot and humid day.

The jungle in this area is very thick and dense. There were many times when we had to use a machete to hack our way through this dense hot humid jungle. I didn't like that the Sirens of the

Machete. They are screaming messages through the jungle of my coming home. An Uncomfortable feeling. We walked for hours and I was exhausted. Just thinking about Which Turn and in Which Moment was I going to die in, and if at all.

Maybe nothing is going to happen to me. It was a Bad Dream. I was worrying all about Nothing Hermes. I don't know anymore. It does not matter anymore. It should.

In fact, I don't know anything anymore. All I know is I am here and now. The Suspense is overwhelming me. There were moments when I was so tired of thinking of what was going to happen to me, or possibly going to happen, that I though I was going to die just from my Mental Exhaustion of methinking.

As I am very quietly walking through an area of dense jungle the birds suddenly stopped singing my friend. Ah, stranger, how strange is this?

This dark jungle with filtered light streaming through the tree canopy became very quite and very still. There is Total silence.

I should have known that something is going to happen at any moment.

I could feel the presence of someone but I wasn't sure. Maybe a God or Goddess or some evil perchance?Could have been a spirit guide. An ancestor watching and waiting for me?

I am usually very sure of myself but the Gods have subtly blinded me. I was exhausted from machete hacking. Walking for hours in this very hot dark and humid jungle.

You know my friend I was Thinking about my Destiny.

I should have been Concentrating on what's going on in front of me.

I have to tell you that as I stepped over some branches into what appeared to be a small clearing, my left foot is caught on a branch for a moment in time. Almost as some evil god grabbed and twisted my foot from underneath the ground to trip me up. Then he quickly let go of my foot.

Suddenly my friend I Had goose bumps all over my body.

I stumbled but caught myself before falling down on the ground, on my face Homer. Now my friend Socrates I was off guard. Out of Balance. Out of Harmony. I had suddenly stumbled into this ungodly clearing.

I did not like this evil position I was in my friend.

I will tell you my friend I was leaning forward. Out of balance. Facing downwards towards Hades. Looking into the ground below. To my right side. I was bewildered and blinded by the Gods.

My friend I should have been looking Straight Ahead were the Gods are veiled and they are waiting for me in The Light.

I had this very uncomfortable feeling that something good or wrong and evil is about to happen. As some strange blessing of the Gods? I gathered myself together.

I noticed out of the corner of my golden brown eye an underground bunker complex of some evil god per chance He is looking straight at me. Oh Shit.

Suddenly my friend I can see there is a black shadow of an evil warrior in the bunker about 30 yards in front of me.

He has been watching me all along as I have been making my way towards him. I can see he has me in his winged bow rifle sights. His golden arrow is Aimed straight at me.

I am thinking, Oh my God I can't believe what is happening. It is happening and it is happening now.

Now my friend Every Motion I am making is going on in a very Slow Motion as the Gods have willed me this blessing. Slow Motion.

My friend I cannot seem to move fast enough through these Clouds of black Fate because I am trapped in this veil of Gods Light.

I begin to turn to my left side swinging my golden winged bow AR-15 rifle towards the bunker.

As I turn and face the bunker this evil one fires his winged AK-47 arrows from his winged bows automatic rifle. I fire a burst of arrows from my winged bow AR-15 rifle at the same time. Oh my God. Everything is in Slow Motion as the Gods have willed it in this good deed.

I can See these Golden Arrows leaving his Winged Bow Rushing towards Me on the Wings of Apollo in a Great Bright Blinding Light that Comets towards me.

I am not seeing anything in this Bright Flash of Clear Light from God's winged bow and it is blinding me my friend.

The Sun Light is Extremely bright.

I have to close my eyes. I cannot see anything.

I can only Feel a sudden freedom in my body and soul and I am flying in this incredible speed of light.

Suddenly I am in the Light.

I am ripped out of my body by two Angels and we are flying into and through this bright Light.

Upwards at an extremely fast speed. Faster than a Rocket.

Faster than Superman.

Faster than a Speeding Bullet.

My body, and mind are melting away as we fly higher and higher.

We fly Into and through the Sun. Suddenly I Am in Heaven.

Oh my God.

CHAPTER 3
Flying Home With The Angels Into Heaven

Miraculously to our surprise the next thing I know is I am released out of my body by two of Gods Angels and we are traveling at an incredible speed upwards into a very clear bright light. The Sun.

The beautiful faces of these two Angels look just like what our ancestors look like. Guardian Angels are usually one of our beloved ancestors. As our Grandmother, Grandfather, Aunt, Uncle, Father, Mother, Brother or Sister who has passed on to the other side and is now a Guardian Angel over us. Very simple.

Angels are radiantly handsome and beautiful with an aura of clear white light all around them. They do not have wings on their backs as most people are lead to believe in Fairy Tales or in Mythology.

In the past the reason artist painted Angels with Wings on their backs is to signify to the viewer that Hermes the messenger of Zeus has sent another of his messengers, The Angels, which are from another place in life called Heaven bringing a message to us from God.

Who else would have a sincere interest in watching over us while on Earth, but an ancestor directed by Gods administrators.

As we are flying upwards I cannot hold on to my body or to anything else in my life. My life is actually melting away as we travel upwards into The Light. I feel weightless and very soft like a feather floating through the air in an upward spiraling motion. As a ballerina spiraling upwards in spiritual inspiration of dance.

The best way I can describe my upward journey into the Light is in this way.

When I was a young boy during Christmas time I would play with the cardboard tubes from the Christmas wrapping paper. As with a telescope made out of cardboard, I would look through our snowy window at the Sun through a Christmas wrapping paper cardboard tube.

I would see the sun and everything all around me where ever I looked. It was fun. Yet now this special light tube that I am flying through is a tube of light full of very Bright Clear Light and is lined with Angels of the Light. We are flying through this tube at an overwhelming speed towards and into the sun of the light. All that I know is I am in the Light.

I have no other sense of reality nor do I remember anything of what I was doing before all this happened. I did not even remember I was on a combat mission in Vietnam. All I can do now is to let go of everything I know in life and go with the Angels flowing upwards into the Light.

Our entire life is flashing by us peeling away as we travel upwards.

Amazingly, We have a feeling of Dejavu.

I cannot look directly into the bright light because it is blinding me from its brilliance, as looking at the sun on a clear sunny day.

I am being gently escorted by our two Guardian Angels and I feel there are thousands of Angels all around me.

My two Guardian Angels are Guarding me and Protecting me as we race into and Through the Light. The only thought that comes into our consciousness is wow.

I can hear beautiful gentle music all around us on this spiritual soul journey.

I can feel we are flying into and through the Sun and I am being purified by the bright Sun Light as we approach Heaven.

The Suns Rays are gently melting my old life away into Light.

I feel we are a part of the universal candle flame, that is using my past life, the wick and bees wax to create us all from the Light. We are Light.

Miraculously as my soul journey to Earth began with Angels in Heaven, I am now flying through the Sun of the Light returning into Heaven with Angels. Wow. To my amazement I am greeted by my father, relatives and friends who are in Heaven. I am crying from joy. I am really happy and overwhelmed.

I realize, Oh my God, I am back home again.

A Modern Parable that I believe can help us visualize our arrival into Heaven.

The Itinerary to Heaven is beyond our control.

Arriving into Heaven is very much as going on a long unexpected airplane ride to visit our family and friends whom we have not seen for a very long time. The airplane arrives at its destination after a long journey. We are tired yet glad to be home. The airplane safely lands on the runway with a perfect landing. We breath a sign of relief. The airplane slowly taxis to the arrival gate. We made it.

The airplane doors open and we get ready to get off the plane. We wonder who is going to meet us at the airport, if anybody.

We are walking along the dimly lit airplane tunnel ramp into the well lighted waiting area for arriving passengers. As we approach the waiting area we are looking for somebody we know but the airplane tunnel ramp is dimly lit.

As we near the doorway to the waiting area we begin to See bright light and people in the background.

We not know who is there waiting for us, if anybody.

As we walk through the Doorway and into the brightly lighted waiting area we See somebody we know. We see Them.

They have been patiently waiting for our arrival on the Other Side of The Doorway in The Light.

We see our Loved Ones. We smile and we cry with Joy. We hug each other. They ask us how was our Journey? We start talking and sharing our life experiences on Earth. They load our luggage into their car and they take us Home. They give us something to eat and drink.

Our father, mother, family and friends are happy with our safe arrival home. We talk for a very long time. We are tired and they take us to our room. We get our pajamas out and go to the bathroom. We brush our teeth and take a refreshing bath. We get into our bed and have wonderful dreams. Oh my God, I am home again.

Classic Parables that can help us visualize our arrival into Heaven.

These Parables are from The Holy Bible and are very appropriate as to how I felt when I arrived in Heaven.

We are positive that these parables equally apply to women and men, young and old. We would like to humbly make a suggestion from our heart for women, men, sons and daughters who read these parables.

First, Please read the parables as we find them in the Holy Bible, King James version. Afterwards you may want to change the words around as man to woman, father to mother, sons to daughters, he to she, him to her and himself to herself for further clarity in methinketh.

We all have a father and mother, and possibly a daughter or son or both and it is Ola Kala with us and God to read these parables in these other ways to feel the Spiritual Love. Grok It.

St. LUKE, 15.

A certain man had two sons: And the younger of them said to his father, Father, give me the portion of goods that falleth to me. He divided unto them his living. Not many days after the younger son gathered all together, and took his journey into a far country, and there wasted his substance with riotous living. And when he had spent all, there arose a mighty famine in that land; and he began to be in want. He went and joined himself to a citizen of that country; and he sent him into his fields to feed swine. And he would fain have filled his belly with the husks that the swine did eat: and no man gave unto him. And when he came to himself, he said, How many hired servants of my father's have bread enough and to spare, and I perish with hunger.

I will arise and go to my father, and will say unto him, Father, I have sinned against Heaven, and before thee, And am no more worthy to be called thy son: make me as one of thy hired servants.

And he arose, and came to his father. But when he was yet a great way off, his father saw him, and had compassion, and ran, and fell on his neck, and kissed him. And the son said unto him, Father, I have sinned against heaven, and in thy sight, and am no more worthy to be called thy son.

But the father said to his servants, Bring forth the best robe, and Put it on him; and put a ring on his hand, and shoes on his feet: And bring hither the fatted calf, and kill it; and let us eat, and be merry: For this my son was dead, and is alive again; he was lost, and is found. They began to be Merry.

Now his elder son was in the field: and as he came and drew nigh to the house, he heard music and dancing. And he called one of the servants, And asked what these things meant. He said unto him, Thy brother is come; and thy father hath killed the fatted calf, because he hath received him safe and sound. And he was angry, and would not go in: therefore came his father out, And intreated him. And he answering said to his father, Lo, these many years do I serve thee, neither transgressed I at any time thy commandment: And yet thou never Gavest me a kid, that I might make merry with my friends: But as soon as this thy son was come, which hath devoured thy living with harlots, thou hast killed for him the fatted calf. And he said unto him, Son, thou art ever with me, and all that I have is thine. It was meet that we should make merry, and be glad: for this thy brother was dead, and is alive again; and was lost, and is found.

St. LUKE 15. 8

Either what woman having ten pieces of silver, if she lose one piece, Doth not light a candle, and sweep the house, and seek Diligently till she find it?

And when she hath found it, she Calleth her friends and her neighbors Together, saying, Rejoice with me; for I have found the piece Which I had lost.

Likewise, I say unto you, there Is joy in the presence of angels of God over one sinner that Repenteth.

This is how I found my self before God in Heaven.

With our arrival into Heaven there is a great joy with happiness And love everywhere.

CHAPTER 4
Heaven Is Very Beautiful

When I arrived into Heaven it is to an Awe Inspiring Estate called The Kingdom of Heaven. The Castles of France and England are shanty cold shacks in comparison to Heaven and Heavens Hospitality.

It is very obvious to us that God Created Heaven with Spiritual Thought and Love.

The first thing I noticed is everything in Heaven is in Peace and in Harmony.

Heaven is the most Symphonic Landscape Spiritual Scenery of Enchanting Mountains Majestic. Melodies of Meadows, Graceful Green Pastures, Lovely Lakes and Rivers and Oceans of Love and with the most Gorgeous Gardens I have ever had the Privilege to Live Within.

All the landscape in Heaven Illuminates in Peace in Love in The Universal Light. Words are totally useless in describing what Heaven really looks like my friend. The word wow works well for us.

The Lovely Spiritual Images I now have of Heaven is this.

A Love I can See. A Love I can Feel.

A Love I can Smell. A Love I can Taste.

A Love I spiritually can Touch.

A Love I can Enjoy in our Life.

My friend, If you would like to now receive these Spiritual Images of Heaven, You will by reading this Good book and breathing in and out all Of these good Images in Peace. When you are ready, we can close our eyes and breath them into our being.

Heavens spiritual flowers are the most Fragrant of Essence's and the Most Lovely Brilliant Flowers I have ever gazed upon as they Radiate the Beauty in Life as Gods flowers of spiritual love.

All of the Landscape and Flowers are the Emanation of Life as their Colors are in Clear Light from Within Themselves. Look closely my friends and we can actually See the Beautiful Flowers Breathing and Dancing in Harmony to the movement of Music and Life. The Luminosity of Heavens Beautiful Landscape with All the Beautiful Colors of the Rainbow are Miraculous and Wonderful to Witness and Play Within.

Heaven is Beauty.

There are many Beautiful Souls in their Spiritual Soul bodies from every country, race and religion in Heaven. Actually there is no race but Souls in God. We are all One Soul.

No matter what one's soul age is, everyone is Youthful looking, Healthy, Happy and Peaceful. Spiritually Consciously Content Being.

There are also many Beautiful Animal Friends Playing in the Beautiful Landscape in Heaven.

The Spiritual Air in Heaven is Spiritually Invigorating. Full of Spiritual Manna and Prana. My friend Please feel free to take a deep breath and refresh yourself now while we are in the Light and in Heaven on this short visit with me and God.

The Clear Spiritual Water's in Heaven is the Best Water we have ever Tasted. Holy Water is True Love. When I tasted Heavens Mountain Spring Water all I could say was Oh my God this spring water tastes so good. The Best.

The Nature of Heaven is in Total Harmony through Gods design of Spirit in Peace in Love in Light Flowing Together like Beautiful Music. As Lovers in Love Kissing Lovely to the Beautiful Music of Love in Their Hearts. Of Course there is Beautiful Music, Song, and Dance in Heaven. Where do you Think it all came from but in Spiritual Methinketh?All the Good Songs, Dances and Music are All first created in Heaven.

The Many Celebrations and Rites of Passage and the many different Wedding Celebrations from all around the Earth in many countries are Created by Gods God's & Goddess's in Heaven. The Gods and Goddess's are Angels too.

There are Gods Minstrels that play their Golden Harp and Lyre's and all many other Beautiful Instruments of Music. They Sing for God and Gods God's & Goddesses in Heaven and for us too.

We Now know All the Good Music in Heaven is Spiritual Inspiration in the Form of Music, and is Created in Heaven, and is the Inspiration of Gods Soul and Love for us all.

For those of us my friend who want to now Receive and Hear this Beautiful Inspiring Music to Sing, and Dance and Play on Earth, We can Receive this Beautiful Spiritual Music now.

Lend us your ear over Here. Cup your hand around your Ear and Listen within Your Inner Ear, and Hear the Beautiful Music Playing now within YOU.

I am positive that if you ask any humble musician on Earth how they really received their Beautiful Music, they would gladly say from Gods Heavenly Inspiration.

As I look around Heaven, there is an Abundance of Everything Good which is God.

By the Way my friend, Do You know What the difference is between God and Good and how God Created GOOD?

A Letter O.

O is Gods Good Thoughts of what Good is with All of the Fine Detail.

My friend If you Believe in the Power of Gods Word, We will now Realize that the difference between our good and not so good is our O thoughts.

Oh, what Good Thoughts do we have of What is Good in our life becomes our good or not so good in our life on Earth. God gave all of us sons and daughters free will. We use our free will to CO-Create our Life on Earth. GOD is GOOD.

GOODNESS is GOD.

We can be as good as we can think for our selves our good thoughts that do manifest each moment of our lives. My friend Good is the same word as God. It just has an extra O to expand the Word God as in the Creation of Something Spiritual into more Good.

By the Way my friend, Everyone in Heaven travels by Spiritual Soul Thoughts. It's is also known as traveling through and with the Light.

One minute we are Here.

The next minute we are There.

Bingo!

One minute You are Here with me and the next minute You are There with God and me in Heaven and throughout this story called Love Is The Door Way In to our mind, body, heart, soul and Into Heaven.

My friend I traveled Spiritually with Angels this Way all throughout Heaven, And even on Earth. Angels travel this way through The Light on Earth because our Earth is actually Spirit-Matter created from Light.

Without the Sun and without The Light there would be no Earth or Life anywhere in Creation. Heaven is GOOD. GOD is GOOD.

Now my friend We do Recollect what the difference is between God and Good. God is Methinkething Good Thoughts. God is Every-Thing Good. All Good is from and created by God.

GOD is G 'O' O D. 'O'. Now my friend with 'O', We Can CO-Create Good too.

Now we go dear friend, Of a Truth no one of mortal men may contend with Zeus, for Gods Mansions and Gods Treasures are Many and Everlasting. Let us Look within our mind. Everything is Within Us, not out side of us. We live within our spiritual body, mind, heart and soul.

The planet Earth is as a spiritual mirror reflection that God created in matter. Some-thing as a carbon copy A Spiritual Hologram of earth. Life on Earth is always changing.

It is a spiritual copy of a part of Heaven, yet it is not Heaven. It's a part of a copy of God's Creation called Life on Earth. Another humble description of Heaven for My Friends Around the World. It is very difficult to adequately describe Heaven because of Words that have limits.

Because we have to use Words and word Pictures to write with, and Words and Paintings do not really do justice to properly express Heavens Spiritual BEAUTY because God is Beautiful Beyond Words.

God is spiritual. Words of Poetry have helped Homer, Socrates, Shakespeare and others describe Life, Heaven and Beauty the best they can. Yet it is really never good enough because deep within our Heart and Soul is Beauty, and BEAUTY is Spiritual in Nature. Heavenly Art So Beautiful my Dear Love.

We are HEAVENS Beauty HERSELF.

Clothed in ETERNAL Garments of Golden Spiritual Love. We Love Your Art.

Your Radiant Eyes are the Beautiful Twinkling Stars Up Above.

Thy Smile is a Beautiful Rosé Pink One of Love for us.

Your Virgin Skin is Olives Oil of Mother God Who Are Thee.

Thy Fragrant Essence is a Lovely Virgin Rose.

Thou Art Beautiful, as BEAUTY is Beautiful of Yourself, No other Art My Dear Heaven is You.

We Love your Loving Heart and Beautiful Smile. Your Loving Soul So Gentle Caring Gracefully for us. How Fortunate and Blessed we are.

For a hapless, wretched soul we have been.

We Look Upon Thy BEAUTY, Thy Graceful Face of Love, That smiles upon us all.

Odysseus I am in Spiritual Love with You.

My Dear Heaven of Grace, Your Art is Truly BEAUTY, That Heals My Soul, And Holds My Heart, Within your Loving Heart. I LOVE YOU.

My friend, Methinking Heavens Landscape is very similar to the Earth's, in that it is Gods Abundance of Love for All of us, that is Good and Even Much More than we know. Heaven is in Spirit Infinitely Spiritually Multidimensional beyond 360 degrees.

What I want to humbly say about Heavens Spiritual Multiple Dimensional-ism is that each and every one of us has our own beliefs as to how Heaven is until we arrive in Heaven in our Soul Life.

Even some methink how we would like Heaven to look like because of our personal beliefs and conditioning.

It would be incorrect for me to say that this is The Way Heaven is for everybody. This is The Way Heaven is for me.

Methinketh this could not nor would not be True until we experience Heaven for your self.

Heaven is a very multidimensional Spiritual Place Within Gods Creation. Heaven looks just like what one might imagine Heaven would look like but beyond our Imagination and Much More Beautiful.

For me or for anybody to exactly describe Heaven as Heaven actually is, would be like trying to describe what Love is or what Gods Entire Creation Looks like, yet the best we can see today is not even the tip of an iceberg of Spiritual Love and Heaven or even our universe and the many other universes we are unaware of.

This Iceberg of Spiritual Love is Ourselves, our Sun, the Earth and all that She holds. The planets that revolve around the Sun, and we cannot even see all that I have just described very clearly at all methinketh. There are many other spiritual worlds too.

There are no words in any language that can actually accurately describe God or Heaven other than possibly the simple word I will humbly draw upon this Sandy Spiritual Kealakekua Bay beach in Kona Hawaii. I will even utter that word and the sound is wow.

In Truth, Heaven is Heaven.

Heaven is All of God in Goodness.

Heaven is The Way Heaven is Created by God. Beautiful. That is the Truth. This is my humble description of what Heaven looks like when I visited Heaven. Wow.

Of course My friend if one other Soul goes through The Light into Heaven and Returns they could possibly Elaborate more Clearly than I am capable of expressing how Heaven is Spiritual BEAUTY and Heaven is Beautiful. Now I pray this humble explanation will help us Feel Good about Heaven and Give us a Sign of Relief as we Exhale All our Fears and Doubts about our Soul Life.

My Good friend, If you Live Your Life and You do your Best to Live In Harmony with God and Your self and with Others and with Nature You may very Well Find your selves Blessed on Earth and Blessed in Heaven One Fine Day Having Supper with God Father and God Mother, Jesus and Gods God's & Goddess's In The Kingdom of Heaven.

If we live our life in Arctic regions, as many good people do, you could see Heavens Landscape as one of the most Beautiful Arctic Landscapes you have ever witnessed with God and Gods God's and Goddesses at your side.

If we live our life in Canada as many good people do, you could see Heavens Landscape as one of the most Beautiful Canadian Landscapes you have ever witnessed with God and Gods God's and Goddesses at your side.

If we live our life in the United States of America as many good people do, you could see Heavens Landscape as one of the most Beautiful American Landscapes you have ever witnessed with God and Gods God's and Goddesses at your side.

If we live our life in Central America as many good people do, you could see Heavens Landscape as one of the most Beautiful Central American Landscapes you have ever witnessed with God and Gods God's and Goddesses at your side.

If we live our life in South America as many good people do, you could see Heavens Landscape as one of the most Beautiful South American Landscapes you has ever witnessed with God and Gods God's and Goddesses at your side.

If we live our live in Europe as many good people do, you could see Heavens Landscape as one of the most Beautiful European Landscapes you have ever witnessed with God and Gods God's and Goddesses at your side.

If we live our life in Northern Europe as many good people do, you could see Heavens Landscape as one of the most Beautiful Northern European Landscapes you have ever witnessed with God and Gods God's and Goddesses at your side.

If we live our life in Russia as many good people do, you could see Heavens Landscape as one of the most Beautiful Russian Landscapes you have ever witnessed with God and Gods God's and Goddesses at your side.

If we live our life in Eastern Europe as many good people do, you could see Heavens Landscape as one of the most Beautiful Eastern European Landscapes you have ever witnessed with God and Gods God's and Goddesses at your side.

If we live our life in Southern Europe as many good people do, you could see Heavens Landscape as one of the most Beautiful Southern European Landscapes you have ever witnessed with God and Gods God's and Goddesses at your side.

If we live our life in the Mediterranean as many good people do, you could see Heavens Landscape as one of the most Beautiful Mediterranean Landscapes you have ever witnessed with God and Gods God's and Goddesses at your side.

If we live our life in Greece and on the Greek Islands as many good people do, you could see Heavens Landscape as one of the most Beautiful Greek Landscapes you have ever witnessed with God and Gods God's and Goddesses at your side.

If we live our life in the Middle East as many good people do, you could see Heavens Landscape as one of the most Beautiful Middle Eastern Landscapes you have ever witnessed with God and Gods God's and Goddesses at your side.

If we live our life in Arabia as many good people do, you could see Heavens Landscape as one of the most Beautiful Arabian Landscapes you have ever witnessed with God and Gods God's and Goddesses at your side.

If we live our life in Africa as many good people do, you could see Heavens Landscape as one of the most Beautiful African Landscapes you have ever witnessed with God and Gods God's and Goddesses at your side.

If we live our life in India as many good people do, you could see Heavens Landscape as one of the most Beautiful Indian landscapes you have ever witnessed with God and Gods God's and Goddesses at your side.

If we live our life in the Himalayan Mountains as many good people do, you could see Heavens Landscape as one of the most Beautiful Himalayan Mountain landscapes you have ever witnessed with God and Gods God's and Goddesses at your side.

If we live our life in Siberia as many good people do, you could see Heavens Landscape as one of the most Beautiful Siberian Landscapes you have ever witnessed with God and Gods God's and Goddesses at your side.

If we live our life in China as many good people do, you could see Heavens Landscape as one of the most Beautiful Chinese Landscapes you have ever witnessed with God and Gods God's and Goddesses at your side.

If we live our life in Indochina as many good people do, you could see Heavens Landscape as one of the most Beautiful Indochina Landscapes you have ever witnessed with God and Gods God's and Goddesses at your side.

If we live our life in Indonesia as many good people do, you could see Heavens Landscape as one of the most Beautiful Indonesian Landscapes you have ever witnessed with God and Gods God's and Goddesses at your side.

If we live our life in Polynesia as many good people do, you could see Heavens Landscape as one of the most Beautiful Polynesian Landscapes you have ever witnessed with God and Gods God's and Goddesses at your side.

If we live our life in Australia as many good people do, you could see Heavens Landscape as one of the most Beautiful Australian Landscapes you have ever witnessed with God and Gods God's and Goddesses at your side.

If we live our life in New Zealand as many good people do, you could see Heavens Landscape as one of the most Beautiful New Zealand Landscapes you have ever witnessed with God and Gods God's and Goddesses at your side.

If we live our life in Hawaii as many good people do, you could see Heavens Landscape as one of the most Beautiful Hawaiian Landscapes you have ever witnessed with God and Gods God's and Goddesses at your side.

If one is a Penguin and lives their life in Antarctica as many good Penguins do, a Penguin would see Heavens Landscape as one of the most Beautiful Antarctica Landscapes a Penguin has ever witnessed with God and Gods God's and Goddesses at their side.

If we live our life all around the Earth as many good people do, you could see Heavens Landscape as All the most Beautiful of Earthly Landscapes you have ever witnessed with God and Gods God's and Goddesses at your side.

My Good friends from around this Earth, this is the best that I can do to describe Heaven while on Earth and give Heaven's BEAUTY Justice and Honor with words that will never really be good enough for me or for you to describe Heavens True BEAUTY.

You will really know for your self, when you arrive in Heaven.

If the Soul Journey to HEAVEN is very important to your Souls LIFE and you want to get out of Hades, You will Strongly in Spirit do your Best in your life to do good deeds in thoughts and actions even if you have to Fall Flat on your Face Doing your Best in this life to come home to God and God is waiting for You now.

When God sees you coming home, God will meet you and Welcome you with love and God hug you and kiss's you, his long lost child. God will bless you and God will give you a good spiritual ring to wear on your hand and a beautiful spiritual robe and good spiritual sandals to wear.

God will have good food for you. All of Gods Goodness is Very Wealthy and very Happy that you have come home. It is all for you.

My friend take a look here in the hot sand where you passed out from exhaustion face down in the heat of the day, In the Desert of life and out of water and you were crying wondering where Art Thou Oh God, thinking I had left you to die.

You thought I did not care about you and your struggle for freedom from bondage from the evil Pharaoh in the land of The Evil Wooers. If you look down again my friend you will see only one pair of prints in the sand that lead here to me. Realize it is Gods foot prints you see who carried you home when you could walk no more.

Yet God saw you coming in the distance and God ran after you and picked you up because you tried your best in your life to do your good deeds in thought and action and now you are here with me. Blessed and Refreshed and your soul is Restored in Truth that I am Loving You.

When you arrive in Heaven you will know what I am not able to say with words other than, I love You.

This planet Earth is like a mirror reflection, something like a carbon copy, like a hologram, it is not really real, but an illusion that is real to you, and you live in this hologram, it appears to be real and solid and constant.

Yet the Earth is continually changing in SpiritMatter. As you are changing and evolving in spirit moment by moment, breath by breath. It is a copy of a part of Heaven, yet it is not a real Heaven, it is Life on Earth.

My Good Friend, HEAVEN is Really the Real GREAT SPIRIT GOD. HEAVEN is UNIVERSALLY OMNISCIENT, OMNIPRESENT and OMNIPOTENT and CONSTANT and in HARMONY and in JUSTICE and in PEACE in BEAUTY and in TRUTH and INFINITE and ETERNALLY ALL GODS GOOD in SPIRITUAL LOVE in The LIGHT. God is The Light. We all live in The Light.

THIS place of being here and now which we are within, is the Spiritual Planet Earth. This earth and all earth's are in Spiritual Material Evolution within Great Spirit GOD.

God has been evolving before what humans call time and will continue to evolve beyond what is called time in Spirit in the Light and so will we if we live a good life in Harmony with GOD and Nature.

CHAPTER 5
The Consul of 9 Wise Men and 9 Wise Women

After visiting with Jesus Christ, my father, my ancestors and my friends in Heaven I was taken before a Consul of 9 Wise Men and 9 Wise Women.

I do understand how people have called this Epiphany a Spiritual Place. Judgment Hall, the Great Chamber of Justice for all.

I would like for a moment in time to also call this Great Spiritual Chamber, The Hall of Self Realization and Acknowledgment within our and Gods Presence.

Within this Holy Hall is Gods Holy Presence of Authority and Justice.

The Gravity of this Great Chamber and the Authority of the 9 Wise Men and 9 Wise Women is Overwhelming in Truth with Gods JUSTICE.

I knew that I was in the Presence of God Himself and Herself within God in Gods Creation being Judged, Gods son, through these 9 Wise Men and Women and in this Great Chamber of Spiritual Justice.

There Really is Real Justice.

There is no place to run to and hide in a Spiritual Judgment Hall.

God is to be feared not man. It is like being before the Supreme Court Justice's of the Supreme Court of the United States of America yet even those justices would want to run and hide and shake in fear of Gods 9 Wise Men and Women in The Great Judgment Hall.

Judgment Hall is Gods Real Court of Law, which everybody on Earth will have their Day in Court God said. I do believe God, do you?

The best thing I can say here in this Soul Odyssey is from the Holy Bible, and Other Holy Books that confirm there really is a Hell and a Heaven and our thoughts and our actions Will Be Accounted for by God with these 9 Wise Men and 9 Wise Women in The Judgment Hall.

My friend This is why in the Holy Bible it say's to Fear God and not man because God is a Jealous God and a Good God. God is Justice too.

Deuteronomy 32

To Me Belongeth Vengeance, and Recompense; their foot shall slide in due Time: for the day of their calamity is at hand now, and the things that shall come upon them make haste today.

For the Lord shall Judge his people, and repent himself for his servants, when HE Seeth that their power is gone, and their is none shut up, or left.

See now that I, even I am he, and there is no god with me: I kill, and I make alive; I wound, and I heal: neither is their any that can deliver out of my hand.

A Wise and knowledgeable soul definitely wants to live their life in Harmony with God and with Gods Good Purpose in life.

A knowledgeable and Wise soul does not want to go to Hell for being a fool on a Washington, DC hill for listening to all the wooers who's fate and utter doom is now sealed by God Himself. Hell is the direct opposite of Heaven and anyplace in between Heaven and Hell is not even fun methinketh.

A living Hell can be worse than death.

A soul, Living in a living Hell in Hades, may even want to die thinking we can free himself or herself, and God will not allow that soul to die, anon to continue to suffer, because God wills this so, because God has Vengeance for wooers. God controls Heaven and Hell because GOD Created them both and everything in between.

God even created the devil who works for God to tempt and test souls on Earth for Gods Good. Because God wants us See Who is Good and Who is not so good. God Knows.

God also wants us to see who is Good and not so good so that when the Day of Judgment which has now arrived upon the Earth, everybody will know the Truth and God, and we all will know, who is a wooer and who is good.

GOD will not be mocked by political evil wooers. God will Smitten thee wooers when ye least suspect His arrival. Even in thy sleep. Even with your secret army all around you. Even within your secret chamber.

For no place nor anything is a secret to God. God is also Invisible and Omnipotent and so are His Angels of Heaven and His Angels of Utter Black Doom.

Methinketh Gods arrival may even be at a secret banquet you are attending to your own political honor.

As Thee lift up thy golden winged cup to thy lips with the wine of the gods within, thy God smitten Thee with good or not so good, methinketh. My friend, Be You not fooled by the political wooers of illusion for even they unknowingly work for God testing everybody in Earth as the devil does. The wooers days are numbered. As so are the good days numbered.

My friend Hell can be an utter doom and there is utter doom for some souls on Earth, Homer, Socrates, and Jesus and many others tell us so, and so does God and Gods God's and Goddesses. Utter Doom is the destruction and the end of a soul who's soul essence is now returned to the soul pool for new souls to be created from by Gods will. God said: So be it.

Now this Great Chamber has a presence and I have this feeling that I am in a Self Soul Realization Court Process and I am also my own judge too. Methinketh for a moment in time I also want to call this Great Chamber, this Judgment Hall, The Self-Realization Hall for the Healing process of Goodness of Gods Good souls.

Because my friend Good can also Happen here in this Great Chamber, like shit happens for the Good Souls who are on the path of life and are learning in Life, life's lessons that what appear to be mistakes, may not be mistakes, yet they are good lessons because we did our best even if we supposedly failed.

Life goes around and around for the good of all good souls to learn about God and about life as the good soul is walking and talking his walk on his majestical spiritual road in life returning home.

This Judgment Hall, this Soul Self-Realization and Acknowledgment Hall is a Luminous Ethereal Spiritual Chamber of Spiritual Light.

The 9 Wise Men and 9 Wise Women of Judgment Hall have the Omnipotence and Authority of God and the Power of God to Judge and Justly and Wisely they do Administer Spiritual JUSTICE.

Ola Kala.

After a while my friend I felt more comfortable and peaceful being before the Consul of 9 Wise Men and 9 Wise Women. I remembered to breath in the Light. My friend The Great Chamber is a Very Bright and Luminous, Oval Shaped and with two-way Multidimensional Spiritual Walls and all Inclusive of a Spiritual Temple in Heaven. I could not see outside or through the walls but God and Gods Angels, God's and Goddesses can and do at will.

The Consul of 9 Wise Men and 9 Wise Women were seated around a large semicircle spiritual bench in Solemn Still Peace. My friend as I stood in the Middle of this Great Chamber before the Consul of 9 Wise Men and 9 Wise Women my life is being reviewed. My entire life is being Projected within a giant ethereal spiritual hologram beam that is in living color.

My friend this is all happening Live in a Beam of Light, as watching a movie at a theater on a Giant Silver Screen yet this screen is a Spiritual Light Beam Screen. A Very Sophisticated Spiritual Movie Theater of God. The 9 Wise Men and 9 Wise Women and I reviewed All of my Good Deeds and not so good deeds of my life.

My friend We were all watching a spiritual soul movie called The life of James John Prattas.

Wow.

I was allowed to See everything in Spiritual Truth. We looked at my Entire Life from beginning to end. My friend, Together We Spiritually See how my Life began from Preconception in Heaven and how I Progressed. How I Evolved to Today on Earth. The Choices I made all Along the Way in my life on this Majestical Spiritual Soul Journey I am on. Very interesting.

Actually my friend the Consul of 9 Wise Men and 9 Wise Women Allowed me to Remember. To Re + Member My Soul Self. To Recollect my Entire Life myself, and the Agreements I Made before Coming onto Earth from within Heaven.

My friend I Recollected what my Sacred Agreements are. What I said I was Going to Do. What I Did Do and what I Will Do. My friend I was allowed to See Why my soul life was on the Path that I was on. Why I Choose for me this soul Path that I was on so that I would Learn about God, about Myself, about Soul life and to Complete certain Tasks I was Given to Do on Earth, therefore by Growing Spiritually in my Spiritual Soul Purpose.

Everything about my soul life was about learning and creating my own good, Gods Good, in my soul life and in Gods Spiritual Life which is All Life and All Good.

My friend I recollected I was on a Spiritual Soul Odyssey on Earth and the Challenges and Circumstances that Befell me From Heaven were for My Own Good Soul, and by so Doing and Living within my soul life, I Learn How to CO-Create Good in my soul life and in others lives with God my father and God my mother and Gods God's & Goddesses.

I learned that every-thing in my life's Soul Odyssey Spiritual Love Story, the James John Prattas story, The Odysseus I Am story, The Love Is The Door Way In, to my Mind, Body, Heart, Soul and In to Heaven's good story, is for my Good, our Good and Gods Good.

My friend There were no Great Emotions Expressed nor Judgments made by anyone on the Consul of 9 Wise Men and 9 Wise Women nor even from myself. The Consul Proceedings were Very Orderly and as a Matter of Fact. No, BS, just the Truth of Life.

I learned that Spiritual Judgment Process is a Self Explanatory Soul Process of Self-Soul Realization built Within our Soul. Being a Child of God, in Gods Creation in Goodness, this Judgment Process In Spirit becomes Self Explanatory. This is the Reason some people Intuitively Know Where They Are Going To Go In Life.

My friend We all know what we have Done in life. Why we Did what we did do. Whether we did what we did Knowingly and Consciously or Unknowingly and Unconsciously. This Consciously or unconsciously, that Knowingly or unknowingly is the Difference Between Going to Heaven or Going to Hell or any place in between, and there are many places of the in between.

My friend In Judgment Hall and depending on the Judgment, there are many things a soul can be turned into besides going to Hell Believe It or not. A small example.

My friend a not so good soul, a human spirit, can be turned into a jackass or mule or a cat or dog or bird or cow or buffalo or chicken or any animal of the Jungles and Forests of Life or Ocean.

Even into a good human soul having to survive and to live their life in the environment they have been born into, as our own family. Anon for another exciting example.

Ask anybody who is pet lover and has an animal friend this methinketh question, possibly even yourself.

When You look my friend into your animal friends eyes, who do you see?

Is not their or your animal friend also a relative?

Is not your animal friend a lover?

Is not our animal friend in a relationship with us?

Is not our animal friend also a soul?

My friend Is not a beast of burden some-one-soul, a spirit, like a Mule or Jackass or an Ox?

Some-one-soul who has been given over to a task master to toil and carry a burden for life because of their good karma? Methinketh my friend.

Is not an animal of the Wild Jungle like a Courageous Brave Heart Lion or a Proud Bangle Tiger named Namaste or a Guerrilla of Gladness or a Gracious Anna the Giraffe or a Happy Hippopotamus or a Majestic Eagle of Great Spirit or an Angel Hawk of Heaven or even any of the other animal friend's of God Poseidon's Great Deep Blue Ocean of Love like a White Shark or a Great Whale or a

Beautiful Golden Dolphin or a tiny little Minnow fish living in a Spiritual Place, a Kingdom of Their Own, That God Created, and In This World called LIFE and In-Bet-Ween LIFE and Among you men and you women and on this planet Earth?

Excuse me my friends yet one more tiny note about soul food that you may methinketh about and that maybe what you are eating from all of Gods Goodness.

My friend, this important note is not to Scare you or Frighten you yet to inform you for you may realize a very interesting thing about receiving our good in our daily food. And my friends even the good that we gave to others in many different ways that we did not realize would come back to us in Health or sickness.

Anon the tiny important note goes like this.

We have your permission to tell you a little story, a parable like this from The Holy Bible.

They cried with a loud voice and said, what have I to do with thee Jesus, Thou Son of the most high God?I adjure thee by God, that thou not torment me. For He said unto him, Come out of the man, thou unclean spirit. He asked him, what is your name?

And he answered, saying, My name is Legion for we are many.

He besought him much that he would not send them away out of the country.

Now there was there nigh unto the mountains a great herd of swine feeding. And the devils spirit besought him, saying, Send us into the Swine, that we may enter them. And forthwith Jesus gave them leave.

And the unclean spirits went out, and entered the swine: and the heard ran violently down a steep place into the sea and were choked to death. And they that feed the swine fled and told it in the city and the country.

My friend I want you to realize that in this tiny spiritual spirit story God exemplifies how Jesus casts out evil.

Where evil goes and that the evil, the devil, and the Legion of devils, in this tiny spirit story went into the swine. Meaning into meat, meaning into food, into whatever God wants it to go into.

They the Legion and they are Many; the Not Good souls, The not good spirits, the devil in them, the our not good thoughts. The our not good deeds Went Into the spiritual ocean of life and choked them to death, only to return in another spiritual way.

Anon this means that this not so good that we people do that becomes evil because we know better becomes a devil in life to some-body and goes into the ocean that is spiritual in nature. That our good will, will come back to us in food and in deed and in life. In many ways that are Invisible to See Gods Hand at Work in Gods Many Multiple Spiritual Dimensional Kingdoms and the Blessing we will receive from God for our good.

Now in this parable and in this tiny little story my friend is about self soul realization. I would like you to realize this is why Good Souls say The Lords Prayer and Ask God to Bless Your Food. Because all food is created in The Light and in Spirit and is good and all good comes from GOD.

Now realize this. If you are a Wooer and you eat meat or vegetables or drink wine or other drinks even water and you have done evil wooer deeds and goings on in life, where do you think all this evil wooers kaka is going to go into other than into the food you are eating giving you your good sickness and disease. Do you really think it is going into the deep blue sea into the fish giving you your good again, or just into the sewer system of life?

My friend just a tiny little methinketh about souls, spirit and goodness. The Many Invisible Kingdoms of the Lord God and what God does with all this good that everybody is creating here on Earth is so that we will realize it does not really matter what we eat it. Yet it does really matter what we are thinking and what we are doing in our life.

My friend, it is very important what we are doing in life and if we are doing any thing GOOD. Because this is THE good we will receive called our Good.

My friend we Methinketh, there are Many Invisible Kingdoms and Multiple Spiritual Dimensions of Life right in the Being Here Now. As our Brothers and Sisters the Native American Indians in their Prayer Say, Great Spirit Bless Me and Mine and All of My Relations.

My friend, who do we think is the real fool on the Washington, DC hill?God or the wooers?Yes, Life is a Real wow.

Yes, our life can truthfully become as the story of Pinocchio.

Anon we must go now my dear lover of life. In many a ways my friend, I Judged Myself more Harshly than anyone on the Consul of 9 Wise Men and 9 Wise Women. As I watched my life go by I asked God to Forgive Me. I Forgave Myself for my Mistakes. I Forgave Others for their Mistakes.

My friends I learned that mistakes are Spiritual Learning Opportunities with what appeared to be the wrong response but it was the right response to learn my souls lesson's and others their soul's lesson's. My life is Very Clear to me Now.

My friend I can Spiritually See and Re + member and Re+Collect' my Life and my Agreements with God and Myself and Others. I can See my entire Life from Beginning to Now from Heavens Perspective in Oneness and in Unconditional Spiritual Love.

My friend by our humble ego dying experience, and this is all spiritual work, and letting go of our past mistakes and the not good deeds we have done in forgiveness and in prayer and in meditation with God, and then humbly re-birthing our self in this spiritual process of soul self realization in Gods Spiritual Love, Goodness Happens.

My friend by our own souls self-realization process and by our ego dying experience and coming before the Consul of 9 Wise Men and 9 Wise Women, we realize we now have the so-called missing pieces of the puzzle of our life, and we can move forward in our life today.

We can now put our life, our spiritual house, into Order and Harmony with God.

We now have a more Conscious Spiritual Awareness of our Souls Structure, Order and Relationship in our life and in God.

My friend so can you if you work strongly in Service to your self soul realization in God and in Goodness. It all makes sense to us now.

Love Is The Door Way In, to our mind, our heart, our body, our soul and in to Heaven. We had forgotten how Good life can Be when we are in Harmony with God. Wow, We have a Beautiful Good life.

Wow we can live our life more wisely today.

The Consul of 9 Wise Men and 9 Wise Women also have the power of Compassion, Spiritual Love, Forgiveness and Healing.

My friend The Council of 9 Wise Men and 9 Wise Women can forgive us or they can send us to hell or back to Earth or any place in between Heaven and Hell to live the hell or good we created for ourselves and others.

The Consul of 9 Wise Men and 9 Wise Women told me I was forgiven and I was free to go to the next step in my souls self realization process. I told the Consul of 9 Wise Men and 9 Wise Women I am thankful that I am forgiven and I have learned from my mistakes being their spiritual warrior sovereign on Earth, the James John Prattas, The Odysseus, the Son of John Dimitri Prattas, and it is my duty defending Freedom and Gods Good and helping others CO-Create their good.

Why not You Consciously and Knowingly help CO-Create Good?

Ola Kala.

My friend I am gracefully reminding you, you may Recollect your Life and that your mistakes are truly not mistakes, but they are lessons in your life that you are learning about as you move forward in your True Soul Purpose.

All Karma is Good Karma when we are on the Conscious Path of Self Realization. All Karma is not good when one is unconscious of their souls Spirituality.

My friend I learned that we all are learning through our Trials and our Tribulations. We are all learning through our pain and suffering which will lead us to spiritual enlightenment if we chose to. If we will it to, until we get it right and move on in life to the next step in our ladder of life, The Stair Way to Heaven.

Just as a baby learning to walk for the first time. Just as our first breath. Just as our last breath. Oh My God.

Forgiveness does not mean that I do not have karma in my life to fulfill, which I do, as everybody does, and this is our Lot.

Our karma is good because it allows us to See Ourselves and Complete Ourselves Within Gods Good Creation.

Homer, Karma is just another word for life experiences.

A-lo-ha! A-lo-ha! A-lo-ha!

Ha! Ha! Ha!

Karma is a history book of ourselves and how we got to Being Here Now. The Akashic spiritual record.

My friend by us being before the Consul of 9 Wise Men and 9 Wise Women we learned about how we judged ourselves when we should be talking to God within us.

My friend I learned to pay attention to Life. It takes anyone in any-body much work at being focused in life. I do not know if a Human can be totally focused 24 hours a day on Earth.

I do know Every-thing means something and sometimes some-thing means nothing.

My friend I learned to pay attention to my thoughts that creates my Good Life, and possibly others Good in their Life. As the One I Love and my Child's life too. In our Business's, and in our Profession's, and in our School's, and in our Church's, and in our Government too. Yet this act of Wisdom & Knowledge takes time to learn and unfold, and with our real life experiences to pay attention to Methinketh.

My friend It is the most challenging and Rewarding thing we can do and it is difficult at best. The more we practice, the better and easier it gets.

Being a Good Mother and a Good Father is the hardest profession on Earth. It takes a tremendous amount of energy to focus on being a Good Parent, ask any Good Child.

My friend we learned about of our thoughts of God, Love, Compassion, Forgiveness, Hate, Judgment, Criticism, Opinions, and Attitudes about ourselves, family, friends, work, school, government, religion and about life in general, including our own life is magical.

All Happens as we Think about Them Methinkeths. We have to Live Them. Why not make them good thoughts? Ola Kala.

My friend I learned that I should think things out all the way through from the beginning to the end, before I act upon my thoughts. This Is Wisdom.

Then my friend, after Thinking Things Out, We See we Really Like Our Thoughts, What we are Thinking about, and if we can Live with them as friends, the Karma we are creating, our COCreation, and See it is Good for we, We can then Act upon our Thoughts, by Doing what we Need to Do, to Get the Good we are Thinking About. Spiritual Thinking into Physical Matter. Is this the same for you?

My friend we Learned a Very Important Part of our Thinking is Visualizing Our Thoughts First and to Imagine Living what we Want to CO-Create By Our Good Thoughts in Conscious Thoughtfulness.

We learned we usually do not want what we thought we wanted in the first place after careful analysis. This Is Knowledge.

My friend we learned that all of our thoughts do create a life of their own. As a dream does, as a fantasy does, as an illusion, as Hope and Faith does, as life will.

My friend we learned to be careful of what we wish for, or think of. Thy Will Be Done.

My friend we learned every-thing that we think about becomes a reality in our Mind-Body and Soul and in our life. My friend we learned that everything a person Thinks about becomes and Idea-In-Spirit Mind-Matter First. Then my friend, Our CO-Creators, the more we Think about a Good Idea Repetitively, and Use Words to Describe our Good Thoughts, the Quicker these Good Thoughts Become Matter. Methinking leads to Being a CO-Creator and CO-Creating our Good.

In other words, our words and our thoughts become our reality.

We learned that all of our personal Ideas become our personal perception of reality.

My friend we learned we create our life situations by our thinking and who knows where and what we shall fall into at times in our life not realizing so many others are thinking about things too. Most Souls Not very consciously thinking we may add.

My friend we learned to be-care-full of what we think about. We do not want Dangerous thoughts to become our life. This is how so many souls get themselves into big time trouble. My friend Are you thinking Rightly Good for yourself and your loved ones?I am.

An example of thinking is all of mans good inventions on Earth do come from a good idea. A Spiritual Inspiration first from Heaven and then they befall upon our mind gently becoming a gift from Heaven. Usually in a dream or while day dreaming or while thinking about something else.

My friend First, the way things happen is when We think about our Good or not so good idea to ourselves consciously. Slowly it settles into what some people call our mind, our consciousness, our subconscious mind or into our God consciousness mind, or into our Christ consciousness mind.

We can even call this Buddha consciousness mind or even Zeus Consciousness mind. Our Great Spirit Souls mind is at work serving us 24 hours a day for our good until we pass on. Even if what we are thinking is not good for us!

My friend Then we transfer our simple thoughts from ideas into spirit-matter by repetitively thinking about our ideas. The good ideas or not so good ideas, and this repetitive stress full idea builds up within us. When it is full IT wants to release itself into the physical world and birth itself, as a woman who is in labor having a child.

Or a couple making Love and are about to have a Really Big Orgasm.

My friend Methinketh is this expressive stress-full idea that CO-Creates Itself by Building itself Up, Creating itself, Making Itself, Living Itself, Writing itself, Drawing Itself, Our Ideas, From Spirit Into Any Material.

Spirit or Matter.

Organic or inorganic. As wood, steel, silicon chips, paper, canvas, elements, chemicals, liquids, orgasms, light, sound, computer, automobiles, dinner or whatever we want from Spirit-Idea-Mind-Matter to Physical matter to Manifesting our Idea.

There are many New Fine Eco Friendly Materials to be Created from the Earth.

We are just beginning to learn how to really CO-Create with Gods Great Spirit. Thy Will Be Done.

CO-Creator. CO-Creating. CO-Creator's.

Universal Karma.

We are Gods Karma.

Ola Kala.

My friend what I am saying is an idea, a thought, be-comes, first from The Light Spiritual Energy, then be-cause's itself into matter. All by thought Spiritual Light Energy Creates Matter.

God Creates Mathematics & All Science's so that we humans can see how God Works within this Spiritual Light on the Physical Plane of Existence called EARTH.

The General Theory of Relativity is a science working in spiritual evolution in the material plain. The Universe, explaining how every-thing is Created. How every-thing is Related. How every-thing is in Order. How ever-thing is in Structure. How every-thing is in HARMONY within God in a PERFECT RELATIVITY.

Mathematics is Spirit in Matter.

Science is Spirit in Matter.

God is Math.

God is Science.

God Is RELATIVITY.

The General Theory of Relativity is working 24 hours a day, 7 days a week, Eternally to explain GOD on this Physical Plain of Existence.

In Spiritual Light, GOD, and all this physical explaining does not matter in Spirit Because God, IS Be Cause. God Knows Be Cause. God IS THE BE CAUSE.

This is what, Socrates, Einstein and The Great Others wanted to further personally explain about the Theory of Relativity and All Science does want this explanation to be simple. It is simple.

It is challenging to explain GOD, Spirit, The Light in Matter.

The Wisdom of The Light explained through any science or math or words is that they All Work Together Wonderfully Well. Be cause God is a Great HARMONY and a Great Mystery and no one science or little author can explain the unexplainable GOD any simpler than I LOVE YOU.

Mathematics and Science explains God in a Material Way, the Physical Way, which is the Spiritual Way. My friend I learned that most of my Life is my thoughts that turn into reality and the same for you. Be-careful. Be-gentle with ourselves.

My friend we learned our thoughts can Bless Us, or Curse Us, and we can even Destroy ourselves.

My friend we learned that as a human race on the planet Earth, the sum total of our thoughts about life, becomes our planets reality on Earth today and every day. Earth Consciousness.

What is earth Consciousness?

My friend Many of our planet Earth's citizens thoughts about God and life are WAY OUT of Harmony with God and with Nature which is obvious, methinketh.

My friend we learned we as a human race actually affect and CO-create our environment in more ways than we are aware of today.

There is a very old saying: I think therefore I am. My friend What Ever we think about, we become. Not only as a person, but also as a Human Race. As a Civilization. As our Country. As our Government. As our planet Earth of good or not so good.

My friend we learned that we can do nothing without thinking about it first nor can anyone.

My friend What ever I or you think about over and over again we become. My friend What ever we think about as a person, family, church, company, country we become.

My friend If we spend a day watching our thoughts, or even if we can do this for 5 minutes which we do not believe you can at your first attempt. We look at all the things we think about, we will probably see, that most of the things we think about are negative, and have to do with our Fears and Doubts about our life as shown on TV.

Mass Hypnosis through TV.

Socrates I know this may all sound funny to you yet it is true.

My friend Every-thing in life is Thought Light Matter.

My friend You may think all of life is solid and hard and concrete like our life, yet it is Spiritual Light fluid thought-matter first, is Spirit-Matter.

It is in a state of continual change just as we are changing breath by breath and moment to moment. One day we will not be here to read this good book again because we are not solid nor is life but Great Spirit God Is.

My friend Life is a Spiritual Dream.

Our Life is also a spiritual dream.

Are you dreaming about your life or are you living your dream life?

Do you know the difference?

My friend I learned I can prove thinking rightly to myself and you can too. Dreams are thoughts.

My friend I can do nothing without thinking about it first. What about you?My friend, You are now thinking and reading these thoughts I am sharing with us, Methinketh this is true?Yes.

My friend Can you Make Love before thinking about it, Making Love, first you Methinketh IT?

My friend Can you make dinner before thinking about making dinner? Thinking about the ingredients you are going to use to make your dinner with. Thinking about how you are going to cook your dinner?

My friend Can you drive your automobile before you think about where and how you are going to drive your automobile? Do you thinking how to use the gas and brake petals? Do you think it is all automatic?

My friend Can you ride your horse before thinking about riding your horse first? Methinketh!

My friend Can you steer your automobile before thinking about how you are going to steer your automobile and how you are going to maneuver your automobile through traffic?

My friend Can you kiss your Lover Lovingly before you think about Kissing your Lover Lovingly Sweet first? Methinketh a Kiss.

My friend Can you work at your profession before thinking about how you are going to work at your profession first?

My friend Can you think wisely before thinking wisely about wisely thinking first?

My friend Can you dress yourself before thinking about dressing yourself and before thinking about what you are going to wear?

My friend Can you go to the bathroom to relieve yourself before thinking about relieving yourself and before thinking how you are going to move your minds-body to get to the bathroom and relieve yourself first?

My friend we learned that what WE methinketh about is most likely, most often, Going to Happen.

My friend I am, you are, we are, The Soul Captain of Our Own Vessel. Our own ship, our own star ship, our own space ship, our own body, our own mind, our own Earth, or whatever you want to call IT.

My friend I learned that it is very important to consciously methinketh good thoughts because They WILL Happen.

Why Live In Confusion?My friend we learned that if we methinketh negative thoughts they will happen. My friend we learned if we methinketh about fears and doubts about our life They will happen.

We learned that if we think good positive thoughts and good goals THEY Will Happen.

My friend Do we know what the difference is between what we Want and what we really Need in life?

No-thing!

My friend Want requires much stress and anxiety verses Need requires less stress to receive our good. My friend we learned that if we Methinketh about OUR Positive Thoughts of Success and Being a Winner with a Good Positive Healthy Attitude They Will Happen.

My friend I learned that if we methinketh negative thoughts for others the same negative methinketh things can happen to us.

My friend Methinketh, if we as a parent think and say negative thoughts to ourselves and to our children over and over again, or if the TV program does, or if the politics does, or if the religion does, or if the fairy tale does, We Will Believe Those Negative Thoughts.

We will LIVE those negative thoughts. We will pass on those negative thoughts, and life styles on to our children.

To their children's children and on for generations of negative soul thinkers. CO-Creating them ALL into a hapless wretched soul and world to live in.

Ah my friend I learned, Methinketh and now you have too!WE CAN Reverse Negative Soul Thinking Process for Future Generations by beginning with ourselves TODAY. My friend we have all have heard the old saying, Physician Heal Thy Self. My friend we learned All of Our Good Positive Thoughts Really Do Create Our Good Life.

My good friend Methinketh that most of us have never been taught how to think good thoughts! How to have a good relationship with God, ourselves and others, or how to be a good soul, or a good parent, or a good lover, or a good friend, a good businessperson or good executive that will create our Good in life.

My friend we learned we can begin to today. Right now to Think Good Thoughts so justly deserved for ourselves for our own good methinketh. My friend Plato, We can all receive Divine Guidance and Divine Inspiration if we ask God to come into our lives through prayer and meditation. Methinketh It.

My friend When I completed my visit with The Consul of 9 Wise Men and 9 Wise Women I was taken by the Angels to visit with Jesus Christ.

CHAPTER 6
My Visit With Jesus Christ

After my visit with the Consul of 9 Wise Men and 9 Wise Women, the Angels took me to visit with my brother Jesus Christ.

When I visited with Jesus he was in a Very Beautiful Spiritual Meadow with Green Pastures and Beautiful Majestic Mountains around Him.

There are Beautiful Animal Friends Gracing the Landscape and Many different kinds of Beautiful Birds Flying all Around. The birds where busy Singing many different Songs as Beautiful Birds do even on Earth.

At times my friend, some of the Birds Sounded to me Like They were very quietly Chirping His Melody name Jesus, Jesus, Jesus over and over Again with their very mellow and very gentle bird chirp that we all hear when birds sing.

Not all of the birds are singing Jesus name. Some Birds sing other spiritual men and women's names and other spiritual stories of Gods Life. My friend, Some of the birds would chirp the name Jesus and there Singing was of a peaceful happy bird chirp beginning with Je and accompanied With a very short subtle almost silent Sus as their bird Inspiration Went Out Into the Ethers in our Spiritual Universe.

There are Beautiful Flowers and Majestic Butterflies in this Meadow.

This Spiritual Meadow Place is where we are Visiting at this Special time. It is Very Beautiful and Very Peaceful. It is a very Restful and Replenishing place.

This Spiritual Place is a very Refreshing Spiritual Meadow. Very much as our beautiful meadows on Earth. Everything all about us my friend is very Colorful and peaceful as a very Beautiful Spiritual Garden Sanctuary.

My friend I can Hear gentle Music in the background coming out from Within this Meadow.

As the Angels and I arrived, Jesus welcomed me with Open Arms and we Hugged each other as brothers do. I was Very Happy and Truly Overwhelmed to be Back Home Again within Heaven. I had not Seen Jesus my Brother for a long time. I had missed Jesus While I was On my Spiritual Soul Odyssey on Earth, yet we did speak every now and then while I was on Earth, Spiritually.

I told Jesus I was so Happy to See Him again and that I was sorry for having to kill people in the Great Trojan Vietnam Soul War as in all the other Great World Wars. Jesus and I both Know, this is The Way of a Spiritual Warrior and All is Good with Him and Me.

Jesus knows that without Spiritual Warriors like Me, a Spiritual Warrior King that I am from Heaven, and all the Other's, My Brothers and Sisters who Give their Life for God, Freedom and Country, There would be NO Freedom or Bill of Rights or Declaration of Independence on Earth for any-body today.

We talked about being a Spiritual Warrior, and many they are from all around this world called the planet Earth. To numerous to mention all, yet here arc a few recent One's that come to my mind, whether a Man or Woman, like King Agamemnon, Achilles, Hercules, Odysseus I am, Alexander the Great, Socrates, Jesus Christ, George Washington, Abraham Lincoln and Gods Friends and Brothers and Sisters of the American Revolution, Civil War and even WWII.

Anon We talked about Spiritual Warriors during WW II with Pershing, Bradley, Marshall, MacArthur, Patton, Churchill, Queen Elizabeth, Eisenhower, Martin Luther King Jr, John F. and Bobby Kennedy, Mahatma Gandhi.

We talked about the Black Horse Regiment Spiritual Warriors of the Black Horse of the Great Trojan Vietnam Soul War who fought with King James.

John, Rex, Doug, Philip, Jack, Swanson, Ray, Doc, Doug, Richard, Ramos, Dennis, Woody, The Hulk, Berry, Harold, Rodney, Paul, Jerry, Wade, Charles, Francis, Robert, Rollie, Doc, Justin, Branson, Brahnsen, Bradin, Patton, Jr., Leach, Hawn, McVey, Raymond, Tex, Jim, Bob, Lynn, David, Ben, McKnight, Bobby, Matt, Mac, Kenneth, Billy, Albert, Bobby, Anthony, Scott, Eugene, Louis, Arthur, Stephen, Richard, Terry, Mark, Luke, Joe, Joseph, Davis, Moses, Grady, Milford, Carl, Homer, Paul, Walter, Norval, Fred, Robert, Steven, Kevin, Douglas, Leo, Glenn, Allen, Wayne, Tom, Martin, Ward, Rubin, Watson, Nick, Floyd, Ollie, George, Darrell, Kevin, Randy, Jeffrey, Terry Julio, Tim, Leslie, Earl, Donn, Kris, or Timothy, Galen, Eddie, Lenard, Allan, Joe, John, Argle, Ernesto, Willie, George, Clarence, Michael, Alex, Andrew, Merle, Jackie, Willard, Ted, Isaac, Sam, Solomon, William, Carlos, Daniel, Rick, Ernest, Bill, Armor, Jonah, Job, Hepler, Lundy, Pittman, Lawrence, Thomas, Lemaster, Reardon, Homer, Larry, Soc, Krueger, Martin, Ted, P.J, Jim, Jimmy, Garland, Michael.

Anon we talked about Maureen the Angel Nurse and all the other Angel Nurse's of Black Horse and Lydia too.

We talked about the good nurses in the Military and Civilian Hospitals and The Florence Nightingale's, Mother Teresa's, The Princess Diana's.

Especially talked about the veterans of WW II, Korea, Vietnam and Desert Storm in Truth in God and Country from All around this planet Earth.

We talked about The REAL Spiritual Warriors, The Real Prince and Princes and Kings and Queens of the Holy Grail, and the Holy Spirit.

A Sacred Covenant in Shinning Spiritual Armor, Agnus Dei.

Consciously and Knowingly choose to Defend Gods Good people on Earth in the Name of God Our Lord and Savior.

We talked about my very important note to you about Spiritual Warriors and if you are not one, realize this important note for your own humility and a humble well being. There is no Higher Position or more Royal Class of Citizens upon this Good planet Earth than the Spiritual Warrior for God.

We talked about how All GOOD Kings and Queens, Princes and Princess, and Presidents, of any Good Country; even whether a Real Country or even a fairy tale country, is a Spiritual Warrior of Good Gods Inspiration Who Actually Personally Fought His & Her Way for God, Country and for Freedom and for the Truth.

We talked about that if they have not fought for The Way for God and the Truth and for Freedom they are NOT true leaders of GOD and Goodness But Impostors and Wooers.

We talked about how you should be Extremely Gracious and Thankful to God in your Prayers and to these Spiritual Men and Women Warriors for your Freedom and Everything GOOD that you have be cause without their Sacrifice to God and Country You would have nothing Good. You would be a Slave.

We talked about how most of you complain and moan and groan and protest that you have rights in life to beg and demand benefits that you do NOT deserve.

You have not earned any good rights in your life for be cause you did not give anything good from your life to Gods Life which is all LIFE. All of your so called benefits will be taken away right away.

We talked about how most you only Take as a greedy taker from what these Holy Spiritual People Gave to LIFE.

You better start GIVING or you will not even have a soul left.

Black Horse Prayer.

Our Heavenly Father, We are professional military men with a mission of destroying the enemy.

At times it may seem that we stray from our ways, but we are striving to bring Peace and Freedom to the World.

We ask your Help in the Battles that face us. Aid us literally to fulfill the Standing Order of this Regiment. Give us the ability to Find the Bastards and the mines, and then give us the Strength and Courage to Pile On, that through our aggressive actions your Peace and Freedom may Truly Come to this Nation and the World.

We ask this through Jesus Christ our Lord. Amen.

Jesus listened as my Compassionate brother would do, knowing how life really is here on Earth.

My friend, Jesus Christ Knows the Truth be cause he also Is a Spiritual Warrior. Jesus Christ came to Earth and Fought for Freedom and the Truth. Martyred by Crucifixion, just like Socrates, Joan of Arc, Kennedy, King, Gandhi, and many men and women and Spiritual Others who were all martyred by a modern bullet of crucifixion, prison or had their assets seized and their life destroyed by the government. Jesus listening to me recounting My Soul Odyssey. All the Good I have done and how I learned from My Own Soul Odyssey. How I Carried Freedom and The Light to All Our Good

People all around this Good planet Earth with My God's and Goddesses and Angels. The True Spirit of Heaven and Mount Olympus & Himalayas and the True Spirit of Aloha. All this is Good and Comforting to Him you and me.

Jesus said to me, everything is Ola Kala and Good. It is Good, and I believe Him and so should you.

We sat down together in this Beautiful Spiritual Green Meadow. We talked all about LIFE and All the Good there is in Gods Good Life on Earth for everybody good. We Thought, Talked, and Shared, the Many Universal Libraries of Gods Knowledge and Wisdom and Holy Inspirations. We talked about how God Father and God Mother Created the many kingdoms within Heaven and within the Earth and All other Universes and Earth's for Soul Living and Learning about Gods Good life.

We talked about the Many Schools and Universities that are Spiritual Consciousness Centers to Spiritually Learn about Universal Unconditional Love, Wisdom and Universal Knowledge in Gods Goodness of All.

We talked about how these Learning Centers are Spiritual Learning Vortex's of Gods Holy Spirit.

We talked about how these Learning Spiritual Centers are also made up of and taught by Gods Good Spiritual Men and Women Souls who are very experienced in God Consciousness and in Gods LIFE.

We talked how every Field of Knowledge which each is a Meadow full of Wild Flower's and Majestic Butterflies of Wisdom & Knowledge is available to All to learn all about God, as God wills it to you through Spiritual Prayer.

CO-Creation to Culture.

Spiritual LIGHT into Physical Matter.

We talked about All the Good Spiritual Sciences.

From Agriculture to Machines and Bio-Machines.

Sports to Space Ships. Technology Tools Weapon's. Spiritual Light Healing Technology to Medical Light Bio-Science Technology. Antigravity Technology to Nano-Light-Technology and the Infinite Applications of Light technology in LIFE on Earth for Goodness.

We talked about how every-thing is Created in Heaven first. Then passed on to good human beings as these Great Ideas and Creations and Good Technologies that all started from one small Idea onto Earth by Prayerful Meditation in Thoughtful Focus as Good God Wills it through good humans by Gods Grace. We talked about how Life on the planet Earth has Many Spiritual Universes and Spiritual Dimensions Invisible to the human naked eye within Life Itself and Within the Earth herself. Universal Oceans of Energy and Ideas, that very few humans have ever explored. By Gods Permission Only.

Top Secret. Crypto. Krypton.

We talked about how LIFE goes on in Miraculous Majestic Ways of Wonder that God has Created for All to Learn all about Gods GOOD LIFE. Our Good life, When we let go and go with the flow of Gods Great Spirit.

As two Beautiful Creating Royal He & She Magnetic Light Beams of Golden Eagles in a Good Royal Dream We Are Living. In this Beautiful Good Royal Fairy Tale We Dreamed. With All of the Good Abundance and Goodness for us to Enjoy in this Dream and the Happy Healthy Good endings and beginning's too.

We talked about how everything is an expression of God How everyone is an expression of God, Him & HER, and how God lives in every-one-of-us. Adam & Eve. Two Atom's as One.

We talked about how most humans beings do not know that God's Soul and Spirit is Inside, Within, each and everyone. In everything, including Atoms and Molecules and other Particles of Spiritual Light.

We talked about how most humans beings think God is Outside of themselves. Far and Away someplace in Outer Space and not on Earth with them.

God Mother & God Father and The Angeles and Jesus and All The Saints are Right Here and Now with each and every one of us. Spiritual Love is the Way on Earth.

We talked about how humans beings think LIFE and All Good is outside of themselves in some Nirvana. When actually their Spiritual Enlightenment of their True Spiritual Nirvana and All Life is with-in our soul in our body which is in Gods Spirit.

We talked about Remembering to Look Within and Breath in and out our Spiritual Love, Compassion and Healing LIGHT from within our Universal Soul Heart of Unconditional Spiritual Love Light of Our God Consciousness within YOU. We talked about how God is The Great Spirit and Soul. We are Gods soul's. The real us.

We talked about how The Great Spirit of God is the Impersonal Good Great Spirit. The Buffalo Spirit, The Great Him Eagle Spirit and The Great Her Hawk Spirit. The I Am within us All.

We humans souls, gods children are the little egotistical personal I am's with big fat egos within God in Nature. Because God made us in his Holy Image and each of us is Unique, my humble Eagle and Hawk Souls and in Nature too and All of My Relations.

We talked because Him & Her Great Spirit, the I Am that I am, works for you All, Gods Children, Gods Good Creations in all body's of Spiritual Love, 24 hours a day, 7 days a week, from the beginning of your lives to the end of your lives, giving you all your Good.

Just as my Good God of the Sun is Shining his Good Loving Spirit of Aloha Light upon you and this Good Earth Giving Life for All, good and not so good, for all to See God Being 24 hours a day, 7 days a week, from the beginning of your life to the end of your life, Truly this is Spiritual LOVE, METHINKETH, ALOHA!

We talked the Be Cause of Adam, Eve and all of our Relations. Please Now Recollect and Realize within our own Good Soul this good thought. When you See Good in your minds-body-eye, you see the Truth. When you Think God in your minds-body you see the Truth. When you Say God in your minds-body you hear the Truth. When you Hear and Believe and Have Faith in God Father and God Mother, You Believe in You Gods Christ Child. You Realize in your minds-body the Truth of God, for yourself, and in your GOOD Soul. Say to yourself.

I am a Winner of Gods Good Will & Goodness. You become a Winner in your Life and our good Winner. You Will Receive a Spiritual Golden Oscar and a Spiritual Golden Globe Award and many More Golden Awards of Goodness.

We talked about how God Placed the Impersonal Christ Consciousness Soul & Spirit within each and every one of you, Gods Children to do as you wills it for your goodness in your Life. We talked about how Christ Spirit Loves you Unconditionally.

Gives you what GOOD you See, Think, Say and Realize within your minds-body and third eye. Within your True Temple of God. Because God Loves you and Gives you the Free Will to Choose your good, as he wills it to you, to CO-Create your own Good through your own choice of your own words and thoughts, and your own deeds to live by and with, till death do you part and reunite in Heaven.

We talked about how Spiritual Love is Spiritual Freedom of your own Choice of your own Will and of your own Words and of your own Deeds. What you Will Creates your own Blessings or your own Doom. What is Karma?

We talked about CO-Creating Good Karma.

We talked about how you are Gods Good Children.

We talked about how you are CO-Creating with me and God in every moment of your lives your lives own Good or not so good, as Christ CO-Creators and 99.99% of you are unaware of what you are creating.

We talked about how very few humans on our planet Earth are aware of Gods CO-Creation Process within Gods Spiritual Love Light. We talked about how most of the human race on this planet Earth are not even aware of much but their stomachs.

Nothing Other than what is going in their greedy minds and giant stomachs. Their unhealthy lustful thoughts of themselves in ignorance and I am Compassion.

We talked about how there are some very enlightened teachers, scientist, doctors, inventors, actors, performers, movie producers, musicians, directors, television personalities, builders, architects, carpenters, plumbers, politicians, trades people and mothers and fathers who use Gods Wisdom and Knowledge on Earth today for CO-Creating Good in their life and in others.

You Can Do It Too!

We Be Caused Adam and Eve and that it is very important for you and All Others to Self-Soul-Realize that God, the I am Within you All, Is in you too. Created in Gods Good Healthy Spiritual Soul Image, Him & Her, Me, you, a Son and a Daughter Christ, Learning to be a humble one as God.

You my Children all are the Children of God.

All of you Christ Children are Created in Heaven.

Your Soul is Created by me God Father. Your Body is Created by me God Mother.

Your Soul is placed within your Body by my Angels by my Will into my Creation of Life and in my Spiritual Love Process of what is called your Birth. Our Beautiful and Healthy and Abundant LOVE Christ Child of God Mother and God Father and The Holy Spirit.

We talked about Being Born by Spirit in all of this Goodness called My LIFE. Called God. All of this God and GOOD and Goodness is a Great Mystery to you if you are out of Recollection of me. If Out of Harmony with me. Becoming ignorant humans and scientist of Me.

We talked Be Cause many of those so called good scientist and professionals, who tell you there is no Sacred Me the Holy ONE, The God Father & God Mother and Our Spiritual LOVE, Our Christ, Our Child You.

They are now gasping and grasping frantically in a paranoid scientific medical schizophrenia. In the darkness of their wretched little vain egotistical minds for any foul air. For any vain proof which they have nothing of. As now being in outer space in their space ship that has an oxygen leak Be Cause God wills it so.

And it is loosing oxygen quickly because they have no Belief or Faith in God, and they are gasping for my Good Air of a Good Life. All the while they a gasping for my air, they are struggling and writhing in pain to explain to themselves in darkness and to you, that they do not really know Who, or What they really are made of.

Or what LIFE is or what even The LIGHT is. Or what is Spiritual LOVE LIGHT or what God is. They are a fool in a black sticky oil pool of ignorance, as they are being sucked down into doom by Poseidon.

We talked Be Cause His Royal Highness the scientist is not good, and Her Royal Highness the scientist is not good, and they are creating not good for themselves and others and will self realize all alone by them selves in their own frigid darkness, that without a soul from me God, they are nothing good without God. This no-thing is but nothing of a black cold frigid darkness and a deep void, a Black Hole in the universe and their black doom of eternal nothingness that they are looking forward to being no-thing.

We talked if it could be, which it cannot be without God, would be, by its own no-thing nature a blind Ignorant darkness, UN-caring, UN-feeling, UN-wise, UN-knowing, UN-compassionate, UN forgiving, UN-healthy, Ugly dead piece of shit that innocent ignorant unconscious unaware scientist think you evolved from Africa. Creating an Illusion. Creating something they do not know.

We talked about how If the Earth is destroyed by a Great Flood which has happened. Or is destroyed by a Great Fire which could happen and every-one and every-body perished on the Earth.

In Time the Great Mother Goddess Earth, Heals Herself Spiritually Again, how do you think little you, the Good children of God, would return to Earth as you have done before Time by Gods will, yet you do not Remember, nor Recollect me because you where Spiritually Veiled by Me GOD to See if you have REAL FAITH.

We talked about how I will tell you this Great Mystery of HOW and WOW. Watch closely. Be patient.

Get ready now. Get comfortable in your Lotus Blossom Velvet Green Spiritual Love cushion and breath in and out my Spiritual Love now. Being here now. Here it is. . . . . . METHINKETH.

Be Cause!

Did you laugh? I did! I am.

We had a Very Big Laugh.

We have to laugh at ourselves sometimes.

We talked about how God is Infinitely Still and Spiritually Evolved Eternally, Yet you may not be without Gods will.

God is in total stillness. Total Silence.

We talked about this so called Evolution Theory without God is in Truth a so called scientific political wooers explanation of a world without God of which they have no knowledge of God.

Nor of who they are made of.

Doubting of themselves and God.

Because they cannot see themselves or who they really are made of from.

Be Cause.

We talked about Gods Spiritual-Matter on the Physical Plane is Evolution in a Spiritual Motion Process as in a Chemistry formula for Penicillin. In what's called TIME. How LIFE is also birth and death. Everything in the middle is spiritual evolution for ever Life Changing.

Our life, and we human beings are the real spiritual aliens visiting Earth for you know no-thing.

We are destroying the Earth with Geo Engeneering, our own home. As the trash we left on the Beach or in our Mothers Beautiful Garden, that our Mother asked us to Carefully and Consciously take care of while She is away with your Father but they will return soon to see how well you have done.

We talked that this Time is This LIFE and is this Spiritual Evolution of Gods Great Spirit Soul evolving in every-thing of whatever is known in the material world and the spiritual world.

As what you hardly see anything of anywise, and you live and experience your life and this is so called LIFE and this Spiritual Evolution of Love is going on for Zillions upon Zillions of years beyond science, scientist, religions, governments and even you and me and beyond the word's that scientist use incorrectly.

We talked in fact of life. There are no good reasons to describe what these political government scientist want to try to describe to us, that is impossible and not true. Because their lives are the proof, that God is Alive and Well and they are not. This is all a cosmic joke on Us!

We talked as a matter of proof to YOU and to scientist themselves, to ask a scientist who does not believe that there is God to stop breathing for 7 days. To place themselves in a 7 foot tall glass cylinder naked in a vertical position, because they of course can stand tall upon their own words of wisdom and knowledge of nothing, in the center of the Smithsonian Museum in Washington, DC for all to watch.

To show you and our citizens and his family and his friends all of his great wisdom and power and his very little knowledge about his life or your life or his loved ones life or his or her children's life which of course will be and is nothing to this scientist because he thinks he is god, and the scientist will be what's called scientifically, DEAD MEAT and a stinking afoul breath.

We talked about METHINKETH as matter of True fact. Spiritual Science Is, every single day, since there has been a body of knowledge called Science, has been and is Continually Proving, that God does indeed, In Deed Exist. In every cell and in every atom, in every Adam & Eve and in every aspect of our life, even of course in the General Theory of Relativity.

We talked about how every Atom, every Cell, every Chemical Formula, every Organic or Inorganic Compound, every Mathematical formula from Simple Addition through Quantum Physics and Linear Algebra to every Musical Composition, every Ethnic Language and even Every Computer Language, every Medical Procedure and Therapy, every Medicine, every Herb, every Scientific Study, every Aspect of Telecommunications, every Study of Satellites and the Stars Orbits, every Wireless Communication System.

Every Use of Sound Waves and Light Waves and Water Waves and Matter Waves, Magnetic Waves, every Computer Program and Computers Themselves, every Economic & Banking Formula and Procedure, every Agricultural Endeavor, every Act of Husbandry, every Aspect of the Oil Industry, every Means of Production from Automobiles to Movies, to Rocket Science, every Outer Space Mission, every Military Weapon Produced, every Act of Law, every Art of Love, every Military Endeavor, every Airplane Flight, every Home Built, even the Crucifixion of Jesus Christ, even me Smiting of the evil wooers has a Spiritually Perfect Structure, Order and Relationship in HARMONY with God Father and God Mother, and that IT is composed of Spiritual LOVE LIGHT to makes IT work!GOODNESS.

We talked about chaos is chaos, and chaos is just flopping around as chaos does, chaos does not have a fixed permanent order, structure and relationship. Chaos cannot be used to create me or you or a movie, computer, a play station, a comic book, an airplane, a television, a light bulb, or even the scientist or even the seat that the sorry Big Okole head of the ignorant faithless blind scientist sits on or the floor he or she stands upon to talk nonsense about chaos.

We talked about that within this Spiritual God Body of Life that God Created, there is All Structure, All Order and All Relationship in Perfect HARMONY within each Cell and Component of LIFE to make it work together in Harmony.

We talked about how every body of knowledge, every chemical formula, even a Light bulb, an Automobile, a Space Walk on the Moon, a Geometrical formula, a Great Pyramid, the Beautiful Acropolis, a Trojan War, a Sky Scraper, the Sacred White House, Buckingham Palace, the Golden Gate Bridge, a Democratic or Republican Party, a Socialist or Communist, a Singer Sewing machine, and even an Electronic Microscope that magnifies a thousand times an Atom, an Adam & Eve, only to find another Inner Universe within the Atom, within Him & Her.

So you can See God and you can visit God at the Smithsonian Institute with Gods thousands of examples of Gods All Perfect Structure, Order and Relationship on Earth that God has Created out of Spiritual Love Light in every-thing, in every-body, in every place and in every Science so that I am and you lovely people can create for goodness for our selves. Thank you my good friend scientist for proving God is alive and well.

We talked about how all this wooers babbling political talk of that God does not exist is a political government wooers joke created by God to see if You believe and know God. Or if you will follow the evil wooers to a black fate called doom.

Aloha, I am seeing a Beautiful Rainbow of Spiritual Love in many majestical colors over Kealakekua Bay, Hawaii on the Big Island of Hawaii. I am seeing the Spiritual Rainbow over you too. God is the YOU in your life. You are the you soul story of God Mother and God Father and Gods God's & Goddess's and Angels too.

We talked about how Homer & Plato call all the you's in LIFE a hapless wretched soul if you are out of Harmony with God and Nature. What do other Saints, Gurus, Teachers from all the other religions and philosophies call somebody out of Harmony?

Malaka.

We talked about God, Our Mother God & Our Father God is The Great Spirit in our Life, ask any Native American Indian or Mexican Indian or Huichol Indian or South American Indian or Australian Aborigine or African Native or India Indian and even my good friends Joseph & Victoria, Cheyenne Eagle Elk of the Navaho Nation.

We talked about from within God All Good is Created by Gods Spiritual Love, The Great Majestical Mystery called LIFE.

We talked about how Gods Breath is our Breath, our Life and our Inspiration. Ola Kala.

We talked about how when WE exhale it is the God breath in us.

That no human can even hold their breath for one day of their little life or a year of your Life without passing out of breath and dying.

Which means little you has no real power worth speaking about or staying power which really does mean you are My Inspiration does it not?

We talked about how when you Inhale Air which is Spiritual it is God who we are inhaling.

The Great Spirit of God known as Spiritual Air, Manna and Prana and that AIR gives us all life moment by moment as God wills it.

We talked about how we breath God In and Out 24 hours a day until we pass on by Gods Will.

We talked about how every-thing in life is made up of God Energy and when we look closely, consciously within every-thing in life, we will see me God. We talked about Gods Creation and All that God Created is Goodness and Good.

Jesus invited me to Supper with Him.

We sat down and we had a Wonderful Conversation and Supper and a glass of The Elder's Good Wine.

The Wonderful Supper is All about Christ's Spiritual Consciousness of Unconditional Love, Compassion, Forgiveness, Healing, Justice, Wisdom and Knowledge in God and about how to live a Spiritual Soul Life on Earth and as in Heaven.

We talked about how many life times have passed by while Jesus and I talked, yet time is nothing in Heaven.

We talked about how all of Christ's Consciousness. That Spiritual Soul Conversation and Communication is in Spiritual Thought Images within Spirit.

We talked about how One Good Spiritual Thought is a library of Spiritual Love books in volumes of Goodness. We talked about how I am now going to call Spiritual Thought Images Love. We Spirited all around Heaven.

Jesus showed me many wonderful things in Heaven and on Earth that I had forgotten about while I was on my soul journey on Earth. Jesus is Gods son and He is living today Christ Consciousness within All. James is Gods son and Jesus brother. James is living Christ Consciousness today within All.

There are Many Other Spiritual Good souls in Heaven who are a living Christ Consciousness also.

We talked about how Christ Consciousness is Unconditional Spiritual Love Consciousness in Gods Wisdom and Knowledge.

Others call spiritual consciousness Buddha Consciousness, Krishna Consciousness, Allah Consciousness, Great Spirit Consciousness, Aloha Consciousness and all the other good words for saying the Spirit of God is within you is Gods Spiritual Consciousness.

Many Good Women and Men Christ's are Talking and Walking and Living these different Spiritual Consciousness on Earth today.

We talked about how I am also calling this Spiritual Christ Consciousness, the I am within me and you, and Living within the Spirit of ALOHA.

We talked about how there are many of Gods God's & Goddesses throughout this planet Earth working and serving God and in many ways seen and unseen in all countries, as Angels in disguise.

We talked about how you are All Gods Children and Jesus Christ is your brother and Mother Mary Christ is your sister too.

How Christ Consciousness is within All of you too, if you will yourself to be in Harmony with God and Nature. We talked about how The distinguishing difference between Holy Souls and unholy souls is what we do with our life.

What we give is what we receive.

We talked about how living my life in Harmony with God, in Peace with myself and Others and Nature, is Good for me. We talked about how Living our life in Balance with Nature in Earth is Good for us and the Earth too. We talked about how sharing our Compassion is Good for us and others. We talked about how Spiritually Loving ourselves and Others is Good for us and others.

We talked about how Forgiveness for ourselves and for Others is Good for us and others. We talked about how Living Within Gods Universal Laws is Good for us and others. We talked about how Thinking Good Thoughts is Good for us and others and is good for you and others to do.

We talked about how taking care of ourselves is Good for us.

Because God helps those who help themselves. Good is Good for me and others too. We talked about how Educating ourselves is Good for us and others.

We talked about how being Strong in Spirit, Mind and Body is Good for me and you. We talked about how being Wise and Knowledgeable about Gods Teachings, Laws and Justice is Good for me and you.

We talked about how having Faith in God and having Faith in My Self is Good for me and you. We talked about how We removed of All of your fears and doubts from your life because you realized all fear and doubt is an illusion and not really your true thoughts.

Fear and doubt is not real.

Fear and doubt is a not-so-good thought. Fear and doubt is no-thing, and that is good for you and others to know and Grok.

We talked about how after removing all of your fears and doubts from your life All is Good. That All the Good that is left within you in your life is All of your Goodness called Success Being a Winner and that is good for you and others too. We talked about how Living in a knowledgeable Faith and Belief in God is Positive, Enlightening and Good for us.

We talked about how doing Good Deeds in Service to God is Good for us and for others. We talked about why Early to bed and early to rise will make us Healthy, Wealthy and Wise.

This means, We do not burn the candle at both ends and this is good for us.

We talked about how the many Holy Books throughout this Earth from many religions and philosophies including the Holy Bible that express Gods Wisdom, Knowledge and Spiritual Laws concerning LIFE, are easily understood when we read them quietly, Consciously and Thoughtfully which is good for you and others too.

We talked about how to Consciously read All Holy books. Thinking in between the lines with a common sense and a rational thinking mind which is good for you and others too. We talked about how learning to read good books with an open mind is Good for you.

There is no-thing to be afraid about in a good book. You never know what Good there is in a good book and What there is to learn from a good book, like a good friend, goodness will guide you and protect you and that is good for you.

We talked about how it is important to read Holy Books and to personally ask God for the Spiritual Meaning Within Each Word and that is good for you. We talked about how All Holy texts have been translated many times over throughout history. From many different languages and countries.

That a Wise and Knowledgeable Soul must look for the Truth and Understand, the Spirit of the Word, the Essence of the Word, which is Within the Word.

As Looking at Petroglyph on a Cave Wall, that I have Scratched Within the Hollows of the Earth's Caves with My Souls Blood, that is a million years old, and that is good for me and you and others too.

2 Examples of unusual translations to help you METHINKETH.

The spiritually weak will not inherit the Earth unless you are a cockroach. It is better to be Spiritually Rich than spiritually poor if you have to care for your family.

Now why would somebody translate these words in the opposite direction? This is the True question you have to ask yourself.

Because they want to keep you weak and down on the ground and a political religious slave. I Am Your FREEDOM.

We talked about how there is no better place for you to go to for accurate Divine Wisdom and Divine Knowledge than to God Himself and God Herself and the Holy Spirit that is within you and that is good for you.

We talked about how Gods Universal Mind, Gods Universal Body and Gods Universal Spirit can be Communed with by you as Gods will it through your Prayer and Meditation and that is good for you.

We talked about how God has placed His & Her Thoughts in Universal Spiritual Centers of Consciousness and how these Spiritual Places are called The Center of Universal Wisdom and The Center of Universal Knowledge and this is good for you.

I talked about how through Gods Grace and Will, we can access Universal Wisdom and Universal knowledge by asking God through our Prayer and Meditation and that is good for us.

We talked about how Ultimately it does not really matter what religion, race, country we started our spiritual path in this life time. Because God and Christ Consciousness, Spiritual Unconditional Love Consciousness, God Consciousness is a Spiritual Way of Living on Earth as in Heaven and Throughout Gods Creation.

We talked about how Gods The Way in Life is Unconditional Love, Unconditional Compassion, Unconditional Forgiveness, Unconditional Healing, Unconditional Justice, Unconditional Universal Laws, Unconditional Universal Order is Gods way in my life. Of course We Use Our Intelligence and Common Sense and Logic in All of these matters. Be not a spiritual fool.

We talked about how everything is evolving as God designed it. We can SEE God in everything evolving if we will just take a look through Gods Kaleidoscope called our Third Eye and even your beautiful healthy new eyes.

We talked about how the Stars up above and All of Gods Children, the Animals in the Forest, the Fishes of the Sea, the Flowers, the Birds, Bees and the Trees, the Minerals of the Earth, and the Air, the Water, the Food, and All of man's inventions are all Gods creation.

We talked about how we are really all no-thing but God.

We talked about how the I Am within us is no-thing but God.

We talked about how I know no-thing but God.

We talked about how we are all on Gods Spiritual Highway in Gods Good life. As spiritual birds flying home to roost in Gods Good nest of Goodness. Right willingly that we fly the right way home through The Light of METHINKETH.

We talked about how the other persons road may look a little different, as the Grass is Greener on the Other Side of the fence. Because you are on your road looking to the left and to the right when you should be looking straight ahead.

We talked about how if you are Looking Straight ahead in your life and YOU See God as your Sun Light, You will see your green path is Straight and Beautiful and Enjoyable, and that all of Gods paths are the same path when You see God.

They just look different and they are different until You walk with God Purposefully with Spiritual Intention. We talked about how to see the difference in Good and NOT Good, in our life.

We talked about what is the difference between Good and Good. O, MY good or not so good thoughts. We talked about how a Good Life is all about how we view life.

What kind of Spiritual Kaleidoscope we use.

Either with our ego's personal perspective or with Gods impersonal perspective and we see oneness in All.

We talked about how It is best for us not to covet another persons path because we will carry their pain's and sorrows and karma too. When our path is less of a burden to carry. As we accept our path, it gets better and better. It turns into The Light.

We talked about how on Earth, All spiritual roads lead to God.

We talked about how All we really need to do is walk a good talk on our Majestical Spiritual Soul Journey. We will find God on Earth as in Heaven. We talked about how it is Good to be our self.

Because we are really unique if we allow our self to be unique. Even in our personal life or job or occupation or custodian-ship.

We talked about how Yes it is true, we are all Gods children. We are the little gods, we children, and Gods Spirit is in us all yet, God is Good.

We talked about how I am very happy to be me I am. I will not be anybody else but me I am.

We talked about how Gods God's and Goddesses are Unique and that is the way God made Us all unique. We talked about how we are all Gods infinite Unique children. Each with Unique Gifts and Talents. With your Own Unique personal Soul Purpose in life.

We talked about how we all have a Free Will in our life.

We talked about how we all have a Choice in our life.

We talked about how We Can Think our Own Good Thoughts in our own Good life. We talked about how we can be Thankful and how we can be Happy and Content to live our own Good life Freely in The USA and in other countries.

To Enjoy our life, it is ours you know, to do with as we please as we follow the spiritual laws. I pray for your goodness.

We talked about how Yes we can emulate Christ Consciousness or Buddha Consciousness or Krishna Consciousness or Mohammed Consciousness, or Mary consciousness, yet it is Best emulated as Your Own Personal Self Christ Consciousness in our own Good life whether we are a President or a Plumber, or a Messiah or Spiritual Healer or Saint and its all the same Humble path remember this.

We talked about how Each person has their own Personal Unique Character and we should Love ourselves for what we are Naturally. In Spirit, Thankfully in a Beautiful, Healthy, Wealthy, Abundant Life. Wise in all of Gods Goodness.

We talked about how Each person in this Infinite Universe makes our life on planet Earth Unique.

We talked about how it does not really matter if you are the Plumber or the President of the USA. Or the Princess or the Prince or Quizzical or the Queen of England of Kindness.

Or the King of Saudi Arabia. What is important is that you are a GOOD Soul. A humble you. Then you are truly unique in life.

We talked about how Every moment in our life is Unique when we pay attention to our life and our breath and to God.

We talked about how Every One of Gods Laws is Scientifically Spiritually Unique.

We talked about how Each Animal Friend in the kingdom of God is also Unique.

We talked about how God Created Each Flower, Fruit, Tree, Vegetable, Herb, Moss, Insect, Fish, Butterfly, Growth, Salt, Mineral in Nature Uniquely Spiritual In The Light. We talked about how Each Cloud in the Sky is Uniquely of The Light.

We talked about how Each Bright Star we see at night in the Sky above is Unique in our life.

We talked about how Each breath we take is Unique and we live another moment of our life. Miraculously, by Gods Grace.

We talked about how Each time We say I LOVE YOU.

It is Unique in our life and in somebody else's life and that is Goodness too.

We talked about how Each time we say I LOVE YOU, it is Unique on the planet Earth and everyone Loves I Love You.

We talked about how Every time you Share & Give a Good Loving it is Unique in our life and in some-body else's life and it is good for us and others too.

We talked about how Every Good Technology we CO-Create on Earth is Unique in our life and Good for us and others. We talked about how Every New Science we discover is Unique in our life and Good for us all.

We talked about how Every Mathematical, Algebraic, Geometric and Physical, and Scientific Equations are Spiritually Unique in our life explaining God and this is Good for all of us on Earth.

We talked about how Every Good Thought and Every Good Word from us is unique in our life. We talked about how Every Good song we sing in our life is Uniquely Good for Us and all life.

We talked about how Good Music, Song and Art is unique and good for all of us on Earth.

Where Art goes, the world goes.

We talked about how If you covet another persons life you will go through their pain's and suffering until you come to Your own spiritual enlightenment of your own True path in life, your Good Soul Purpose. Become your own Super Star in our Universe.

We talked about how Gods Attitude is Impersonal. Begging will not work. The truth will work. Honesty will work. Humility will work.

Service will work. Good work will work effortlessly.

We talked about how Gods Attitude is Unconditional Love.

You have your Good, I have my Good, We have our Good, All together We are All Gods Good.

We talked about how we can read the Holy Bible and many other Holy Book's. Even Homer's The Odyssey or Plato's Socrates Apology and you will See, Feel and Hear God talking through All of them.

We talked about how there Is only One Unique God. I Am.

We talked about how God express's Himself and Herself through every-body and every-thing with Unconditional Spiritual Love Light on Earth.

We talked about how some of us on Earth may Understand and See God Consciousness, Christ Consciousness, even as Buddha Consciousness, or even as Great Spirit Consciousness, or even as some other Holy name of God Consciousness as The Spirit of Aloha Consciousness and this is Good.

Yet All True Unconditional Love Consciousness is God Consciousness manifested through we human beings, and our Animal and Plant friends in our environment on the planet Earth.

I am in Methinketh and with no disrespect to anybody.

Because I believe we are all doing our best and this is good.

We talked about how we can travel to anyplace on Earth and ask any Wise and Knowledgeable person from any religion, who is Jesus & Mary Christ and they will tell you he is the son of God, and she is the daughter of God. More people know Jesus & Mary Christ than anybody else on Earth.

This includes The Good President of the United States of America, The Good Queen of England, The Good King of Saudi Arabia, The Good Emperor of Japan, The Good Chairman of China, The Good Queen of Holland, The Good President of France, The Good President of Germany, The Good President of Russia, The Good President of Italy, The Good King of Greece, or all the other Good Presidents and Good Chairman's of Many Good Countries including all the Good Prince and Good Princesses of the Kingdoms and Countries around the Earth that are Gods.

This also includes the Good Head's of the Eastern Orthodox Church, or the Good Head of Judaism, or the Good Head of Islam, the Good Catholic Church in America, Good Protestant Church, Good Baptist Church, Good Lutheran Church, Good Mormon Church, Good 7th Day Adventist Church. The Good Head of the Buddhist, of the Good Head of Taoist, The Good Pope of Rome. The Good Dalai Lama.

We talked about how many people on this Earth are not aware of their Soul Consciousness or the souls existence within them Because they have Lost Their Way from God in life. They do not know how to even find their own Soul, Heart or Mind. They know where their stomach is.

We talked about how Christ Consciousness is God Consciousness, is Spiritual Love Consciousness and this consciousness is The Path and The Way and it is called:

Love Is The Door Way In, To our Heart, our Mind, our Body, our Soul and into Heaven.

We talked about the Spirit of Aloha.

AL OH A.

A is for the Aloha meaning greetings, welcome with love.

L is for Launa meaning friendly, a feeling from the heart.

O is for Olioli meaning pleasure, of being helpful and kind.
H is for Hauoli meaning happy, the happiness of sharing.
A is for Akahai meaning humble, in giving and serving.
A-L O-H A!

CHAPTER 7
Where is God Consciousness On Earth?

We learned from Great Spirit that our spiritual teachings are Universal truths from God.

As a young man Jesus Christ traveled from Israel to Greece and around the Mediterranean area and back again to Israel to become a Master of knowledge and Enlightenment as any Spiritual Being would have done of this time period.

From Greece to Egypt and from the Middle East to India to China is where the Major Centers of All known knowledge on Earth existed at this time. Also within these countries is where the Major Trade Routes of the world were connected and existed then and even till today.

These routes of commerce and Spiritual knowledge historically extend from Greece to all the other Mediterranean Coastal Countries including Egypt, the Middle East, India to Europe and to the America's and to all of Asia.

Through time these Power Centers of Commerce and knowledge have shifted from country to country.

Example.

Great Spirit may very well all have started in this Golden Age in Greece in Atlantis.

Then spread through the Mediterranean, Turkey to Rome moving to England and then shifted to Europe when England Ruled the world. Great Spirit moved to the USA after WW II.

Very important note. This is the Highest Alert since WWII in Modern times Shit is going to hit the fan.

Lately there has been a major shift of the Means of Production, Finances and Natural Resources world wide to Communist China.

Why?

Most people think a nuclear war is impossible today. Wrong!

California is being dried up due to Geo Engineering Watch. org.

Rome fell, Greece fell, France Fell, England, Scotland, Ireland, Norway, Denmark and Japan fell and the USA can fall in this economic war and we can be taken over by the Elite who run then world on all sides of the game board. They already have control for many years.

They tell the Russians, The USA, China, England, Germany and France what to do.

Germany has revitalized the Third Reich again and The Third Force of The Elite Royals is maneuvering secretly world wide.

Look how China's military is pushing Vietnam, Philippines and Japan all around by force.

This is very unusual considering China would not be a world power at this time in history unless there is a Secret Strange Conspiracy and Hidden Agendas of the Third Force as we Witnessed in Germany during Hitlers Rise.

Communist China has been built up to become number 1 Military ECONOMIC POWER IN THESE TIMES. 2017.

The Global ELITE rulers showed the world with their destruction of The World Trade center 9/11 as a Symbol they have total control of the USA.

Ask yourself why? They want to take over the world today. China is today largest military. Russia and Iran also a Conspirator acting Naive. We have enemies within our borders and in our White House and State Department.

Should we have Methinkeths about this event?

Yes. Very Important considering something Big Militarily is Going to happen within the next two years by Russia and China against the USA. We are going to win. It will not be easy. I have played Russian Roulette. I don't believe any other world rulers have. I would win. They will lose. Fear will stop them dead cold.

The creation of the Reminbi as a new world Reserve currency to challenge the USA. Financial Markets are going to get very exciting in the near future.

The dumping of USA Treasury notes by the Russian and Chinese to crash America. We are at War with China and Russia, Middle East and even the Euro. They plan to destroy The USA and Rule the world.

Their goal is If America falls it will be the end of Freedom world wide. The danger is in America is that we have treason in the White House, Senate and House of representative. We have been invaded by evil wooers in sheep clothing.

Realize if The USA falls and this is possible. Where would we go to live in Freedom. Russia, China, Mexico?

Are the powers that rule the world Elite and Communist. Being that they control all markets of commerce world wide?

All the other countries through out history were built up over hundreds and even thousands of years like Greece, Egypt, Rome, France, Spain, England, Russia, Italy, Middle East, India, South America, Mexico, Australia, The Four Tigers and China.

Keep in mind that all of the most important centers of Enlightenment and Education were spread from Greece, India and to Asia at this time in history.

Christ's comprehension of all the religious teachings of his era reflect from his travels to Greece and are exemplified in his understanding of Gods Words and in His teachings. Homer was here before Jesus and Buddha.

You can ask any of the good teachers and good leaders of Buddhism, Hinduism, Judaism, Islam, Shintoism, Lamaism, Confucianism, Brahmanism, Sikhism, Great Spiritism, Christian, etc. , and you will hear them All acknowledge that Jesus is the son of God and Mary Christ is the daughter of God.

They will also tell you that they are sons and daughters of God which is true.

We are all the sons and daughters of God when we live in Christ Consciousness.

It just depends on what we do with the life God gave us.

God said.

You will know them by their fruits. By what we do.

You just might not know right now you are Gods son or daughter in your heart yet it is true unless you have fallen out of Harmony.

Give this Thought some time.

You will feel and see that it is true when you are in touch with God within yourself. God is talking to you right now. The Truth of the Spiritual Matter.

The reason Jesus Christ is known as a King of Kings on Earth and in the Kingdom of Heaven is because Jesus gave up His life for everybody on this Earth at this time in history in The Way that he did. This was not easy nor effortlessly.

This was Jesus Christ's mission on Earth as a Spiritual Warrior like the other Spiritual Warriors who come to Earth for God.

Jesus & Mary and other men and women Christ are the son's and daughter's of God who Willfully came to Earth.

They willfully gave up their life to bring you all of Gods Good Words, Gods Compassion, Gods Forgiveness and Gods Healing and for Resorting our soul.

All The good things from our God for those of you who have faith in God.

By your Faith and Belief in God you are healed now.

Jesus did not have to do this act of compassion nor do you have to do any Act of Compassion. Acts of compassion are a Personal Choice.

There was Nobody else but Jesus in Heaven who volunteered to come at this time and bring Our Gods Words to you here on Earth because Humanity had lost The Way.

Jesus knew what was going to happen to him before he came to Earth as you did.

As a youth Jesus, Mary and the Other Christ's where veiled from much that was to happen to them until the time was right. Just as it is for anybody else who is going to go through a lot in life.

We can imagine if it was us and how we would feel about coming to Earth being the Emissary Son of Our Lord God father and mother.

To bring the Word of God to a whole bunch of Unbelievers on Earth. To know that we will be Humiliated, Mocked and Crucified at the prime of our youth by our own people.

Later to have some of our friends crucified too. Wow.

Not what most of us, nor any of all the other good religious teachers, would call Having a Good Day. Nor did any of the other religious teachers or leaders do this Act of Unconditional Love and Compassion at this time. Others in the past have as Socrates.

As a matter of fact, if we look around today, we will not see the Good Pope or the Good Dalai Lama or any other Good religious leader or Good political Presidential leader doing what Jesus did. Because they do know they will be Crucified by their own people.

The Conspiracy, Treason, and Crucification of Gods Messengers on Earth. Very Wooer Political as it is today.

No, you will not because they do not have The Faith to give up their life as Jesus did.

This is easy to see and we do not have to be Rocket Scientist nor Einstein to see why.

They do better talking political rhetoric than living the life that Christ did and does do today.

This is why Jesus is a Son of God and know as a God.

I do not believe we will see a Pinkies worth of healing work from them because they just don't have the ability nor the Blessings from God that Jesus does. They are the wooers.

I am not saying this in any disrespect to those leaders. Because I think they are doing their best and a wonderful job being an evil wooer.

I am just pointing out the facts and The Spiritual Truth.

As a matter of fact, the only religious or political spiritual leaders that come to my mind in the last hundred years to Move a Body of Peoples Souls and be Crucified by a bullet is Mahatma Gandhi, John F. & Robert Kennedy and Martin Luther King, Jr. They walked their talk. Jesus walked His Talk. Mary walked her talk.

The evil wooers Corrupt others with their political rhetorical talk.

All the others talked good but walked the other way when God called them to give up their life and to come to Earth and to do Gods Will as Jesus did. Our Life is Gods Life. Is it not? Who gave us life? This is the difference between a Political Coward and a Spiritual Hero.

You do not have to be a rocket scientist nor Einstein to figure all this religious and political stuff out.

The Truth is self evident.

This is all very simple if fact. We can see why nobody but Jesus the Christ and other good Christ Spiritual people did do Gods Good Will on Earth at this time in history. We have to give up our life to gain a life. It is as simple as that statement. Period and the end of the discussion. No excuses.

What do Combat Veterans from The USA and all countries give up? Their Life for all of us to live in FREEDOM.

HEALING is NOT a very difficult and complicated Spiritual Work. Healing Work is an Art from God and it does come easily. It is not easily learned without great pain and suffering. Nor does the Spiritual Work come to just anybody.

Only to those who God Blesses them with HIS Spiritual Gift of The Art of Spiritual Healing.

There is a Tremendous amount of Personal Sacrifice to become a mover and shaker of the people, Gods people, as Abraham, Isaac, Jacob, Moses, Jesus, James & Mary, Mohammed, Gandhi, Martin Luther King, Jr., John F. Kennedy, and others through out history have done.

This is Jesus Christ's mission and it was not easily accomplished by others who have no Faith in God.

Jesus and the Other Christ's Purposefully worked with their Mind, Thoughts and Soul. Focused on God Father and Mother, Their Great Spiritual Fountain of Youth, Great Spirit, The Holy Spirit.

No other Son or Daughter of God has given his or her life for us all under these very difficult of circumstances. No other Son of God has ever accomplished this Enlightened State of Oneness with God at this time in history. Accomplishing at the same time Gods Miracles Working through Him as He is Walking and Talking on the Earth as in Heaven.

No other messiah nor religious leader has ever been crucified by his own people and have the world acknowledged He is the Son of God.

No other messiah but Jesus Christ Healed the people with Gods Compassion, Forgiveness and Grace as Jesus did do with The Spiritual Light from Heaven within Him.

All the other Good Teachers did good deeds for God. They taught what they saw and heard from God. They lived their lives as a good example to others who need help. Some of them also gave their good life for God.

They did their best in their life as we should also do.

Some of these Good Brothers and Sisters are Gods Good Children from many Different Religions and Faiths.

Some Modified Gods teachings to fit their Environment and to Serve their people from whatever country or land they were from to Keep the people from Straying to Far and Away from the Spiritual Truth.

All Spiritual Enlightened Teachers including Jesus Christ never started a Church nor a Religion. Men built Church's or Temple's or Mosque's afterwards in their name for prayer to God in Thankfulness. Politics Conquered religion to Control People with fear.

Every Enlightened Spiritual teacher who has come to Earth has always said that our Body is our Temple. The Earth and Nature is our Church and that God lives within All of us today.

We learned from Jesus Christ that the reason so many people around the world have opened their hearts to Him & Her and do accept them Open Heartily as the Son of God with Gods Truths and Gods Way is because everybody knows that all Truth, Wisdom, Knowledge, Compassion, Forgiveness and Healing come from God.

Our Christ's are Our Messengers from God. Some call them Angels from Heaven. Jesus and Mary Christ lived Gods miracles in life on Earth. Jesus and Mary Christ want to remind you, that you can do what they did in your own way in your own life work. You do not have to be crucified for doing good deeds.

Jesus and Mary Christ want me to Remind you that Greater Deeds Others Shall Do Daily.

Jesus and Mary Christ would like me to remind you that Everybody is a Child of God. Just like them. They are like you and me. Other than by their Faith and Belief in God. They did do Goods Good Works, and so can you. If you chose to work with God.

Jesus and Mary want to remind you that you must have Faith in Yourself and in God and believe God. God will guide you and protect you with Gods Angels. God will Work Miracles through you as God wills it. Because God has a Covenant with you who chose to do Gods GOODNESS.

Jesus and Mary Christ want me to remind you that if YOU have the Faith of a tiny Awesome Mustard Seed that is in the palm of your hand you will move mountains too. Just like children in a Sand box move mountains of sand every day having fun living in faith, that all is for their goodness, which it is.

Jesus and Mary walked the Earth and they continue to walk the Earth in Spirit Today.

Jesus and Mary Taught the people and they continue to Teach the people in Spirit from within their souls. Jesus and Mary healed the sick. Comforted and Forgive souls for God. They continue to do so around the world personally, and through Angels and through the Holy Ghost, the Great Spirit, God. Methinketh Humbly, Being Respectful yet as an example on Earth.

More people know who Jesus Christ, is than The Good President of the United States of America. The Good Queen Elizabeth of England, The Good Pope John Paul, The Good Dali Lama, The Good Mr. Bill Microsoft Gates, The Good King Fahd of Saudi Arabia, Moses, Good Yahweh, Good Buddha, Good Vishnu, Good Mohammed, Good Chief Joseph, Good Chief Geronimo, Good George Washington Or Abraham Lincoln, Mother Teresa, Good Martin Luther King, Jr or John F. Kennedy, Good Jacqueline Kennedy, the Good Mr. Steven "ET" Spielberg, the Good Mr. George Yoda Lucas, The Good Mr. Billy Graham the Evangelist, or any Good Movie Star or anybody else Good on Earth.

As another matter of fact. The only other Aspects of God known more than the unknown name of God, and the name of Jesus and Mary Christ, and their other Infinite Manifestations around this Earth is the SUN and the MOON. Him & Her and their child Mother EARTH.

I went around the world to see for myself.

I have not visited all countries yet. I walked the Himalayan Mountains from Pokhara to Jomsom and the Good people know Jesus Christ. They are Hindu. I visited Japan, Vietnam, Burma, Thailand and the Good people know Jesus & Mary Christ. They are Buddhist and Moslem.

I visited England, Holland, Spain, Germany, Belgium, Luxembourg, France, Switzerland, Austria, Liechtenstein, Yugoslavia, Greece, Italy, Ceylon, Azores and the Good people know Jesus & Mary Christ.

I have meet many Good Arabs, Good Muslims and Good Saudi Arabian citizens who know Jesus & Mary Christ.

I have meet many Good African people and they know Jesus & Mary Christ.

I have meet many Good South Americans and they all know Jesus & Mary Christ. I visited Mexico and the Good people know Jesus & Mary Christ. They are Christian.

Even the Good Huichol Indians who live in very remote mountain villages in Mexico know Jesus and Mary Christ.

I went all over the United States of America and the Good people know Jesus & Mary Christ. I visited with the Good American Indians and they know Jesus & Mary Christ.

The reason so many good souls know Jesus & Mary Christ is because Jesus & Mary Christ and their Angels Spiritually Visit many souls around the world 24 hours a day Consoling, Forgiving and Healing Gods good people, us.

The teachings of Christ Consciousness is the Culmination and the Sum Total of all of Gods, Thoughts, Words and Teaching from all religions that God gave to us the people of Earth through out all time.

Christ's teachings are the Essence of all the Good Thoughts and Words from God.

Christ's teachings are the Essence of all of Gods Universal Laws from all religions that God Gave to the world so that we will live in Peace and in Harmony. In Health and in Wealth with God in our Goodness.

Christ's teachings from God are the most Simply Said and Taught Spiritual Teachings in the world for us all.

Wow, what a Miracle today, Simplicity.

When you think of what Jesus & Mary Christ did do, and said, we will realize why Humanity has filled many good Public Libraries, Colleges and Universities with good books of Spiritual Wisdom & knowledge from their good words and Deeds.

Jesus & Mary Christ's teachings are the Essence of Gods Good words and they are very simply stated.

Love one another as we love our self.

Treat one another with Respect as we would want others to treat us.

Anybody can understand what it means to Spiritual Love.

Anybody can understand what it means to have Compassion.

Anybody can understand what it means to Forgive.

Everybody on the planet Earth needs Forgiveness.

Almost Everybody needs Healing.

Anybody can understand Love.

I Love You.

Everybody needs LOVE.

LOVE is also Spiritual LOVE which is Union with God.

Yin and Yang.

Man and Woman. Together being in Oneness and in Spiritual Love, CO-Creating Love.

We learned from Jesus & Mary that everything we do is for our own Good in life. We learned that all Good Souls in Spirit Believe in Peace, in Love, in Compassion, in Forgiveness and in Healing.

We learned that all Good souls are all coming to Christ consciousness which is God consciousness which is Unconditional Spiritual Love Consciousness no matter what religion we started with.

All paths of spiritual love lead to God.

Ultimately it does not matter where you started on your spiritual soul journey. What is Important is that you started.

You will probably at some time in your life Read a part of, or the whole Holy Bible and you will probably say the Lords Prayer.

Ultimately it does not matter which Good Prayer and which Good meditation you do. Or which Good works you do. Or which Good spiritual fasting or dieting you might do. Or which Good healing therapy you do.

Or which Good dancing you do. Or which Good water you drink, or which Good drink you drink. Or which Good air you breath, or which Good healthy dieting you do, or which Good loving you do.

Or which Good exercise you do, or which Good mantras you say. Or which Good fun you do, or which Good compassion you share. Or which Good songs you sing, or which Good food you enjoy.

Or which Good traveling you do, or which Good deeds you do.

Or which Good abundance you enjoy and share. Or which Good I Thank You God you say. Or which Good spiritual teacher you study with, or which Good mantra words you say.

Or which Good I love you, you say to others and yourself. Or which Good Church you go to, or which Good Temple you go to, or which Good Mosque you go to or which Good Tee Pee you go to pray in.

Be Cause our Omnipresent, Omniscient, Omnipotent God Father and God Mother and Gods Christ Consciousness is in every-body and in every-place and in every-thing from Heaven to Earth.

We humans have been spiritually evolving for a long time. We have been learning about God for a very long time. We will continue to do so because God is Eternally Evolving us through His Creation.

We are Gods Creation. We are a part of Gods Creation.

There is never a boring moment with God. We will enjoy the Good in our life if we believe and have faith in God. God Wills it. Good is God. The Choice is ours.

There are many Wonderful Things to explore in Gods eternal universe. There are many marvelous kingdoms upon the Earth that very few men and women have yet explored that are for us to enjoy for our Good life.

Our Animal friends will tell you They Live in a very magical world of Nature.

We need to Develop your Spiritual Eyes to See Gods Many Kingdoms for our enlightenment, knowledge, enjoyment and for our own Good.

Life is for Learning about Ourselves and God. Enjoying our life with all of Gods blessings that he has given us. Our FREEDOM comes from God. SLAVERY comes from POLITICS.

FREEDOM in Our Life is for CO-Creating Our Good with God.

Give me Spiritual Freedom, or Give me Death.

Most of us are only using one or two of our blessings, and our talents, that are our unique tools Hidden Within our souls Treasure Chest and Guts for our Success in our life.

If we open our heart and our mind and our body and our soul to God we will see within us, and all around us Gods over Flowing Spiritual Love, Abundance and Goodness that God has given us all.

It is True, Our cup runneth over.

We also learned, If we are not careful and we are living way out of Harmony from Gods laws and Nature, and not doing good deeds for ourselves and God, there is also many life times of Hell to enjoy and that is not fun, it is hell.

We can get out of hell and live in peace on Earth Today!

Our Father and Mother which Art in Heaven, Hallowed be thy name. Thy Kingdom Come. Thy will be done on Earth, as it is in Heaven. Give us this day Our daily bread. And forgive us our debts.

Lead us Out of Temptation.

Deliver us from our own ignorance and into your Land of Milk and Honey. For Thine and us Is the Kingdom, and Power, and the Glory for Ever Amen.

So my friends be of Good Cheer. Being in Happiness. Being in Health. Being in Wealth. Being in Abundance.

Being in Spiritual Love.

Being in Harmony.

Being in Enjoyment.

Being in Spiritual Wealth and Abundance.

Being in Compassion. Being in Kindness.

Being in Love.

Being in Methinketh.

Being in Healed.

Being in Youthfulness.

Being in Fun.

Being in Wisdom.

Being in Knowledge.

Being in Goodness.

Being in Harmony with Nature.

Being in a really big explosive orgasm called Spiritual LIFE.

Being Here Now in Peace, in Spiritual Love and in This Clear Light.

Amen.

CHAPTER 8
Mans Inventions

I learned God has given you and me the gift to CO-create with Him & Her good creations.

There are many inventions that truly are good. There are some that appear not so good yet they have gotten us to here and now. We have learned?

God has given us Free Will and a Choice in how we live our life and what we will do with our will and our creations.

As we look back in time to the present we can see the evolution of our human creativity from Heaven to Earth. We can see that when we were spiritually birthed out of Heaven to Eden.

Life is Good until we were sent out of Eden to live on the Earth and to learn our THE Way. It was not because we did not believe or listen to our Father & Mother God.

We were Tempted by Doubt and Fear of the Truth of Gods Eternal laws that were given to us from the beginning.

We learned to live by our own efforts and our own creativity by trial and error. By our faith as any growing child will do when He or She leaves home.

We Will Find our way.

Even Gods children have to make their own way in life. There is no better way than to earn our own way in life and pay our own dues.

This is the True Spiritual Way.

Chop wood and carry water is Zen.

Do our own work.

Paint our own spiritual mental visualization painting of our life.

Sing our own song.

Dance our own dance.

Play our own tune.

Write our own book of our spiritual life.

Sign our own Declaration of Independence.

Sigh our own Bill of Rights.

Live our own life in the Kingdom of God. We will meet others who have also done the same as us.

In time we learned to forage through Nature for Sacramental Plants. Make our tools for our own good.

As time evolved through thousand of years we found our selves in a very Enlightened and Sophisticated world.

Life is good. We created everything by Thought that we have today.

Mans mind is highly evolved in methinketh.

What we could Imagine and Think about we created for our good. Very much as things are today. We are still evolving to reach this Specialized spiritual place we have been to before the world was flooded and destroyed by God because we fell out of HARMONY.

We destroyed ourselves through our own miss use of our spiritual gifts and Talents from God.

We destroyed the Earth by our actions.

The Great Mother Earth and God have their own ways of Clearing Things Up for their own good and for our own good since most of the world population, about 99.9% is unconscious of who the really are.

We can understand how we became Greedy and Self Centered.

We forgot who gave us our breath, our unique gifts, and what they were really for. Their true soul purpose. Which is to give our selves a Good life and to share with others our Good life. To purposefully work and to enjoy life the best we can.

Through our own greed as a human race we started to forget God and started to believe we are God that believed in other false Idol gods, just as the Egyptian Pharaoh's.

We miss used all of our talents and gifts and our love. We miss used compassion and forgiveness for our selves and others.

We turned ourselves into an egotistical self serving Vain People with hidden political agendas of greed through our own economic, religious and political vanity that has nothing to do with God or the Good of life.

Today we all can clearly see that we are headed to the same fate of Self Destruction by our own creations unless we do something about realigning our selves with HARMONY which is realigning our selves with God Spiritually.

Let us look at a small part of our past history and what we created.

We created tools, homes and villages, fishing boats, canoes and small sail boats that were non polluting and in harmony with nature. We walked everywhere. Everything was Good at this time.

Then we captured and harnessed men and our animal friends against there will and we used them to work for us. Slaves.

We made them haul our carts and wagons that we created and burdened them with the things that we created.

We used our slaves in armies to carry weapons of destruction and to kill others even their own country men at their own life expense just as today.

We made men to row our large cargo vessels and war ships through out history and to till our soil. So be it.

Evolution.

Then we became More Vain and Lost Our Way and decided to use people as slaves and have them build enormous temples and palaces to gods that do not exist for vain monarchs and queens for self serving purposes that really had no value other than to use human lives in vain and to appease false gods hoping they will enter their heaven which does not exist.

There will never be any eternal wisdom, knowledge, love, compassion or forgiveness from God in these temples. They are only architectural and mathematical and physical wonders that we humans created and goes to show us what we could have really create if we used this knowledge for good.

What most people feel in these temples as a presence or an energy is the presence and energy of mathematics, physics and matter put together through architecture creating man made vortex's.

The only Truth there is in these temples is about how people believed back then in history.

How people suffered in vain by disillusioned kings and queens with their high priests with false beliefs to false gods that never acknowledged them. They all personally suffered. Karma.

They All died leaving us a history of how they failed in life by miss-using their breath, their unique gifts that God gave them to create good in their life and for others, their citizens.

Let us look at the Great Pyramids of Egypt, The Acropolis in Athens and even those Mexico Aztec and Mayan Temples or any other Great Man Made Architectural Temple.

These Pyramids and Temples are a great example of how Sophisticated and Enlightened certain humans were about Mathematics and Physics and how to use magnetic energy to move matter with this powerful electrical energy.

Obviously much of this knowledge is not available today because we will miss use it as the Pharaoh's, Kings and Queens and others did because they became evil wooer leaders.

Real Spiritual Kings and Queens and leaders that are blessed by God have available to them the powers of God to do Good for their Kingdoms and their people to Prosper and be Blessed with this Gift of Enlightenment. The Holy Grail.

Do we see any political leaders who have this gift on the planet Earth today?No.

We are miss-using our technology today. We are seeing the Signs of Gods Hand and Foot Print already on the face of our Earth through the many natural disasters that are accelerating daily.

God is Talking.

Mother Nature is Talking.

Are we listening as a human race? No.

All of the Spiritually Sophisticated and Enlightened Wisdom & Knowledge of Gods Ancient Ones, and Gods God's and Goddesses is here and now. Those who have it and know how to receive it and use it will not give it out to anybody because God willed this so.

This Knowledge is guarded and Protected by Angels.

The NWO is self destructing itself for miss using Wisdom & Knowledge against free peoples of all countries and against Nature and all of Her Relations.

Their Leaders and their families are dying daily to Karma disease.

Looking at history and the miss-use of our talents the Great Pyramids and other Great Temples are built at a great cost of human suffrage and loss of life.

A great waste of knowledge and resources that could have taken the human race to the next level of Spiritual Enlightenment and Goodness that is Good. The New Golden Age.

The Wooers do not want this to manifest on Earth today.

Because they will lose control and they will implode into nothing.

They will be arrested for Crimes Against Humanity.

Just as Hitler and The SS Nazi's where tried for their Crimes during WWII.

Mathematics, Physics, and the Sciences are to be Used for our Enlightenment. Not for enslavement.

This is why the human race has been cursed because of what the evil the wooers have done with this knowledge.

They wooed many to vote for them. The Devils Temptation. They miss-used the sacraments and the knowledge and they got fried on their way to doom for their deeds.

There are World Revolutions going on all over the Earth today. The people are sick because of the wooers. The wooers are a Cancer to humanity. For their deeds they also received their Karma from God.

Just look around the planet and see what has happened to them and theirs and to their citizens in every country. It is the Truth.

It is in our face can we see it? Yes.

Anon now, History repeats herself so get ready for shit to hit the fan.

Spiritual Boom!

The Egyptian Pharaohs died and were mummified having everything sucked out of them. Their treasures of gold were left to the grave robbers, private collectors and to the museums for everybody to remember what Christ said.

It is easier for a Camel to pass through the Eye of a Needle than for a rich man to enter the Kingdom of God.

There is nothing wrong with being Rich.

Rich is Good.

It is not a sin to be Rich.

It is uncomfortable to be poor.

The Truth of this parable is that God is within us all and knows all.

We do not have to abuse our people, our environment, and our unique mathematics, geometry, sciences and physics to build a great temple to worship God.

Or to channel Natures strength to us, as some Star Wars LAARS weapon and LHC Reactor or HAARP Program.

Because God is already Here Within Us and within everything on Earth. God has always been with us from the beginning. God is Life.

We have forgotten the truth and The Way.

The real question for us to answer is are we with God?

Be Cause.

There is no Star Wars weapon to defend anybody or any country against God Smiting them to Smithereens if we self destruct because of vanity, power and greed.

Not even the Aliens can stop God. We can. God is here first and then he made little us. We Live in God.

We did not make the Sun, the Earth nor God. We humans have no real lasting power. Nor do Aliens.

We humans cause more damage to our environment and to Nature than any other species on Earth.

There is an Evil Alien Force on Earth controlling many people and countries today. It is the evil wooers.

They look like we do.

They are morphed to look as we do.

They are not good.

They are evil.

The are here to Mine and Poison all of Earths Resources and to enslave the citizens of Earth to work for them.

They pay their political slave citizens of Earth with their Monopoly Fiat money.

It is not Gold.

It is paper money that they created from nothing.

Since they control all of the world today they have persuaded everyone on Earth to accept it.

They claim their Treasury Notes are good and for all countries to accept them as Legal Tender.

They Control all governments today.

All citizens of Earth must use their money or Credit Cards or we will die from starvation.

Their money is not backed by Gold, Diamonds or Rubies which have real historical value. It is their Federalist Reserve System of The Alien Wooers.

God is Testing us all to SEE what we are going to do. How are we going to get rid of this alien evil wooer Third Force from the planet Earth.

We humans come and go, yet God is always Here and Now.

We live in Gods Creation.

We live in The Light.

Everything is Light.

God is Light.

We cannot even control our breath other than to keep breathing until God takes our last breath away.

Most people are scared to death of when that day will arrive. Because they will have to face God, so be good my friends!

The Truth is that we cannot take our gold with us. Freedom is very Important. Only our good deeds travel with us to Heaven.

This is why we are talking about doing something good for yourself and your loved ones while you still can.

Life is changing very quickly.

You will notice time flying by.

Many people are waiting for God to show up any time now. Many spiritual people are getting ready to move into another spiritual dimension soon.

We are Moving more closely into The Light. There is a reason for all this excitement.

Something very big is going on.

I don't want you to do something for me, I am doing good.

I hope this good book is good for you to help you CO-Create your Spiritual FREEDOM and goodness and share it with others today.

I want you to do something good for YOURSELF, Your Family, Friends and GOD.

I am doing good.

Yes, we can set up a Monetary Trust's for ourselves and our loved ones and we should take care of us and them. We pray and hope that we and they have the strength, knowledge and the common sense, and intelligence to use spiritual wealth wisely because it is Gods Wealth and we are gods custodians. Gods wealth used wisely is a Blessing. Gods wealth used foolishly is a curse.

We can also Share some Wealth to Others and to Charities if we want to help people. Or to Spiritually Serve a good cause or God.

After we have arranged our lives and if there is any money left over.

In truth money comes from God and Spiritual Love and our good thoughts. We are custodians of Gods wealth.

We are not to be a Christian Muslim Jewish Buddhist Hindu or whatever Scrooge with our money. Nor are we to be a FOOL on a hill squandering it like we witnessed in the Dot. Com days.

Most of us forget where our breath of life comes from and so did the Pharaoh's. God is our breath of life.

It is amazing how many people still follow the life of the pharaohs only to have the same fate of doom.

God through Moses had to come to Egypt to FREE the Jewish people.

Because.

And it Happened in the Process of Time, that the king of Egypt died, and the children of Israel sighed by reason of the bondage, and they cried. Their cry came up unto God by reason of the bondage.

Exodus 3.

Then the Pharaohs and Egypt really began to suffer for what they did to humans for not doing good, being selfish and greedy and cruel.

There are many countries who suffer today needlessly because of their self serving leaders not doing good for God and his people.

These vain leaders enslave and drain their own people.

They ruin their true natural resources for their own greedy and self serving hidden political agendas. They open hidden off shore bank accounts. Build large palaces and secret armies to protect themselves from their own good citizens because they are evil wooers and false leaders.

They are afraid the people will eat them alive, as if God hasn't already given them their good. I am sure he has, because God is swift, and you can't see inside of these leaders heart, mind and body as to what Karma has happened to them.

Just ask those who work for them or their family members and they will tell you the truth.

As we look around the world in every country on Earth we will see who they are.

Do you want to see a miracle on CNN?Yes.

It is very easy to see who are the wooer leaders and who are not because Gods True Good leaders are working doing good in very humble ways.

They have taken off their royal garments and holy vestments and put on their gardening clothes and they are in the streets of their countries doing good for their citizens like Good Princess Diana.

Oh my God.

Here is a challenge to Good CNN, Good ABC, Good CBS, Good NBC and all the other Good Television stations around the planet Earth.

Do you want to see the power of God at work in every country in the world today? Yes.

Do you want to see who is Gods Good leaders and who is a wooer leader LIVE on CNN as the world watches TV?Yes. Good!

Then you will go get the Good children of every world leader whether they are a Good President, a Good King, a Good Queen, a Good Prince, a Good Princess, a Good Chairman, a Good Senator, a Good Member of Congress, a Good Pope, a Good Lama, a Good Indian Chief and even the Good CEO's of all the worlds largest corporations. You will ask their Good children to ask their Good parents LIVE and on Camera for the world to witness.

Who father and mother is really the boss?

Is it you or is it GOD in your life and in our country?

Then, quietly, patiently, wait for the answer while the camera is showing all the facial expressions and body language of these Good world leader for all the world to see. Even their Good children's faces. Even their Good citizens faces.

All waiting for their Good leader, their Good parents to answer. As Good you will be waiting too. Holding your Good breath in anticipation of the Good truth!

While WE have this Good world leader televised LIVE for All the World to SEE and HEAR the answer, we will see God do amazing things not only in those Good leaders lives, but also in their Good countries, and in their Good citizens lives, and in their Good employees lives, for all the Good world to witness the Good power of GOD live on Good CNN!

I am GUARANTEEING You Good, and the World Good, that YOU will be AWESTRUCK for life by the Good power of GOD and so will be the world leaders!

Humpty Dumpty sat on a wall.

Humpty Dumpty had a great fall.

All the King's horses and all the King's men, Couldn't put Humpty together again.

You can do it Good CNN. It will be Fun. World Leaders Live of CNN.

Are evil wooers in your country not wearing their gardening clothes. Are they not in the streets and in the hospitals and in the schools helping their Good citizens?

Why not?

You can visibly see that evil wooers live a life of Hades on Earth no matter how much they have taken. Or how many secret soldiers they have around them because they all are in a living Hades.

They will never be happy unless they give up being a wooer. God is not a fool on a hill.

God is invisible to most people. There really is a Heaven and a hell on Earth. Be Wise and Acknowledge in the Lord God. Be Cause. God lives within you and You live within God.

God can be anybody's worst nightmare when we least suspect his arrival. Like a Good Hungry Lion in our face when we open the door to the bathroom in the middle of the night like in a nightmare.

Anon after a while we created machines that use petroleum oil products for automobiles, trains, ocean ships, airplanes and rockets. We created Nuclear Reactors.

Yes, these machines did our work for us in greater capacity to produce more work. Some souls FREED themselves from slavery. Today, many souls are still slaves to economics and to mental hypnotic television and environmental pollution.

Many people are still sex slaves and abused children world wide.

We polluted our cities with poor geo engineered air quality to create poor health, emphysema, lung problems, allergies and sickness of abundance.

How many people are sick and don't know why?

The wooers disease's. The Curse of the evil wooers!

How long can you live without clean air and water and food?

We have polluted our cities, our environment and our water and air systems. Geo Engineering of our total Human Earth life is dangerous. We are heading for Bruising.

Chemical Trails spread and HAARP world wide. People and Animals and Nature getting sick.

Our Aquifers polluted with Fracking oil explorations. Diesel fuel auto and truck emission gases.

Toxic waste emissions, petrochemical plastics, medical and animal waste in river and sewer water systems.

Chemical man made residues to the point that humans, animals, nature, and marine life are polluted and toxic and sick.

Fukushima Radiation. Katrina. EXXON Valdez. Chernobyl. ETC.

9/11 and Many Wars.

Agent Orange deaths, disabilities, deformities in Vietnam and USA Veterans. Desert Storm Veterans Chemical Poisonings on both sides of the fence.

We are a sick people manipulated by the evil wooers.

We have polluted our water systems above and below the Earth to our own detriment. How long can you live by drinking polluted water?

Ask Odysseus I am, he will tell you the Truth.

Not very long.

No Air only minutes. No water maybe 3 days.

Today look at all the bottled water we all consume around the world. Water cost as much as gasoline in some countries today.

If the water isn't polluted why do you buy and drink bottled spring or purified water?

Our oceans are polluted to the point that way out in the deep blue sea we see enormous areas that are miles long of floating plastic garbage dumps and petroleum oil slicks and tar balls all over the Atlantic and Pacific oceans, the Mediterranean coastal areas and the Baltic seas and in the Middle East and throughout all of Asia.

It is truly disgusting.

We humans are the slobs of the Earth for greed and ignorance.

We have been brain washed by the evil wooers.

We have become possessed by our on vanity, greed and secret political wooers agendas that we cannot see ourselves because of the oil tar balls in our eyes and of all the Geo Engineering pollution in our air, water, earth and food.

Most of the human race eat polluted food.

Most of our minds-bodies have stopped to function properly on the planet Earth because of the toxins in our food and from the pollution in our cities. This is one reason many people and animals are sick with Cancer.

Many have lost their heart and soul and do not know how to find it.

It is possible to find and heal your beautiful good mind, body, heart and soul right here in this good book. FREEDOM!

We are addicted to our own pollution because of our greed and we chose not stop and change for our own Good.

We are a caged human animal living in Polluted Cities.

Ask your self, Why?

How sick do you have to become either personally or in your families or in your nations or as a human race and on and in our Earth before it is much too late?

Why do you make excuses that you don't know why?

The Truth is in our faces.

The reason we are sick as a Nation is because of ourselves and the way we think as a Nation The USA.

The way we do things politically. The way we live personally and as a family and as a country and as a planet Not in Harmony with Nature and God.

This pollution, this ignorance in bounty, is what we as a human race have done with Gods Good Bounty on Earth.

No other animal has done this good.

Mirror Mirror on the wall, Who Evelyn is the most beautiful Wooer of them all?

We will arrest them all.

CHAPTER 9
There Is A Solution

We as a human race have to expand our horizons within our spiritual minds. We learned we can chose to make a difference in this world that we live in.

God asked me to ask our Good Kings, Good Queens, Good Presidents, Good Chairman's, Good Rich or Good Poor, where do we think you can hide without God seeing and hearing everything you think in secret, say or do in private?No Place.

God does know you and he expects you to do good as leaders of Gods countries and citizens.

You do want to go to Heaven don't you?

There really is a hell and a Heaven. Most of us have already gotten a little taste of what heaven and hell is like by living here on Earth.

I am asking any Good King, Good Queen, Good President, Good Chairman, Good CEO, Good Wealthy and Good Elite, Good Rich and Good Poor, who is the boss in your life really?

It is not you. It is the Good God within you.]You may fight God. You will lose.

Ask any Good leader in the world today who is the boss. Them or God, and you will know the truth and where they stand and why things are as they are in your country.

Go ahead and do not be afraid of men and women, be afraid of God.

Ask the Good Queen of England, ask our Good President, Ask the Good Germans, the Good French, the Good Dutch, the Good Greeks, the Good Jews, the Good Moslems, the Good Asians, the Good Mexicans, the Good Spaniards, the Good South Americans, the Good Canadians, the Good North & South Africans, the Good Australians, the Good New Zealanders, the Good United States of America, the Good Swiss, the Good Chinese, the Good Austrians, the Good Russians, the Good Balkans, the Good Italians.

Ask anybody Good and hear what good they have to say and watch what good instantly happens in their lives and their good country and we will all know the good truth and so will they.

There are no good excuses for not doing Good today with what we know. Unless you claim the devil made you do wrong and you are ignorant and possessed. You ask God to please forgive you for being a wooer, you better ask God for help now.

We learned that you wooers who administer empires and own empires of Finance and Technology and Banking can and will diversify their portfolios and yourselves and CO-create a nonpolluting life with the technology and the machines we have for your own GOOD and the GOOD of All on earth.

We created everything else good through out time and we will create the good in our life time also. It is only a Natural. We can creates good.

Good will created good will.

We will CO-create good because deep down inside most of us, in our soul, all is GOOD. We all want our good.

Yes, we have had to do whatever we had to do to get to Be Here Now.

Now that We Are Here we can through our good will create the good that we have in our mind and heart and soul.

We are all very Unique and very Talented and the Best is yet to Come.

I personally know that in each and every soul there is good inside of you all.

You can CO-Create good when you will it, so be it. We learned we can and will create a better life for our own GOOD or our lives will perish in vain.

We learned we as human race will create antigravity nonpolluting modes of transportation. We have seen them from Heaven.

We can apply ourselves and ask God for Divine Guidance and Inspiration.

As CO-inventors, engineers, industrialist's and scientist's with God we can ask God and receive the knowledge from the Spiritual Light on how to create the good in our life and the good machines for our own good on the planet Earth. We can also miss use them to our detriment.

We learned that we good leaders and good industrial moguls will have our wealth multiplied a thousand times for creating good in life.

We who do not do Good will perish as things of the past and be forgotten.

God said He will have others take our place in life, if we do not pay attention to Him & Her, God.

History has proven many times over that many others including Kings, Queens, Presidents and Moguls of Commerce, have gone and will go by the wayside for being out of HARMONY.

We will change our use of oil to nonpolluting technology and stop geo engineering or we will die from our own pollution.

Oil is not worth killing for or dying for when there is a better way. We learned that the oil industry is coming to an end as the Whale Oil Industry and the dinosaurs did.

In fact, The Industries New (IN) that are forming in our industrial moguls minds today are vastly more wealthy and prosperous than oil ever dreamed of becoming.

There is zillions of dollars to be made from nonpolluting technology in antigravity vehicles for transportation alone. There is zillions of dollars to me made using Light Waves for Technology in Health and Medicine.

There is zillions of dollars to be made with Light Waves Technology in Communications and Business. We see this today.

There are endless of Industries New (IN) in technologies to explore within Gods eternal creation. Life is very multidimensional. There are many universes unexplored right here and now if we would only open our eyes and even our third eye and look and ask God to show them to us.

The many polluting industries including the oil industry of today are like what the Whale industry used to be in the past, they are dying.

We can suggest to anybody who wants to be apart of a New World Revolution of CO-Creating Good, that this is the time to ride the Lightwave of the Future Today.

Start Methinking and Start Receiving and Start CO-Creating Today.

We learned we will create an entirely New and Better way to live life on Earth by Default and Due to Un Foreseen Disasters. Way Over The Top!

We as a human race do have a choice. We can go with Gods flow or we will perish.

Recollect It has all happened before.

We can live the Good life or we can die from our own Rigidity and from living in the past that does not exist anymore today. Life is changing right before our eyes, will we take notice?

Life is like our breath. We have to take it now, and enjoy it. It is Gods breath. Because later we do not know when later is. We will have to let our breath go and breath again.

We Keep on breathing Good thoughts and thinking Good thoughts and Doing Good thoughts and we will keep on enjoying life until Gods Angels come calling.

We learned we will get our good by thinking good thoughts and by our own good actions, we want to. Life is good if we look for the good.

We learned we all have been blessed with Gods Good if we will only look for the Good first within ourselves and in our own lives and all around us even in Nature.

There are birds, bees, flowers, trees, oceans and rivers and mountains too and many things Good to enjoy in life.

Some Good things in life are free.

They do not have to be expensive to enjoy them.

Here is a Free Treat.

We can look in a mirror and say: I Love You, I forgive you.

This is a Beautiful New Day. We Begin A New Way Today.

You can say to somebody else, I Love You.

See how GOOD they will feel. They will smile.

As you think so shall you be. Think love, think health, think wealth and abundance, think fun, think compassion, Laugh!

Think forgiveness first of ourselves and of others.

Then think of how you really want your life to be. How to enjoy your good life while you can.

YOU never know when YOU will be called by Gods Angels. When it is our Time it is our Time Unannounced.

We learned that eventually we will realize that all of our good is here and now within us today. We are here today. What WE have been thinking about.

Let's all begin to think good thoughts for ourselves and our loved ones, our Nation and for others less fortunate.

How many good thoughts did YOU think today?

It is NOW the time to think good for ourselves, our loved ones and our neighbors, our business, our profession, our country, our Earth and our good life that God has given us all.

Do not wait until you are dying.

Please make it good for YOU.

We all Deserve The Best.

It is all about us to CO-create our good.

Very soon we will travel through Spiritual Light beams.

We will use our mind to Co-Create good today and everyday.

Today we will realize that Christ means Sun Love and God is within US all.

CHAPTER 10
God Father & God Mother

After my visit with Jesus Christ the Angels brought me to my Father and Mother God. My father and mother hugged me and, and I hugged them. I am so happy to be back home again.

I had not seen my parents in what appeared to me to be a very long time. Yet there is no time in Heaven.

Being on Earth I forgot at times that they and my Guardian Angels are always with me. Guiding and protecting me and you too. They do watch over me all of my life and continue to do so even today. In Spirit.

I just forgot that they were with me because of my environmental human conditioning. Because I let the chaos of life get to me as so many of us do. At this juncture on my soul journey in Heaven there was no need to say I am sorry to my parents because I am already forgiven.

They understand all. They have lived all. They are all knowing. They are All. My Father and Mother know everything about our life and All LIFE. They see everything in our life just as their Sun & the Moon does. Everything we do is recorded by the Spiritual Archives which is a spiritual history book.

Everything is always Ola Kala and Good with our ever loving and knowing Good God parents who unconditionally love us all. Our parents in Heaven know how life is here on Earth because everything in life is created through them and we are their children. God is all of LIFE.

All of our life is an expression of God through us on Earth too.

Because we are all One in Spirit, Mind and Body.

We can look at our LIFE and this Godly creation called LIFE as WE are CO-Creating LIFE with God as unusual or strange as this may appear to you.

Life can be beautiful or crazy and anything in between.

There is only One family on Earth as it is in Heaven. This is our God family. All is One. God is One. We and life are all within One God One Life.

I Am, you are, we are All together One big spiritual family on Earth as it is in Heaven.

God really lives within every one of us and in all life. All there is, is God.

Gods Electrical Spiritual Energy creates The Light.

All that is good in our life is Gods good. We are born good in spirit.

We are born spiritually good.

This is a good reason to realize that what we do to others we are doing to God and to ourselves.

This is why in the Lords prayer WE ask God to Forgive us our debts.

In some of us God is more visible. Others may See a good person because we listen to God inside of ourselves. We do the best we can for ourselves and God. What Good anybody sees in anybody is really Gods Good that we see in our self too.

While in others whom we see very little of good in a person or no good at all as in some diabolical persons is Gods will. God is Silenced in them because they have closed themselves off to God within themselves for whatever their personal reasons may be.

They have chosen and They have created for themselves their life this way.

This is the karmic role they are manifesting. This is the karma they are paying.

This is the lesson they need to learn in their life's lessons as we all do. Very much as closing themselves off into a basement without any air, water or sunlight becoming Crazy and Insane and living in a living hell on Earth.

I am saying that most of us humans do not know what the animals know.

Some people on Earth just do not care to accept that we are one big family because of bigotry, hypocrisy of race, religion and education.

Heaven is not some Milk Toast Place where everybody is sitting around the segregated pool at some fancy Mauna Kea Beach hotel in Kona, Hawaii with palm tress blowing in the wind being waited upon by beautiful half naked Hula men & women with voluptuous bodies bringing us a Pina Colada, Martini, Gin and Tonic, Johnny Walker, Ice Tea or a Pakololo joint.

Nor are there angels flying around singing to you that you are holy and saved and good because you are a Christian or Buddhist or Muslim or Indian or whatever you think you are other than humble spiritual souls, Gods children.

Because, only God is Good.

God Father & Mother share their Abundance of Unconditional Spiritual Love with us, their good children, so we can create for ourselves our own goodness.

God does not create our good. We create our own good or not so good with our thoughts, our words, our deeds and our actions.

Every one of us good children are self made by ourselves.

Every one of us good children will also judge ourselves when you look into the mirror of life every day.

Because the Mirror on the wall will not lie to us. We do have an aware consciousness.

What we see in our selves is what we are.

What we have thought of and what we have done. This is what we will receive for our good deeds. We can change all of what you see. Make Mo Betta!

This is why God gave everybody freedom of choice and our personal self directed will power to create what good we will. I humbly suggest that after reviewing your lives in private and you look to see what good and not so good things you have created in your life you may want to think about creating some good karma to live and enjoy because life is very short. Is it not?

YOU may want to ask God for forgiveness. YOU may want to forgive others who have hurt you.

Most difficult of all is, YOU may want to forgive Yourself.

The only true religion in Life or in Heaven is Unconditional Spiritual Love.

Yes, there is a Jesus, a Mother Mary, a Buddha, a James, a Joan of Arc, and many good men and women souls who live in Heaven when they are not visiting us on Earth doing Gods Good deeds.

The real truth is there is only God within us all who is called by our given name as we are called James or Mary or John or Niki or Angela or Abraham or Sarah or Adam and Eve or Jilli.

The only government in Heaven is Gods Spiritual Law, Order & Harmony. It is called Peace of Mind.

The only God in Heaven is One God and God has billions of names all around this Earth. One of them is YOU.

The Real Divine Light of Wisdom and Knowledge in Heaven is Self-Realization & Enlightenment of God.

Heaven is our home away from home were we come to Refresh our selves in Spirit, in Peace, in Spiritual Love and in Enlightenment.

Then we go off to live and learn about all the wonderful things that are available to us all to do.

We can study and learn about Gods Infinite Creation and all that is possible for us to create. We can Educate ourselves about how to live a good spiritual life which nobody taught us how to do.

We can learn how to be a Good Parent which nobody taught us how to do.

We can learn about Good Husbandry and being Good to our animal friends.

We can learn how to Be Here Now which nobody taught us how to be.

We can learn to be a Good Lover that nobody taught us how to be and enjoy love making with our spouse or our lover or our friend.

We can learn how to Spiritually Love ourselves and how to spiritually love others who Love us. We can learn about Compassion.

We can learn about Understanding.

We can learn about Forgiveness.

We can learn about Healing our selves and others.

We can learn about Communication.

We can learn about Spiritual Service.

We can learn about Work.

We can learn about CO-Creating Abundance and Wealth and how to be a Good Custodian and Administrator of our and Gods wealth on Earth.

We can learn all about Great Spirit, God.

We can learn all about Creative Visualization.
We can learn all about Matter.
We can learn to be a Good Spiritual Warrior.
We can learn about all the Elements.
We can learn all about Air.
We can learn all about Water.
We can learn all about The Light.
We can learn all about the Earth.
We can learn all about Science.
We can learn about all Mathematics.
We can learn all about Chemistry.
We can learn about Philosophy.
We can learn about Poetry.
We can learn about Words.
We can learn about being a Leader.
We can learn how to be a Good Politician.
We can learn to be a Good Minister.
We can learn how to be a Good Hunter or Fisherman.
We can learn about the Good Means of Production.
We can learn about being a Good Industrialist.
We can learn how to be a Good Banker.
We can learn how to be a Good King & Queen.
We can learn how to be a Good Prince & Princess.
We can learn how to be a Good Human Being.
We can learn how to be a Good Environmentalist.
We can learn how to be a Good Lawyer.
We can learn how to be a Good Advocate for the poor and the enslaved.
We can learn about Light Machines.
We can learn about Medicine.
We can learn about being a Good Doctor.
We can learn about Good Herbs.
We can learn about the Ocean of Love.
We can learn about the Stars and all the Universes that are within Gods creation.
We can learn to Play Good and have Fun.
We can learn about Sports.
We can learn to Sing Songs and Play Music.
We can learn to Dance.
We can learn to CO-Create Art.

We can learn to CO-Create and CO-Invent infinite Good Technologies for Humanities good.

We can learn to do Miraculous things here on Earth and in all the other wonderful universes that God has created in this Eternal and Infinite Universe.

Many of you good souls will return to Earth and other spiritual places and universes thankfully and live many good life times enjoying life.

It is a misstatement to believe you are going to Heaven to do nothing.

That is just being lazy and wishful thinking. Yes, you will rest in Heaven for a while.

Yes, it is True in Psalms 23

God maketh me to lie down in green pastures. God leadeth me beside the still waters. God restoreth my soul. God leadeth me in the paths of righteousness for His name's sake. Yea, though I walk through the valley of the shadow of death, I will fear no evil: for thou art with me; thy rod and thy staff they comfort me. Thou preparest a table before me in the presence of mine enemies; thou anointest my head with olive oil; my cup runneth over. Surely goodness and mercy shall follow me all the days of my life; and I will dwell in the house of God for ever.

Yes, Psalms 23 is true if, We have Faith, Believe in God Mother and God Father and work spiritual hard in life being good. It is not for the lazy. Some times we work effortlessly. If we go to Heaven we can learn to work smarter and wiser and with less effort. To spiritually prosper with more abundance to enjoy our good life.

We can also learn to do simple things and enjoy our life with less if we chose to live a simple life.

When I looked around and saw how wonderful life really is and how many wonderful opportunities they are for us to explore and to challenge us I was very Happy.

It is wonderful to come to Earth and CO-Created with God a beautiful and spiritually exiting life on Earth as it is in Heaven. There are endless possibilities and things to do and learn about. Education is wonderful. You can now begin to explore all the wonderful things there are to do on Earth.

For those of us who enjoy Spiritual Service and having a Soul Purpose and Intention in our life CO-Creating and doing New, Exiting and fun projects, it may take many life times to explore all we can do with God at our side.

Once we see that everything is for our Good to enjoy and to live our good and to create our good we can see that we are very fortunate to be Gods children. Because God is Truly Rich and Abundant in everything Good. Everything good is for us to enjoy and to play with in a Balanced and Harmonious way.

There is a Time When Life is really as a Giant Playground and it is the Biggest Spiritual Amusement Park any of us have ever witnessed anywhere in any universe on any planet especially Earth.

Life is a Miracle.

Our Life is a Spiritual Soul Journey, an Odyssey.

Life is a spiritual dream we live in that god created.

We are all on a majestical spiritual soul journey called LIFE whether we like it or not.

How many of us late in life look back in our life and realize we missed so many opportunities to live the life we really wanted to live?

How many of us had difficulty making up our mind or could not make up our mind because somebody else told us what to do in our life?

They lived their life through your life. They made all the decisions for you. You are today living their life instead of your own!

How many of us had difficulty making a decision because there were so many choices? We realized we could not do them all in one life time.

We had to make a choice because of survival? We have not missed anything yet because we do have a choice to start a new life that we can create today.

First we do have to acknowledge our life. Where we are today with Total Acceptance before we can go on to CO-Create a New life.

Acceptance of our life is a fundamental issue.

We need to be REAL and Honest with our selves.

If we are unhappy doing what we are doing, say so and acknowledge this to yourself and to God within you.

Our life up to today is our Karmic path of the Past that brought us to The Present. By accepting our life and our lessons in life with unconditional spiritual love, forgiveness and compassion we can now move forward.

Yes, there is karma. Yes, we cannot escape it.

Yes, we will have to pay our dues and complete our karma.

If we do not do it this time around, we will have to do it the next time around.

Yes, we will Create New Karma and this is Ola Kala and Good.

Because this is how we learned about our life and Life called God.

This is why God Created All Life because life is good. It is about learning about Life and especially God.

We are the Odyssey.

Yes, it is true that those who have created crimes and injustice against humanity will have to pay their karmic dues moreover return and live those injustices themselves, their own karma. Nobody can escape our own karma.

Nobody can escape God. Yes, forgiveness is Here and Now because God does forgive us but we have to ask God for Forgiveness. Will you also forgive yourself?

Will you allow yourself to be reborn into a new spiritual life with Gods help? Yes, goodness becomes you.

Like any good child that realizes their mistakes, we will replace our mistakes with right action and we will continue on in living our good life.

Our mother told us, do not touch the stove top. It is hot.

We want to learn.

It is not that we did not hear her or listen to her.

We wanted to know the truth personally.

We touched the stove top with our hand.

Ouch!

We burnt our hand.

Ola Kala.

There is nothing wrong in living our karma. It is called taking responsibility for our actions. In thinking about our karma we realize our mistakes and our injustices unto ourselves and unto your fellow human beings are spiritual learning lessons.

We can choose to make amends and do good works and deeds starting today because we want to live a Good life.

Being a wise soul that you are you can easily see that most of us create from our unconscious ignorance instead of from our conscious thoughts, a life of pain and suffering we where taught.

There is no such thing as unconsciousness. Unless you have been Brain Washed or Hypnotized by The Evil Wooers and It is an excuse to be lazy.

All this is forgiven by God by doing good works and deeds.

Most of us do not do crimes against society consciously.

Those crimes are created out of ignorance, anger, pain, frustration and a disbelief in God. Yet most of you do abuse or have abused in the past or present either orally or physically your love ones.

Most often yourselves more viscously and inhumanly.

How many of you look at someone with Stink Eye?

Yes, it is true I was a soldier and I have killed in war. I have done many stupid things. I have said many stupid things. This is life. I have also rescued Vietnamese children and enemy soldiers. I have also helped many men, women and children around this Earth. I have contributed economically, spiritually and physically to schools, churches and hospitals. I thank God I also gave up my hapless wretched life in the Great Vietnam Soul War. I have also orally abused and done many stupid acts that I am ashamed of.

I have asked God for forgiveness and you can to. I have spoken with God in private and so can you. We all make mistakes this is the way we learn. Yet this is the path I walk and I talk and I do. This is the path that I chose and that I needed to walk upon to learn these personal spiritual lessons in my life.

Who knows, you may have been a cruel Warrior or President or King or Queen or Prince or Princess or Banker or Senator or Mother or Father or Brother or Sister or Pope or Lama or Merchant or Minister or Police officer or Jailer or Prisoner or Teacher or Healer or Teenager or Pauper or Industrialist or Environmentalist. Or whatever you are at this time at this juncture in your life that you are living today. You are living your karma, well and good for you, because without a life you got nothing my friend.

We all have to learn our lessons and this is good for all of us children of God on Earth. This is your path and you should realize it is good.

You do not know another way to learn but the hard way at this time in your life.

Soon you will make it easy and effortlessly.

Today I pray we have learned a New Way by reading this good book and this love story called PTSD Heroes Odyssey, Love Is The Door Way Into our mind, body, heart, soul, and into a Good Life. This New Way is Very Simple to understand and do. Nothing is easy at first.

Because of our past conditioning, we keep on trucking. It will become easier and more effortlessly and we will CO-Create and Receive our GOOD.

This is Scientific. This is Mathematical.

How many of us learned about life through Divine Wisdom and Knowledge first without any pain and suffering?Nobody.

As Christ said We are All Sinners and I do believe God.

How many of us good children learned to walk without falling down?

How many of us good children never burnt our hand on the stove of life?

How many of us good children never hurt our siblings because we did not know better?

How many of us good children never hurt or blamed our parents for things we did not understand and we judged them severely instead of ourselves?

How many of us good children never stole a thing in our lives as even candy or a cookie?

How many of us good children were never jealous or coveted our brother or our sister for having things we also wanted but we did not have it because it was not our time or we did not deserve it?

How many of us good children never bullied others around and later became leaders and politicians and abused everybody with your power?

How many of us good children never mistreated an animal or our own pet or a friend because we were mean and angry and frustrated and we didn't know how to be kind to ourselves and others?

How many of us good children were never selfish and we didn't what to share our good?

How many of us good children were never greedy and later continued to be greedier because we learned to be greedy from our family because we didn't know better and hurt all those around us and we did not care?

How many of us good children never slapped or abused or hurt our relatives, our brothers, our sisters, our friends, our child, in some way and later closed our hearts becoming meaner and heartless because we did not know better?

How many of us good children lived our parents lives and were molded in their likeness and we hated them for not allowing us to live our life and we are now living a life we hate and this life we are living is not really our own true self?

How many of us good children are so phony that baloney meat is more real than us?

How many of us good children are a Prince in this world and yet we are spiritually poorer than the poorest pauper and you could do better?

How many of us good children are a Princess in this world and have a Heart of Gold and you can do better than Princess Diana did?

How many of us good children are a Queen yet insensitive and in denial of the spiritual truth in your Kingdom and you could do better?

How many of us good children are a King yet insensitive and in denial of the spiritual truth in your Kingdom and you could be better?

How many of us good children are in positions of power and have corrupted our selves because almost everybody else is corrupt in positions of power and you think it is the right way to be and you could do better?

How many of us good children are on The Financial Street's of Commerce World Wide and you have hardened your hearts and taken the money from the innocent who trusted you and you could do better?

How many of us good children are Military men and women who have served a government and a commander who is as phony as baloney and you did as he or she commanded you and you are living in shame and you could do better to speak the truth and not do what they command you to do for the sake of freedom and the truth in your country?

How many of us good children are an insensitive Leader of a Country and have appropriated millions for war and peanuts for the Infrastructure of Health, Education and Welfare of our citizens and country and you could do better?

How many of us good children sold your soul to the devil, like the evil emperor in the Star Wars movie who used your hate, your fear and your doubt of your self and God and now you serve him instead of God and you could do better to free your self?

How many of us good children are a King and Queen of our country and have buckled under the pressure from International Banking wooers to serve the elite few instead of our millions of good people that God gave you to protect for God and you could do better and overcome the wooers as Odysseus did?

How many of us good children live a life we really do not want to live and are afraid of our own fears and doubts of success to live the life we really want to live today and you could do better?

How many of us good children have polluted our mother Earth with your Corporations trash and waste and your machinery of greed and thinking you will get away with your deeds and not ending up eating your own poison and you could do better?

How many of us good children who authorized the use of Agent Orange to kill others and defoliate and contaminate mother Earth and her good children and her good animal friends and plants in Vietnam and think you can get away with your actions and go to Heaven instead of Hell when you could do better?

How many of us good children who support war and killing when God said Thou shall not kill, think you will not pay for your deeds and you could do better and find a peaceful way if you methinketh?

How many of us good children in Secret Government's think that your hidden secret agendas from your own fellow citizens and God are really hidden in secret politics and in secret orders and in secret religion and in the secret military and in secret banking and in secret education and in secret health care and in secret medicine programs and it will not come back to you and your families and you will end up cursed and sick living your own secret painful agendas in this life time and you could do better?

How many of us good children are in pain or in disease, either mentally or spiritually which manifests physically in your bodies because you have not forgiven others and your selves and because of your not good thoughts of good and you could do better?

How many of us good children have never hurt our neighbors and others and you never said you are sorry to them personally or even in spirit and you could do better?

On and on we good children go on learning all about US and God, and really it is All about God. Be cause everything Good is God and everything not good is created by mans ignorance of God.

Now we hope you can see that there is a much to learn about and a much to live about and there is very much GOOD to create and that is GOOD Works and GOOD Service for you to enjoy.

YES, we good children may even be surprised that when we do good works WE will be Happy with ourselves. You will enjoy yourself and your life and others will Respect You and you will even have fun!

God Blessed You and Me, All of US, to do Good with our lives because really it is Gods Good life too. God is Successful and a Winner. Just look around the Earth and see what a success God is.

You want what God has.

God knows that in time all Good things will work through us because we want our Good. We are Gods Children!

Just as we want our Delicious desert and we love it because good is GOOD.

I am positive that if we good children chose to be a winner we will be, A Winner in our life.

I am positive if we good children chose to be successful we will be, A Success in our life.

I am positive if we good children chose to enjoy our lives we will, Enjoy OUR Life.

I am positive that if we good children chose to do good we will, Do Good in our life time.

I am positive that if we good children chose to move the mountains of fear and doubt in our life, we will have All GOODNESS in our life.

Fear and Doubt is an illusion to keep us from being a winner and successful.

I am positive that we good children can easily realize that our breath is our life force and energy and it is Gods breath too that we breath in and out God until our time has come.

I am positive that when God sends his Angels to us good souls and tells us that it is time to give up our Soul life we will come to God and we will receive a New life in Heaven when God chooses to do so.

I am positive we good children do not have to be a rocket scientist nor Einstein to realize we are a soul, Gods breath, and God is the I, AM each and every one of us.

I am positive every good religion in Earth says this same good story about Life.

Love is the door way into our mind, our heart, our body, our soul and into Heaven.

As I stood with God in the middle of Heaven I realized that I must be dead or very close to being dead and I was amazed in this miracle.

God asked me if he could show me something and I said yes.

God said, look over here James.

And I looked Up.

God Opened the Heavens and I could see everything God created.

The Earth is floating in the Heavens in total Peace and Harmony with all the other Stars in Gods Creation.

I can See in the middle of Gods Creation the Sun with all the planets and stars Revolving around His Sun.

I can see Gods Sun is really Gods Beloved Sun radiating Unconditional Spiritual Love Throughout ALL of Gods GOOD Creation.

Gods Sun is called LOVE, The Christ, the One within us all, our soul. Gods Sun, The Light gives us All Life. Our Sun shows Us The Way in Life when the world would other wise be very cold and dark and lifeless without Gods Sun.

I am sending my Sun to you.

He is Me.

I am.

The Christ, the I Am within us all is Pure Unconditional Spiritual Love.

The Good Sun shines upon us all equally.

God asked me what do you see James?

I said: God all I see is Good.

God said: GOOD.

God said: Every-Thing is God and Every-Thing is Good.

All I can See God is in Peace and in Love and in Harmony with you God.

I do not see chaos.

I do not see war.

I See and Feel Peace.

I do not see any of all of mans injustices against humanity and the Earth.

All I can see is God in Perfect Harmony.

God said: Good because All is Good.

God told me: It is us his unconscious children who create all the pain and suffering and famines and wars and sickness and disease and hatred and corruption and governments and religions and ignorance that creates all the NOT good in peoples lives on Earth.

Good will always exist in Gods Universe because Good is God.

Good is a Spiritual State of Mind. We can be In Goodness or we can be out of Goodness. Goodness and Good always exist in Harmony in Gods creation.

God said: All his Good is Being Here and Now and Good will always be available to us Here and Now when we chose the Good in our life.

When we good children chose to get into Goodness and think good thoughts and do good deeds, our good will manifest in time in our Good life.

When we good children chose to live in Gods Harmony and in Peace with ourselves and with Others we will live in Peace on Earth.

When we good children chose to live by Gods Spiritual Laws of Spiritual Love, Compassion, Understanding, Justice and Forgiveness of ourselves and others we will also have a Spiritual Healing.

When we good children chose to stop polluting our Earth, our Mind and our Bodies, our Air, our Water, our Food, our families, our friends, and our Animal friends, we will live in Good Health without disease and we will be Happy and live on a Happy Earth.

When we good children choose to use our Free Will to choose the Good in our life, and in Life, we will have the Good that is in The Light and so shall we have the Good on Earth for Us all.

When we good children realize that what Good we give, goes around and around and comes around again to us, we will Enjoy and Give goodness in our life to all.

When we good children realize that Good is the Natural State of living life for a good human soul and all the Good that there is in Life is Good. WE will be Happy. We are Happy.

When we good children realize that a good life is Abundantly Good in Health, Wealth and in Richness in All Ways, WE will be a Winner and Successfully Enjoying our life.

When we good children realize that if we are living in a hell we created, and we are suffering, because we created our hell on Earth, and we realize that it appears we have lost our soul and our heart and our mind and our body, and we are in mortal pain, in sickness and in disease, it is never to late to talk with our Father and Mother God in Heaven in Spiritual Prayer.

It is effortless! It is easy!

We can do it!

It is The Spiritual Key to Our Doorway to FREEDOM!

We can humbly ask God for Gods Forgiveness because we have self-realized our mistakes, our own learning lessons in life that we choose.

We Do need Gods Compassion, Understanding and Forgiveness and Healing because we have a great need to Restore and Replenish our soul. Unless we can heal ourselves without God. I question that we have the Power.

We can live our life with Peace of Mind by now doing good instead of not so good. As a child who says I have learned from MY mistakes from miss-using MY unique gifts and talents that God gave ME.

One day we will realize that our Job is a job and it is not the real you. Our Job is only a job and we are all Gods people.

The king is a man and the queen is a woman.

The prince is a man and the princess is a woman.

The carpenter is a man and the mother is a woman.

The President of the USA is a man and his wife is a woman.

The Statue of Liberty is a Symbol of Spiritual and Political Freedom. She Stands Tall for Gods Freedom in the USA because we good citizens believe: In God We Trust.

The Earth is our Spiritual and Material God Mother. She Gives us all our Bodies. Our Bodies are Her bodies.

Gods soul rests within us.

Our Mother is our Holy Church, our Holy Temple, our Holy Mosque and our Sacred Tee Pee. All of our Abundant Goods in all of our life come from within our Mother Earth. As we her child birthed, comes out from within our mothers body, a Mother Earths Woman's body, our Mother Earth.

We the child Need Milk and Honey and Water and Food and Clothing and Toy's to Play with and all the other goodness from our Mother Earth. She, Spiritual Mother Earth, IS Holy God.

Anon WE better take GOOD care of Her and Respect Her or She, Our Mother, will give Us, Her Child, a GOOD WHOOPING that you will never forget in our whole life!

WE will deserve it if you do not listen to our Mother & Father God.

God MOTHER Feeds and Clothes Us All on our Planet Earth.

The Food we Eat.

The Air we breath is Hers.

The Water we drink is Hers.

Our fine clothes and shoes we wear are Hers.

Our automobiles and airplanes and the petroleum that fuels them are Hers.

Our refrigerators and stoves and showers and baths and towels are Hers.

Our televisions, stereos, CD's, computers, fax machines and cell phones are Hers.

ALL the Good Things in LIFE are Hers.

The White House is Hers.

The Congress is Hers.

The Senate is Hers.

The Supreme Court is Hers.

Anon.

She holds within Her Hands All The Holy Papers that are very Important to us in America.

The Bill of Rights and The Declaration of Independence are from within Her Heart, Body and Soul.

SHE is GOD and SHE is GOOD.

The money we so worship and enslave ourselves for are Hers.

The lumber and bricks and electrical wires and plumbing we build our homes with are Hers.

The weapons, bombs and the Agent Orange poisons we kill our own kinsfolk with are made from Her.

She can turn them against us Her Children at Her Will. As Like a Raging Volcano, worse than an Atomic bomb. A New Black Invisible Plague that chokes us All to death into utter doom.

We throw our poison's in our Own Mother Earth's Face. Because of our own venomous disrespectful gratitude of a selfish brat attitude. We are thinking we can do what ever we want to do to our Mother God. We will NOT for long because Her Patience has run out of Her.

She Loves us very much, and how we returned to her, Her Love in Vain. She Will return to us our own nothingness!Ask Any of HER Good Daughters if this is not TRUE.

Everything that we humans use to create goodness in our life is from within our Mother Earth's Body.
O.
Oh.
Oh My God Mother She Is Mother Earth.
GOOD.
O.
Oh.
Oh My God.
She is our Mother Earth.
BEAUTY is Her Name.
These Blessings are Her Goodness.
Her Sky is our Inspiration.
Her Mountains are our Vision Quest.
Her Meadows and Forest's are our Resting Place.
Her Oceans, Lakes, Rivers and Ponds are to Baptize and Cleanse,
Our Soul's Life within HER HEART, MIND, BODY & SOUL.
Her Love is our True Natural SOUL Way of Being.
Her Stars Above are for our Direction and Way.
Her Ocean is our Ocean of Unconditional Love.
Her Animal Children are our Friends.
Her Birds Sing us Songs of LOVE.
She Is Beautiful as BEAUTY IS.
BEAUTY is Her Name,
She is Mother Earth.
Oh My God. Oh. O. GOD.

Anon the present condition of our life on our planet Earth is the total sum of all the conscious and so called unconscious unconditional acquiescent good and not so good thoughts of over 7 billion human souls.

These good and not so good thoughts of ours today, and in each and every day, are being manifested in our daily life as we know, Live in and understand it.

Today, our thoughts can actually affect our environment of life on the planet Earth.

A small strange example about Mother Earth and what we do to her.

Please and pardon the language yet it is affective.

Let us assume for a moment in time you are a man who is a new wretched hapless wooer oil salesperson living in a dark, cold apartment in the Manhattan. You have not been able to sell any Wooers Oil and you are starving to death.

You just started in this Job and you want to be as successful as the Rothschild's and Rockefeller's.

You have come to the Wooer Oil Merchant's in Manhattan hoping to sell some of your oil products but nobody wants to by your wooers oil from Baghdad because it looks as if there is sand in it from the Desert Storm war. The merchants are wondering could there be soldiers body parts in the oil.

It is late in the afternoon about 6:01 p.m and it is raining and you have to get to the subway station to get back to your dark, cold, depressing apartment on the other side of Manhattan. As you walk out of the last oil merchants office in downtown Manhattan and you realize you will have to walk through Central Park in the dark to get to the subway station entrance on the other side on the Park on 86th street.

You are carrying a few ugly depressing heavy oil cans and by accident for some unknown reason, on your way to the subway entrance, walking through Central Park where poor people like you hardly ever visit from Wealthy Manhattan you slip and fall in some big stinking dog shit because you are not looking where you are going in life.

By accident a beautiful woman who is also walking through the Central Park feels sorry for you and helps you get up on your feet. She happens to have some paper towels in her artist bag and gives them to you to wipe off the kaka from your face, hands, heart and body because you do stink afoul.

Majestically by accident you meet this Gorgeous Beautiful Good Woman who is in disguise as an Artist in blue jeans and tennis shoes carrying an artist bag. She does not look like She is Wealthy or anybody special, but she looks clean and she looks just like any other artist because she has paint on her blue jeans.

By accident she takes a liking to you and things are looking good.

She is thinking, who knows, maybe we can be friends.

One day she comes over to your dark stinking pad, and she sees you do not have much wealth but you do possibly have love and she kind of likes you, and SHE has Compassion for you, and in HER mind, SHE is Methinkething.

Well, I Do not Need Wealth. I am Wealthy, What I need is LOVE.

I could make him a really RICH MAN, but I will not tell him I am WEALTHY as of yet. Because I want to See if he has any Spiritual Love and if he is really kind, gently and good. SHE wants to see if he LOVES ME or is he just trying to fool me as all wooers do.

You, a man, a wretched poor arrogant wooer snake oil peddler being an ignorant soul, blinded by your own vain ego, pollution and drugs, not thinking well, not seeing well, not thinking well or respecting that possibly as a person, or even as a woman, SHE is important to you or even in Life.

Yet majestically invisible like the Goddess Athena, SHE is not only important, SHE is a Very Important SOMEBODY. She is Mother Earth as an Artist Painter. She Knows everybody in the wooers Oil World.

Because you are blinded and drugged by your own mental political business pollution, you say, act and treat Her, your new found friend like some white trash artist drug bag.

You mentally and physically stab and trash Her all over HER Spiritual Body and bruise Her and even orally hurt HER.

She leaves your dark stinking cold apartment in despair as so many good woman have, bleeding from angry mental knife wounds and bruises all over her body crying Oh My God.

She calls Her Father, who happens to be The GOD FATHER of New York. SHE tells HIM Everything about your little wretched soul and job. Where you live in Manhattan and HE is PISSED OFF to the MAX.

Now you the oil man wooer being drunk on your egotistical greedy and political pollution, thinking you are powerful victimizing this innocent good Mother Earth Woman and Her Children on Earth do not yet realize, YOU are in BIG TROUBLE.

You have bucked the wrong daddies girl and you are going to die a terrible death.

In fact, you will wish you could die now, if you only knew what was going to happen to you. Now this Wonderful Beautiful GOOD Woman that you did not realize, nor think that your very survival in life depends upon Her Mother earth.

Her Healing Spiritual Love, and Her Abundance, and Her Wealth of Goodness all come from Her. Because in her invisible disguise as an Artist she was invisible like the Goddess Athena is and SHE is a Very Rich & Wealthy & Powerful Woman, but you to not know or see SHE isThe Wealthiest Woman in the Whole Wide World.

She Is Mother Earth as an Artist in disguise.

Anon now what kind of good love do you think you the wooer oil peddler is going to get from HER & HER GOD FATHER & HIS SON'S?Now you Can feel that HOT double bladed machete on your little tiny head cant you?

Men and women can make a choice to choose to think good thoughts for ourselves that does create our good in our personal and professional life.

We men and women can choose to do good deeds.

Good Thoughts and Deeds will CO-Create and Build Up our Self Esteem.

A Good Positive Attitude and Good Optimistic Thoughts will create a Positive Outlook on our life because our Goal is to CO-create a Good life for our Self.

As we realize as a human of the human race on the planet Earth that we are the Captain of our Ball Team.

We can create a little bit of success or a whole lot of good Success by our actions, thoughts, visualizations and dreams of well being in Harmony with God.

The more good thoughts we have the better life becomes because we are creating good.

If you evil wooers want to self-destroy yourself as a planet as you have in the past, and have God Take UP the Good Souls to Heaven and make the Ocean Rise Up and flood you wooers out and cleanse the Earth again, it will be done.

If you want to self-destruct and bring fire and brimstone down on your wooers head it will be done to you.

If you choose to blow your self up with nuclear bombs and chemical viruses it will be done to you wooers.

If today we want to heal ourselves and our planet Earth as a human race, as citizens of the Earth and of God and of The Spiritual Light, as custodians of this planet Earth and of Us and our Animal Friends lives too, All 7 billions of US, Will have to Consciously make a choice to Open a Door called Love Is The Door Way Into your Mind, our Body, our Heart, our Soul, our Peace, and our Good Health, our Wealth and our Harmony for thousands of years, or we will become wooer looters and perish as a race and have to start all over again.

The choice is ours.

The majestical golden spiritual ball is in our court.

How will you play the game of Love Life?

What will you CO-create for your self today?

Will it be not so good or Real GOOD Love?

You do not have to be a loser! We Can Become a Winner.

You can make a good choice!

I am choosing to serve myself Good Spiritual Love. I am A Winner.

You Can Be all you can be by CO-create With God.

The further we go into outer space and away from your Mother Earth, the more we learn. That the further we go into an outer space, and further from the truth we will travel from Mother Earth, God Mother is that we All human animals need oxygen (Air) which is Gods Love Light, Manna and Prana.

How will we live without spiritual air in an outer doom in a space ship being a test monkey in an experiment of weightlessness of nothingness having no more purpose than a prisoner Chimpanzee that is in a medical space station experiment that is obviously going to perish from the stress. Of course it is our chose.

We know we can see how beautiful God created the All of the Universes with all the Stars floating in HARMONY.

Why not live our life in Harmony too? We do not have to be a monkey prisoner for Dartker Vadernut building his Black Star Ship of Doom that ultimately will Self Destruct by a great heat wave from Gods Sun Shining Bright Light burning away all the little wooers of the evil emperor as Directed by God.

As the Astronauts will testify to you as they fly around the planet Earth, Our Mother Earth, the Earth is Very Beautiful. The Moon is Very Beautiful. All the Stars in Heaven are Very Beautiful and in Peace and in Harmony and The Sun is Beautiful. Oh My God Mother is Truly Beauty Herself.

Anon yet, without Gods Air and Water and Food and even His Space Ship it can All become a very ugly doom in outer space if we are out of HARMONY with God.

These are the things I See.

These are the things God spoke to me about.

These are the things I learned and shared with you my friend.

After looking at all the wonderful things God showed me, God closed the curtains of Heaven and we stood in silence.

I realized that I could stay in Heaven if I chose to.

I had this feeling within me that even though Heaven is my home and is wonderful and beautiful, I wanted to come back to Earth and Complete, A Spiritual Task to bring us the TRUTH about FREEDOM, and I told God my feelings.

God asked me why would I want to go back to Earth now that I am back home?

I said to my Father God, now that I Spiritually See how things really are, I want to go back to Earth and to help you.

God said: James you don't have to go back to Earth but if this is what you really want to do, so be it.

As my father God said: So be it, He showed me my New Path that I am to Walk and Talk and Write and Spiritually Paint for you. This New Path was not going to be easy.

I was going to fulfill my past karma for all I had done in my previous life and that was Ola Kala with me.

I was happy and willing to fulfill my Sacred Contract with God.

My New Life is truly being a majestically spiritual wealthy and abundant Soul tour all around this Wonderful Earth and all the way back into Heaven.

This time around it is going to be one of peaceful gentle learning and fun exploration of Gods many universes in the Be Here Now on Earth. God said, I will learn all about my Father & Mother Gods Creation called Life through my own self realization and experiences.

I will humbly learned through my own pain and suffering early on in my own life and now I have come into Enlightenment and Peace and Love and Enjoyment and Abundance and Fun while I am here on Earth.

I will learn how to use my own weaknesses and lessons in life to CO-Create Spiritual Strength and Good Deeds for myself and others.

I will learn about the importance of my prayers to my father & mother God. I will learn how to use Gods Spirit of Creative Visualization, Prayer and Meditation.

I will learn how to use The Healing Arts and Physician Heal Thy Self through my own healing crisis's of sickness, disease, pain and suffering which I have over come into Health and peace of Mind today.

I will travel around the world many times as a Successful Hero with a Thousand Faces being my own great Artist learning and sharing Light, Love & Aloha.

I will have all the Abundance and Wealth and fun in my life and I will share my Abundance and Goodness with others.

I will be Guided and Protected by God and God Angels and I will be Teaching others about The Light in Education, Love, Health, Wealth, Fun and God. I will learn about Being In Spiritual Love and Loving Others Being Spiritual Love.

Then God said: Surely Goodness and Mercy Shall Follow You James All The Days Of Your Life and You Will Dwell In The House Of The Lord Forever. Amen.

We hugged each other and I cried.

Anon then as In the Beginning of my Odyssey to Heaven, the Angels picked me up and we flew through Heavens Gate and through the Bright Sun Light and onto the Earth through and with The Eternal Aum Sound Reverberating In Reverence Of Omnipresent Omniscient Omnipotent GOD. Wow.

I would like to ask your permission to tell you a parable.

Three Little Bird Story of Justice.

A story that I adapted from Mr. Gerry Spence and the story goes like this:

Once there was a wise old man and a smart-aleck wooer boy & girl.

The boy & girl were driven by a single desire-to expose the wise old man as a fool.

The smart aleck's have a plan.

They each had captured a small and fragile bird in the forest that sings beautiful songs.

With the little bird cupped in each of their hands, the children's scheme was to approach the old man and ask him, Old man, what do we have in our hands?

To which the wise old man would reply, You have a bird, my children.

Then the boy & girl would ask, Old man, is the bird alive or is it dead?

If the old man replied that the bird was Dead, the smart aleck's would open their hands and allow the bird's to fly off into the forest.

If the old man replied that the bird is Alive, the boy & girl would crush the little bird's inside their cupped hands, and they would crush it and crush it until, at last, the bird's where dead.

Then the boy & girl would open their hands and say, See, old man, the bird's are dead!

Anon so the story goes, the smart-aleck boy & girl wooers went to the old man, and they said, as planned, Old man, What do We have in Our hands?

The old man replied, You have a bird, my children.

Old man, the boy & girl said, their voice's dripping with wooers disdain, Is the bird alive or is it dead?

Whereupon the old man looked at the boy & girl with his kindly old man eyes and replied, The bird is in Your hands, my children.

Dear Women and Men, our soul and our life and the life of our planet Earth is in our hands.

CHAPTER 11
Health or Sickness

We are Spiritually Well.
We are Spiritually Healed.
Be Thankful to God and The Holy Spirit.
Health or Sickness are easy to See within our selves.
Health or sickness are within our minds-body.
We are Not our minds-body. Our body may be going through ruff times but we are not our body. We use our body to live in this dimension on Earth. We can direct spiritual energy into our self to support our healing. Herbs are very good friends.
We are really a Soul living within our minds-body.
Our minds-body is our home on the planet Earth.
Our soul is Living in our minds-body Temple.
Health is Harmony.
If we are living our life in Harmony within God and Nature, We are Spiritually Very Healthy.
If we are living our life OUT of Harmony within God, we have sickness. I have Compassion for you.
It is all very simple to understand.
Our mind-body is a biological-machine.
Example.
A human body is very similar to an automobile.
An automobile and all its many parts has Structure, Order and Relationship all built within itself being an automobile.
This is why it works. All the parts work in Harmony.
If we Maintain and Repair our automobile properly and drive it consciously and safely on the roads and highways of life our automobile will serve we well.
A human body has Structure, Order and Relationship all built within itself being a human spiritual light body.
All of the organs and all the parts of our body work in Harmony. This is why it works.

If we Maintain and Service our human mind-body properly and use our human mind-body properly and drive our mind-body Consciously and Safely on the Roads and Highways of our Life, our human mind-body will serve us well.

Our Health is in our hands. Our health is within our Souls minds-body.

What have we been thinking about?

Are we thinking LOVE or are we thinking HATE & ANGER?

All this GOOD thinking we are Doing in methinketh is the difference between HEALTH and HARMONY or sickness and disharmony and disease.

What have YOU been doing?

As a Planet this is all true.

As a Family this is all true.

As a Business this is all true.

As in Hereditary this is all true.

As Generically Genetically Engineering this is all true.

As a Society this is all true.

As a Culture this is all true.

As a Country it is all true.

As a Nation this is all true.

As a Government this is all true.

As a Religion this is all true.

As in Spirituality this is all true.

As Health, Wealth and Abundance this is all true.

God Created the Spiritual Human Mind-Body to Naturally function Properly in Harmony with God and Nature, as God made us in Gods Image.

All human and all animal bodies need Good Clean Air, good Clean Water, good Clean Food, good Clear Sunlight, and a good Loving Environment to live in to maintain good health. Anything less than good, and to what degree of more or less of Good CLEAN Air, Water, Food, Sunlight, and Loving Environment, Is the difference between good health and not so good health.

This will be the Environment we live in.

This is very simple to understand.

Is your environment, your home, your neighborhood, your work place, your city, your state, your country polluted?

Then You Live in an Unhealthy Environment.

What else Other than Sickness do YOU expect to have?

If your environment is polluted, Who, What, When and Where they polluted your environment? Use your Common Sense!

Oh God Help US ALL see more clearly in The Clear Light.

Nature is in Perfect Harmony with God. God Created Nature Spiritually and Materially Perfect.

If we look at a forest or a jungle or a meadow or a mountain or the ocean in its Pure Natural State that God Created it in BEFORE man came to Earth, We will See that Nature is Naturally Healthy and Abundant and in Peace and in Spiritual Universal Harmony with God. So are All the Animals that live in Nature and All is Beautiful. All is GOOD.

Since the arrival of we humans to the planet Earth the Nature of the planet Earth has changed from Healthy to unhealthy. Because of what some of the evil wooer have done to Her that has ruined Her Physical Nature.

NOT HER SPIRIT NATURE, this is impossible.

Not all of the alien souls, WE humans, have done this Riotous Destructive living. Some human souls know how to live Spiritually in Harmony with Nature.

The Native American Indians and many other Indigenous human souls who have Respect for Her and Her Abundance live in Harmony with Her.

They live a Thankful, Happy and Healthy In an Abundant life. Because SHE, Mother Nature is Abundance with All that is GOOD.

What has happened here on Earth is that when we humans were brought to the planet Earth by God, We were ALL instructed by God on How to live in Harmony with Mother Earth and God.

Gods Children, We humans, Were given a Sacred Agreement and The Holy Covenant and The Holy Commandments to live by on the planet Earth by God.

Similar to By Laws in Real Estate,

The Bill of Rights, and The Declaration of Independence.

They are all embedded Within our RNA and DNA Spiritual Codes.

Similar as Computer Codes and Algorithms.

These Covenants and Commandments, were placed within the souls of every human and animal by God Father and God Mother by Gods Angels.

Because these Universal Laws are Gods Spiritual Laws for humans and animals to live with in Harmony with God and Nature.

Because all humans and animals are Gods Creation, Their Children, and all of their Relations and everything God Created is GOOD.

Historically, we can find these Holy Covenants and Commandments in the Holy Bible and in other Holy Books all around the Earth.

We can Look Within our self and find the Covenants, Commandments and Sacred Agreements.

Gods Holy Sacred Agreement, Covenants and Commandments are not hidden secret agendas nor are they a secret from anybody on Earth or in Heaven.

They are easily found and easily read and easily understood by any human who wants to Recollect what Gods Agreement, Covenants and Commandments are All about concerning the human race.

We, a member of Godhead, that has been brought to Earth to live OUR life within Gods LIFE have these spiritual agreements and laws for guidance.

What has happened before and what has happening today is that there some of us who have become evil wooers, wooed by the evil wooers, and betrayed God and the rest of us good people.

These wooers are the Evil Greedy Wooers on the planet Earth. Wooers are some of Gods own children, who have lost their mind, heart, body, soul and The Way from God Consciousness and Gods Covenants and Commandments and are out of Harmony with God.

They have become an Evil Alien Third Force on the Planet Earth as we all have Witnessed What happened in Germany during WWII with Hitler, The SS and what happened to The Jewish people.

Because they do not believe in God anymore.

Because of their own Self Idolatry and Egotistical greedy thinking, being lost in a black sea of ignorance, and having their own wool pulled over their own eyes by their own doing, by their own deeds, by their own thinking, they have become conspirators and traitors to God and Our Country.

I do not judge them because they are innocent as all wooers in sheep's clothing say they are.

God wills them their good because God is the Giver of ALL Good.

These evil wooers think foolishly they are god, and that they created everything, and they are evolutionary superiorly ignorant of themselves, thinking everything is theirs to do as they think.

A Major error on their part.

The wooers became the Dark Evil Alien Force, becoming an Invader Third Force in their own ignorance to their lost sold soul.

Betraying their own Families and their own Friends and their own Neighbors and their own Business's and Associates and their own Country and Our own planet Earth and to all of their Relations and to God. Not Good.

Anon these evil wooers started to worship themselves as being creative and talented and powerful and secretive and hidden agendas in Dark Illuminate Mystery's as false Idol gods do.

They have no real power but their little egoism with Scabs of Scale upon their little tiny wretched faces. SS Pin Heads.

Anon they built enormous glass temples and gathered fools gold and diamonds and hoarded they peoples wealth and squandered the peoples wealth upon themselves in riotous living.

Forgetting God and The Sacred Covenants.

Being drunk on Gods wine. Thinking it is their wine.

They became Fat and Ugly eating Gods Buffalo's thinking those Numbered Ox are theirs to do what ever they want to do with.

God and His Angels are patiently waiting for them all to arrive at the great banquet for the wooers that has now began.

God is watching the maidens serve them their Good Karma wine. God is waiting for the moment the evil wooers raise their Winged Golden Cup of Doom to their lips for their Utter Doom is now Upon Them all.

When they all Least Suspected Gods arrival at their Banquet Hall on the planet Earth.

Because of all these good deeds that the evil wooers have done, God has Blinded Them and Smitten Them.

God has given them not goodness and has hardened their heart for their hypocrisy.

Because God is a Jealous God and He has Vengeance because God is also Justice. God knows All because God is Omniscient, and Omnipresent and Omnipotent.

God has always had a Spiritual Plan from the Beginning of Creation.

Because God is Creation.

God has tested his own creation in the beginning. God tested his own children before he released His Program called LIFE.

Just as the military testing a rocket or a computer company testing a computer software program or an automobile crash test.

Because God has already tested his creation, God knows there would be a Rebellion.

A Soul Stars War.

A battle between the good souls and the evil wooers.

Between the Greedy Dragon and Bear and the Noble Eagle.

Because the Eagle is God in Heaven, Great Spirit, and the Dragon and Bear is the greedy wooers writhing and devouring all the good people on the Earth in their own greedy Black Hole of Red Communist Void.

The Noble ever wise Penelope said: Never can their be fame in the land for those evil wooers who devour and dishonor the house of God.

Why make this a reproach?

Behold our Spiritual Guest is Great of Growth and Well-knit and Avows Himself to be born of the Sun of a good Father.

Give him the Polished Bow that We may see that which is to be.

Thus I will declare My Blessing and it shall surely Happen.

He shall String The Bow, and Apollo does now grant him to be renown all over the whole world.

I will clothe Him in a Golden Purple Mantle and Doublet, the Godly Raiment.

I will give him a Sharp Javelin to Defend against the evil dogs and evil men.

I will give him a Two Edged Spiritual Light Sword and Golden Winged Sandals to bind beneath his feet.

I will Send him Safely and Protected with my Angeles wherever His Heart and Spirit bid him to go.

The Spiritual Eagle is Carrying in his Mighty Claw Lighting Bolt's from Zeus.

Anon the Eagle Will Smitten the Dragon and Bear upon his tiny SS Pin Head with Zeus Lighting Bolt's that are a Mighty Bright Blinding Light.

The little tiny SS Pin Head of the Dragon and Bear Bleeds Open as a waterfall and the Brains of the Dragon and Bear Crackled in the Flames as his whole body Writhed all Around the ground for all to witness his nothingness as God and the good people Rejoiced in Justice.

Anon God Knows that Wealth and Abundance is Gods Spiritually Created Through Spiritual LOVE. To be given to those who God so chooses. To give Goodness to all who are good. Because God is the Giver of All Good and Goodness because God is Good.

God knows that all good things whether they are children, food, clothing, home, tools, money, business, power, position, military, governments, religion, countries, and the planet Earth all require Conscious Responsible Administration by Spiritual Administrators.

Soul people like you and me, who have been placed into these Positions of Responsibility as Custodians of Gods Goodness to have good and to do good deeds with Gods Goodness.

If we do not do good we will be removed one way or another by God.

Anon God knows the Devil will Corrupt the Ignorant and Greedy souls.

Whether you are a King or Queen or a Prince or Pauper or a President of a country or the Princess of a Pond or an Industrialist of Commerce or a Carpenter or a Plumber or a Secretary of State or a Private or General in the military or a Senator or a Congressman or a Seamstress or a Cook or a Fisherman and his Wife or a Pope or a Lama or an Artist or whatever anybody's job is because God created the Devil to do just that purpose of using TEMPTATION.

The Devil serves God well.

God created the Devil Program to test us all.

Anon God knows that the wooers will Rebel against HIM & HER. God will give them utter DOOM because God created everything GOOD.

God will DELETE their Program into the TRASH BIN.

Boom!

TRASH BIN NOW EMPTY.

We are wondering what does this body of knowledge have to do with health and healing and how we can now Heal our Self and have a Healthy, Wealthy and Abundant human mind-body that is in HARMONY with God and all of Gods Goodness my dear friend.

Well, I will tell us now.

We are Spiritually Healed by our Faith in God. We Are Well In Spirit, Mind and Body. We will always be Well in Spirit Because Spirit Is God.

We are Well if we live our life in Harmony with God.

If we have not lived our life in Harmony but want to live in Harmony then we are Healing our souls mind-body and this is good.

Everything happens for a Reason and for Learning about life.

It is all about US and God.

We can change our life through Prayer and Action.

This book is about US and for US and to US ALL.

This Good Book is about US.

This Beautiful Human Spiritual Soul, a Stranger's from a Strange Land, and This thing called:US.

My Personal Example.

I was wounded in the Trojan Vietnam Soul War. I was smitten with an AK-47 bullet right through my left elbow.

The bullet shattered my elbow into approximately 50 pieces and broke my arm above and below the elbow joint. I had malaria and hepatitis. I also had blood poisoning from the bullet. All of this Smiting happened all at one time in the Trojan Vietnam Soul War.

I spent six months in the Army hospital. The Army tried to amputate my left arm off my body against my will.

I had to Escape from Ireland Army Hospital to save my arm and my soul. I got to a Pay Phone and called two US Senators from Indiana to come to the Ireland Army Hospital to STOP the Army from amputating my arm against my will. To please rescue me and my left arm that is apart of my souls minds-body.

Shit Happens.

I was basically what we would call dead. I was in terrible shape.

I Looked emaciated, skinny, and boils all over my body the size of golf balls and very yellow looking from malaria.

I lived in a bed for three months and then in a wheel chair for two months as in the Born on 4th of July movie.

When my mother visited Ireland Army Hospital at Ft. Knox, KY and asked where is her sons bed looking at me not realizing it was her son because I looked so bad, she freaked out screaming.

I am also adding to my personal experiences for karma depth of methinketh.

My brother who was a Marine committed suicide after returning from the Vietnam War.

My step sister who was born mongoloid and with a heart problem died at eight years old.

My father died of a heart attack right in front of me when I was eight years old at home at his own party with family and guest present and my mother screaming for help.

I was not what you nor anybody would call a happy puppy. Living my Karma.

I was living way out of Harmony in my life back then before joining the Army and going to the Vietnam War.

All of it just depends on how we look at something that we have experienced.

I am healing my souls minds-body left elbow and arm and this is good for me.

Shit Happens in Life.

Forest Gump said, My mama always said, You never Know what you are Going to get in Life's Box of Chocolates.

Next.

Structure, Order and Relationship Our Beautiful Structure.

OUR beautiful minds-body has beautiful spiritual structure.

We can see our outer structure if we look into a mirror. Mirrors do not lie.

We can see our beautiful outer minds-body, our beautiful body's soul shadow, our beautiful silhouette with all of our beautiful features.

We can see our mind-body's beautiful hair, our beautiful head, our beautiful eyes, our beautiful eye lashes, our beautiful eye brows, our beautiful ears, our beautiful nose, our beautiful mouth, our beautiful teeth, our beautiful tongue, our beautiful neck, our beautiful shoulders, our beautiful arms, our beautiful elbows, our beautiful wrists and our beautiful hands.

We are all beautiful.

We can see our beautiful chest, our beautiful nipples, our beautiful navel, our beautiful stomach, our beautiful hips, our beautiful genitals, our beautiful thighs, our beautiful knees, our beautiful legs, our beautiful ankle's and our beautiful feet, our beautiful heels and our beautiful toes.

If we Look In a Mirror and turn around we can see our other beautiful back side. If we look real close and bend over we can even see our beautiful rear end and our beautiful okole.

We are Beautiful!

If we close our beautiful eyes and pray and meditate and use our beautiful Spiritual Third Eye, We can look within our beautiful self and see our beautiful self from within ourselves.

We can see and visit any beautiful cell or beautiful part of our beautiful structure and converse beautifully with it. Try it, you might like it and impress your beautiful self with your own beautiful inner vision and spiritual strength.

Our Beautiful Order.

OUR beautiful minds-body has a beautiful Natural Spiritual Order built within itself. There is a beautiful Harmonious Order of all the beautiful Components within our beautiful minds-body.

All of our Beautiful Human Biological components are Naturally in Harmony within themselves and with each component within our beautiful selves and God.

This beautiful order is composed of many beautiful parts like our beautiful skeleton system, our beautiful organ system, our beautiful nervous system, our beautiful arterial system, our beautiful eliminatory system, our beautiful digestive system, our beautiful glandular system, our beautiful cellular system, our beautiful blood system, our beautiful circulation system, our beautiful brain-mind system, our beautiful reproductive system.

We are Beautiful.

All of our beautiful human biological parts Naturally work together in Beautiful Spiritual Harmony as they were created by beautiful GOD to be functional and in support of each other as a hub with spokes and rim of a great beautiful Cosmic Magic wheel that rolls along in life.

This is our Beautiful Spiritual Anatomy in Harmony with God.

Just as a wooden house or a wagon wheel or an automobile or a light bulb. They work well and so do we.

Our Beautiful Relationship.

OUR beautiful minds-body has a natural beautiful healthy relationship with all the other beautiful parts that make up our mind-body's beautiful home. Every beautiful component of our beautiful minds-body is composed of beautiful cells that beautifully join together to make a beautiful living component.

As an example our beautiful heart is made up of beautiful heart cells that have a beautiful life and a beautiful consciousness all of there own as all other components in our body do. Our blood system is composed of beautiful blood cell that join together to make a River of nutritious blood.

Oxygen, with Manna an Prana are within our healthy blood cells that nourishes us all.

These beautiful cells actually have their own beautiful mind-body consciousness. These cells know their beautiful purpose in life and they also have a beautiful memory. Within all cells there is a spiritual life force known as God that gives them and Us all life, a beautiful life.

This spiritual life force known as God is in Perfect Harmony within itself and within all of our cells and this is why every component works Naturally on its own and in Harmony with God and with All of our other beautiful components in our beautiful minds-body.

Anon As long as WE Respect our beautiful minds-body and Consciously Think beautiful Nourishing Good Thoughts with our beautiful Mind, and nourish our beautiful minds-body properly with healthy beautiful food.

Breath good clean beautiful air, drink good clean beautiful water, exercise regularly, say our Good beautiful prayers to God, and live in a good clean healthy loving environment, playing and having fun, singing beautiful songs if we chose to, go dance with a friend, laugh good, share good beautiful love, be thankfully good, WE will be Healthy Naturally beautiful.

Our GOOD Health.

We Are Naturally Healthy.

Sickness and disease.

As we realize that our beautiful soul lives in our minds-body home, our beautiful Temple, we will realize that God also lives with US in our beautiful home.

Every beautiful cell of our beautiful minds-body is in perfect Spiritual Harmony with God naturally. Sickness and disease begins by OUR thoughts and how we live our life in our minds-body on Earth.

Because of where and how WE live in our personal environment, We can be Healthy or sick or anyplace in between Health, Sickness and Death.

There is a beautiful saying: As we Breath, so shall we be.

As we Think, so shall we be.

As we Say, so shall we be.

As we Eat, so shall we be.

As we Do, so shall we be.

As I methinketh, therefore, I am, My Methinketh.

What does all this Mean and How does it affect little 'O' beautiful Us?

Let us look at OUR beautiful life.

We are born into a household we call our beautiful family.

Our beautiful family lives in a Castle Estate, or in a home, or in apartment, or in a cabin or in a tent, or in an automobile, or in a trailer, or in the city park or in the street.

We live either in the city, the country, by the ocean, in the mountains, in the plains, desert or in a beautiful meadow or by a river.

Every place WE live in has an environment that is good or not so good.

As an Example:

We could be living in the pristine beautiful country.

We could be breathing fresh clean air.

We could be drinking good clean water.

We could be eating good organic food.

We could be working on a Farm or Ranch or in a Beautiful Office Building or Royal Castle or Family Estate with fresh air and plenty of sun light away from industrial city pollution.

This all sounds wonderful and beautiful.

We are happy because this is GOOD.

Good.

Ah yet my friend, let us consider for a moment how OUR health could possible change for the worse in different psychological mental environments. Or even Electrical Environments.

If in OUR beautiful Castle home or Corporate work place or Factory there is any kind of environmental pollution we will get sick.

Or as another mental pollution, we are being orally abused and or physically abused and or continually criticized or traumatized in some other way, We begin living out of Spiritual Harmony with our own spiritual soul self love.

WE begin to think that We are Not respected and loved as a person, as a human being, which you are not in this example.

Very much like a beautiful fish out of water.

Usually We will start to think of what is wrong with US.

We start THINKING about trying to change ourselves, Out of Fear and Doubt of ourselves, To become someone or somebody or something else, other than our own beautiful natural true spiritual soul self.

Just to please the person or persons that are abusing US.

We start to change our spiritual mental perspective on life and of our own beautiful naturally wholesome self and self esteem to one that is not natural, beautiful and wholesome.

We start BELIEVING the words of criticism and abusive actions and We see ourselves as not being loved, not beautiful, not happy, not successful and definitely not a winner in life but a prisoner developing PTSD.

From THE ongoing abuse, We begin to believe, there is no God because this would Not be happening to us or our personal or work or societies or evil government environment.

We become the abuse and consciously mimic the abuser and become a codependent of abuse by being worn down over time.

Some of us souls live our whole life in this ugly environment.

OUR reasoning being, that if there is a God, this abuse would not be happening to beautiful Us.

WE start to change our beautiful self.

By changing our true self, WE loose our true self in this defensive act to survive and protect our self.

SURVIVAL.

Internally in our minds-body, by our own thoughts, We start to hate ourselves and hate the other's who are abusing us, mostly out of self-survival and justly so, Not to like our abuser.

Now We have become what We do not want to LIKE.

Those who abused us really do not know what they are doing because they are spiritually mentally sick in their minds-body believing that they can abuse us or anyone because they want to.

Those who abused US are usually acting out and living their life upon US out of their own painfully ignorant family or Religion or political conditioning that they have received from their parents, family, friends, strangers, government, secret orders, church.

Even though they are wrong in what they are doing to US. They also had to endure abuse at some time in their life because they learned this abuse someplace and from someone.

They are consciously thinking of what they are saying and doing when they are abusing us. They claim they are unconscious because it is buried deep within them. True but an excuse.

As an Example Think of what the Nazi SS soldiers did do to the Jews and Gypsies and many others. Russians, Chinese and Japanese Governments did to millions.

This is a global problem.

Think what has happened to millions of innocent women who became sex slaves.

Or gay people who have become sex slaves not knowing why they are.

Most of this kind of abuse is really happening consciously yet they will claim it is unconsciously. Believe it or not.

The only time it is not unconscious abuse is when the abuser is a professional torturer.

They are in the military of any governments, or in Cartels of many different kinds of drug organizations, or even in some religious orders that are roaming the Earth torturing somebody for something whether it is information, property, pleasure or a phony confession to make them feel good. Gang mentality.

A considerable amount of this abuse is really our past karma getting back at us believe it or not. What goes around goes around until we stop the wheel by right action.

I am knowing this may be difficult for some of us to understand especially if we do not believe we have lived before.

I want us to KNOW that we do NOT have to accept abuse, nor should we even think about accepting abuse if we can leave or even run away to FREEDOM.

Now that we understand and know how abuse is cause and if it is in our personal environment and if abuse is happening YOU, get UP and GET as FAR and AWAY and as FAST as YOU CAN from abuse and abuser to SAFETY & FREEDOM.

Now we all know we have lived through abuse and we have survived.

WE can go on with our beautiful good life, without any past regrets, knowing beautiful YOU are now FREE.

Thank God and Yourself.

This is the reason WE are born into these families.

Strangers in A Strange Land?

Yes.

I know it does not seem fair or right but this is the way karma is or otherwise our life would be different.

As the Beetle Paul said: This is Your Lot!

Anon and we could have been born to the Good Queen of England or Scotland or France or Germany or Mexico or Columbia or Africa or Australia, or New Zealand or Belgium or Russia or Norway or Sweden or India or China or Japan or Netherlands, or Greece or Korea or Vietnam or Iraq or Afghanistan or Iran and received a beautiful royal handsome abuse.

Who really knows which is worse?

We do know that we do not really want to live in somebody else's beautiful shoes.

The grass always seems greener on the other side of the fence.

If we do live a good life this time around, and clean our life UP, We may very well get to be born next time around into some very thoughtful, kind and loving beautiful family and We help CO-Create this beautiful time around.

We may even be reborn today into a totally NEW LIFE we CO-Create because we deserve to live a good healthy abundant safe life.

Many good souls have just gotten up and split.

What good goes around really does come around.

It is important to think before we act or do anything isn't it beautiful?

FEELING GOD.

Because we are experiencing this pain we become critical because we are searching for an answer to OUR pain.

As beautiful young children growing up in our family nut homes that is in a strange reality our parents or relatives homes are our legal custodians of us until we are of age to leave home.

If we are married to somebody we thought we knew, WE really are stuck and have no chose but to do as commanded and take the abuse and suffer.

Burying OUR pain and Our HATE and Our ANGER someplace deep within Our minds-body heart and soul.

This is all WE can do until WE leave home, workplace, office, factory, church, government, cartel, gang or country.

Unless Gods healing comes to our family by a miracle, and the abuse stops, and the love begins and this is ALL possible we must continue until we can get to FREEDOM NOW.

Our beautiful minds-body is were OUR painful memories of abuse and hurt, Anger and Hate are hidden and stored within.

We can bury all this PAIN in our beautiful heart, in our beautiful liver, in our beautiful ball bladder, in our beautiful stomach, in our beautiful intestines, in our beautiful colon, in our beautiful prostate gland, in our beautiful ovaries, in our beautiful lungs, in our beautiful breast's, in our beautiful brain, in our beautiful nervous system, in our beautiful bones, in our beautiful joints, in our beautiful skin, in our beautiful eyes, in our beautiful ears, in our beautiful throat, in our beautiful nose, in our beautiful arm, in our beautiful knee, in our beautiful leg, in our beautiful foot, in our beautiful joints, and even in our beautiful bone marrow.

WE can even bury all this pain anyplace within our beautiful body minds-brain or soul.

All of this Pain, Anger and Hate that WE have stored in OUR body, OUR Church, OUR Temple, OUR Mosque, OUR Tee PEE, Can very easily be turn into SICKNESS, CANCER, AIDS and many other so-called incurable DISEASE.

Many of US have closed off OUR beautiful hearts from OUR feelings.

Many of US cannot Cry Anymore.

Many of US cannot FEEL anymore, and WE are Numb.

Many of US are all shriveled up inside our heart, soul, mind and body.

I am and do know that, We all do want Healing Spiritual LOVE, To Come Into OUR Life Now.

I am now Recollecting Happy Beautiful Us.

We do have a beautiful Heart of Gold.

Given to Us by GOD.

Right within our beautiful soul self.

We can Breath this beautiful LOVE In and Out.

We can FEEL our beautiful Heart Opening Up, and Radiating beautiful LOVE, Compassion, Forgiveness and Health to beautiful YOU.

YOU could not feel our beautiful HEART before now.

ALL the beautiful Spiritual Love that is Within beautiful YOU.

Because YOU had buried your pain, and your feelings.

So deep down within your beautiful minds-body-heart and soul.

Hidden in so many places from all to see. From all the abuse YOU have suffered.

In OUR beautiful life, It took US COURAGE and a little bit of spiritual time and energy.

To bring our PAIN to The SURFACE. NOW WE FEEL OUR PAIN.

THIS IS HEALING US SPIRITUALLY.

Ola Kala.

Now WE can Spiritually RELEASE and BLOW ALL OF OUR PAIN OUT of OUR MINDS-BODY-HEART & SOUL INTO THE SUN.

THIS WILL CLEAR OUT OF US, all the NEGATIVE ENERGY.

OUT of US For Ever.

OUT of OUR Good LIFE.

WE CAN BREATH FREELY FOREVER MORE.

Thank you GOD.

'O'

Oh.

WE had forgotten that beautiful Spiritual Love is within US, And all around US saying to US. Please forgive and go on with OUR beautiful life.

HEARING GOD.

Many of Us had closed off OUR ears and WE cannot Hear Well because WE only heard abusive and negative words.

I do not blame YOU, I forgive you and I know you can Hear Well now.

We do not what to Hear anything but what WE want to Hear and this is, I Love You.

Before, We could not Hear God, Talking to Us, From within Us, To Love Ourselves, To go forward with our life.

To CO-create the life YOU really want to live.

Because YOU were afraid, To come out of the closet, Because you might get hurt again.

I Am understanding you.

Your Hearing is healed and you do Hear Well, I Love You.

SEEING GOD.

Many of Us could not see God well before Now.

Because We only saw abuse and violence.

I do not blame you, forgive YOU and I know YOU SEE Well Now!

I know We only want to See what We want to See.

We do not to see violence and abuse.

We want to see Spiritual LOVE.

WE could not See that Spiritual Love Is All around Us, Nor in others, Nor in Nature Reminding YOU, YOU are not alone.

YOU can See Well Again, I Love You.

Being SPACED Out of HARMONY into HARMONY.

Many of US have become hypocrites and bigots and critics of the highest order.

We judge ourselves, others and even God.

We say mean, nasty and dirty things which are our DEEDS to ourselves, and to others all around US.

To those WE love, and to OUR families, to OUR friends, to OUR fellow workers, and to those WE do not understand, even to God.

Everything WE say in HATE and ANGER actually manifests within OUR life FIRST.

These nasty remarks and DEEDS that WE make are Poison Arrows to OUR loved ones Mind, Body, Heart, and Soul Wounding or Killing our Love Ones.

A Sick Attitude is unwanted, undeserved, cruel, and unusual punishment.
We Will Pay For Every Word That Comes Out of our Mouth!
Words Deeds Are Very Powerful!
WORDS can Bless US All.
Words can Curse US ALL.
YET who is really being blessed or curse?First of All, It Will Be ourselves.

Our unkind Words and Deeds will actually manifest in our minds-body, heat and soul as sickness and disease GUARANTEED!

IF WE SAY and DO, Mean and Nasty Things to Our love, to our children, to our family, to our friends, to our Fellow workers, to Innocent people, to our Country Tis of Thee, WE are in Sickness.

Bad words and deeds thought inwardly in Our mind about others or spoken outwardly to our loved ones, are only going to make everybody who can RUN from US, run away from US faster than a Speeding Bullet, Faster than Superman.

Even worse than that, they Close OFF their hearts to US.
As the Gates of Heaven They Will also be Closed to US.
WE all want to be Loved and Respected.
Even to those who WE do not even know.

We say and do mean and nasty things to them and about them, only returns to US, To become OUR very own, Sickness and Disease.

Call IT Cancer, or anything you want.
It is our good words manifested to US. So we should enjoy IT, our Karma, our goodness.
IT those Magic Words, our Words, is Truly the Power of the Word and God. ~ God said so.
Words of Love are in Perfect Harmony with God who lives within every cell of our minds-body.
God lives in every organ of our minds-body.

When We say, I Love You, to our Love, to our children, to our Family members, to our friends, to our fellow workers, to our World, WE make them All Happy, because WE Love THEM.

LOVE rushes back to US, A Thousand times Revitalizing and replenishing every cell in our Heart, And in our minds-body.

WE are Now Happy.
THEY are Now Happy.
LOVE is Happy LOVE.
Love = Love.
LOVE Heals ALL.
Love is Compassion.
Love is Forgiveness.
Love is Good.
God is LOVE.
We are Love. We All Love, One Spiritual Love. O.

Even the devil wants to be loved for his evil doings of temptation, and fear and doubt about Gods Good life and creating the Illusion to sway US into not saying, I love You to every body who WE do LOVE.

The Devil does not get any love. Be Cause he does not know what spiritual love is.

There is NO Human Being, Nor Animal Friend, Nor Plant Friend, Nor Mineral Friend, Nor Molecule Friend, Nor Atom Friend, Nor Anything in life, That does not Like LOVE.

GOD is LOVE. God is Good. Ola Kala.

Oh GOD, O.

An Example of Not Good Deed Words.

Now WE can all realize that good and bad words do have power.

I will give US small example of some words and phrases that are mean, nasty and dirty deeds that many of US may have heard OR WE have even said to Ourselves and to Others that have given THEM and US Sickness and Disease.

Please excuse me for this example yet it is necessary for understanding the power of negative words.

I hate you. I hate them. You are stupid. They are stupid. You are an ass hole. You are a buck up. You are a bastard. You are a bitch. You son of a bitch. You are a son of a bastard. You are a failure.

You couldn't fight your way out of a paper bag. Be a man. You are a sissy. You are a queer. You are evil. You are ugly.

You are an ugly duck. You only think of yourself. I cant stand you. You are cheap.

Your nose is funny. Your teeth are crooked. I can't afford you. You are eating me out of the house. I am broke because of you. You never help me. Look at your hair.

You can't do anything right. You are dumb. You can't cook. You can't clean the house right. You don't know how to make love. You can't do anything right.

You are a mess. You are a dog. You are deformed. You are a duffer. You are insane. You are crazy. You are incompetent. You are an imbecile. You are a moron. You are a scum bag. You are a whore.

You are worthless. You dishonor me and your family. You are an animal. You are a mistake. You are a little shit head. You are abnormal. You are a pig. You eat like a pig. You drink water like a horse. You are a donkey. I abhor you.

You make me sick. You smell. Did you wipe your but. You are a misfit. You are unaccountable. You are a maggot. You are a thief. I can't trust you. You are a Republican. You are a Democrat. You are a Communist. You are a Socialist. You are a Royal Ass Hole. You are a rat. You are on the left. You are on the right. You are a hippie. You are sick. You are a slob.

You are as daffy as a duck. You are absurd.

You don't know what you are doing. You don't know how to dress. You won't amount to anything. You are cursed. You are possessed.

You can't make anything work. You don't know what love is.

You are heartless. You cant feel. You cant hear. You cant see. You are inadequate. You are shit. You are lower than low. You can't be my child. You are a bum. You are an alcoholic. You are a drug addict.

You are bucked now, etc.

Forgive me for this example.

How would WE feel if somebody said that to US and WE had to listen to those words day in and day out as many people around the world do?

Would WE Not get sick?

An Example of GOOD Word Deeds So Now, WE do realize that good and bad words DO have Power.

I will give US an example some words that are GOOD that many of US may have said to Yourselves and others that have given them and US LOVE, Health, Happiness, Enjoyment and Success in our life.

I Love YOU God. I Love YOU. You Are GOOD. You Are Beautiful. You Are Beauty. You Are Handsome. You Are Very Kind. You Are Very Thoughtful. YOU Are Thankful. You Have A Big Heart. YOU Have A Golden Heart. You Are Very Smart. You Dress Well. You Are Very Organized. You Are Very Clean. I LOVE The Way You Love Me. I Love Your Smile. You Have a Beautiful Smile.

I Love Your Touch.

I Love Your Eyes. You Have the Cutest Nose. You Are Happy. You Are Healthy. You Make Me Happy. You Make Me FEEL Happy. You Are Very Neat. You Have A Beautiful Voice.

You Sing Beautifully. You Are Wonderful. You Are Well Groomed. You Have A Wonderful Fragrance. You Dress Beautifully. You Are Well Mannered.

You Are Compassionate. I Love You Dad. I Love Mom. I Love You Brother. I Love You Sister. You Are Well Spoken. You Come From A Good Family. All Of Your Relations are Good.

You Are A Winner.

You Are Successful. You Are Well Appointed. You Are Forgiving. You Are Healed. You Are Loved. You Are Well Behaved. You Are An Angel. You Are Intelligent.

I Love You God Mother. You Are Thoughtful of Me. I Love You God Father. You Are An Excellent Cook. You Are Well. You Are Healthy. You Are Strong. You Are Brave. You Drive Well. You Think Well.

I Love YOU Jesus. You Sew Well. I Love You Mother Mary. I Love You James.

I Love you Angela. I Love you Jilli. I love you Stathie. You are Organized. You Work Well. You Administer Well. You Build Well. You Are Well Intentioned.

You Make Me Laugh. You laugh At Yourself And At The World.

You Are Easy Going.

You Are Comfortable to be with. You have a strong mind. You have a spiritual mind.

You Have A True Soul Purpose. You Say Your Prayers Well. You Pray Well. You Meditate Well. You Have A Good Mind.

I Love You Grandmother. I Love You Grandfather. You Have A Good Body.

You Have A Good Soul.

You Are A Child Of GOD.

I AM Proud Of YOU.

You Make Me Laugh.

You Make Me Smile.

I Love You Cousin. I Love you Aunty. I Love you Uncle. You Really Are Well Meaning. I Love You Uncle.

You Are Well To Do.

You Have A Creative Imagination.

You Are Spiritual. I Love You Aunty. You Have A Good Instinct. You Are A Leader. You Are Balanced.

You Are Talented. You Are Intuitive. You Are Focused. You are Strong.

You Can Do It.

You Are Good. You Are Well Founded. You Are Well Heeled. You Have A Good Mother. You Have A Good Father. You Are Wise. You Are Knowledgeable.

You Are Protected And Guided By GOD. You Have two Guardian Angel Always With You.

You Have A Treasure Chest Of Unique Gifts and Talents Within YOU To Create The Life YOU Really Want To Live.

You Are Inventive. You Are Creative. You Dance well. You Make LOVE Well.

You Play Your Instrument Well. You Write Well.

You Are Gifted. You Are Blessed By GOD.

You Are In Harmony With God and Nature, etc.

How would WE feel Hearing these words day in and day out that most people around the world Do Not hear?

Wonderfully Good and Healthy and Happy and Successfully We Are.

CHAPTER 12
A Good Hollywood Movie

We now go on with OUR Good life CO-Creating Goodness. In whatever WE chose to Methinketh about.

As WE think about our Good Life & Health, WE realize we have So Much To Be Thankful About.

WE Learned to forgive ourselves, and Others. We Go on living our Good life.

WE realize that our Thoughts and Deeds are and do become US, And Our life.

WE Are The Good Captain, Of Our Good Life.

WE Are The Good Script Writer Of Our Good Life.

WE Are The Good Producer Of Our Good Life.

WE Are The Good Director Of Our Good Life.

WE Are The Good Actor Of Our Good Life.

WE Are On Our Own Good Stage Of Our Good LIFE each and every day.

Let Us Spend Some Spiritual Quite Time Methinking, Visualizing and Writing in detail about Our Good Life Story.

Let Us Spend Some Spiritual Quite Time, Visualizing How, WE Want To Live Our Good Life.

As Our Own Good Script Writer, Let us spend some Quite Time.

Writing Our Good Life Script, As WE See It, Within Our Mind, Body, Heart and In Our Soul.

As Our Own Good Producer, Let Us Spend Some Quite Time.

In The Planning And Organizing, Of Each Step, Of Our Good Life's Movie, That WE Will Produce.

From The Beginning To End, Within Our Mind, Body, Heart and In Our Soul.

As Your Own Good Director, Let Us Spend Some Quite Time.

Visualizing Each Set And Setting, Of Each Segment Of Our Good Movie.

As It Will Be Filmed, With Our Good Actors Passionate Performance, Within Our Mind, Body, Heart, and In Our Soul.

As Our Own Good Actor, Let Us Spend Some Quite Time.

Within Our Own Inner Souls Spiritual Magic Mirror Of Life Rehearsing Our Good Part.

Until WE Become The Part, In Our Own Life's Good Movie.

What A Beautiful Good Movie.
WE Created WithIn OUR Spiritual Life, Within Our Mind, Body, Heart and In Our Soul.
Now Our Good Life Movie is a Wonderful Success.
Shown All Around the World.
WE and OUR Movie and OUR Friends have been Awarded a Golden Oscar in Every Category of Film that The Oscars have to Award US.
 Everybody Loves US.
OUR MOVIE BECOMES A GREAT EPIC CLASSIC MOVIE AMONG THE WORLD BEST!
WE Are A Winner.
We are VERY Successful!
We Want To Commend US and Congratulate US, On A Job Well Done.
God Blessed US.

CHAPTER 13
My Return to Earth

As the Angels and I flew through the Gates of Heaven, through The Sun, through The Light and onto the Earth.

I could hear this beautiful eternal omnipresent omniscient omnipotent sound of Aum in reverence to God everywhere and within everything.

The Sound of Aum was within everything and everywhere.

We remember everything is vibrating to the sound of Aum.

It is incredible. Aum is as all of life is Aum vibrating within All.

I can hear beautiful singing and music in the background of the Aum sound and vibration.

The Angels have gently returned me to the Earth.

I felt like I was a feather floating down on to a beautiful flower resting in a beautiful green pasture meadow with very bright diffused spiritual light.

I did not want to move or open my eyes.

I just wanted to Feel and Bathe in this very peaceful beautiful diffused white light with gentle music playing. My entire body is vibrating to the sound of Aum.

Suddenly, gently, just waking up, I realized I was in my body.

I slowly started to move but I couldn't.

Just like being frozen in a deep dream. I felt as a Rip Van Winkle slowly waking up from a long sleep.

I was starting to feel what it was like to be in a body again. I did not remember why I felt this way.

I felt this wonderful warm moist wet water sensation all over my body.

Almost like being in an old claw foot bath tub taking a relaxing warm bubble bath in a beautiful green pasture all alone and in private.

This wonderful feeling also reminded me of when I was new born baby peeing on myself laying flat on my back.

My pee just shooting out of my body up into the sky. I can feel the warm pee flowing on my legs and the pee feels wonderful.

When I began to try to move in my body I felt very unstable, out of balance and very fluid.

I know this may sound crazy to you, but I felt like I was Jell-O!

Have you ever taken a piece of Jell-O and held it in the palm of your hand wiggling it?

This is exactly what I felt like.
Oh I felt So Good.
I felt So Wonderful.
I felt like I was floating In a Warm Ocean Of Unconditional Love.
As floating in Kealakekua Bay.
I was thinking to myself, This is Heaven.
I was in Awe!
I am floating In Bliss In The Great Ocean of Nirvana.
I unexpectedly woke up.
I was astonished.
I was totally taken by surprise.
What is going on?
I didn't know where I was?
For some Profound Spiritual Reason, unknown me at this time, Most of my memory of Heaven, and what God spoke to me about, And the New Spiritual Life I was to Live, was within a sealed golden book within my soul.

I felt as if I was enclosed within a very delicate silk material that is wrapped around my body.
I was thinking to myself, Where am I?How did I get here?
All of a Sudden I heard a Very Laud Bang!
Methinketh, what is this sound?I know I have heard this sound before. Then I heard it again!
Bang, Bang, Bang and a very loud BOOM!
Now I heard many loud gun shots and machine guns firing and soldiers yelling.
I was wondering What's going on here?
Where am I?
As I looked around to see what is going on I realized my body was laying flat on the ground. I am facing upward into the bright sun light.

I was in shock. Wait a minute. This isn't Heaven!What am I doing here?Where am I?
This is all unforeseen, Homer.
Socrates, I did not recollect all this at this time. This is totally unexpected.
I though I was going to get a New Spiritual Body.
Oh My God!
I am wondering what is this warm wet sensation I am feeling?
I looked over to my left side. I see my blood is gushing out of my arm like a water fountain all over me and upon my face. It's coming out of my left arms elbow. Oh my God.

I try to move my arm but I cannot move my arm. It feels like Jell-O. My arm just flops over as a wet noodle. There's no strength in my arm. I can't feel my elbow or the bones in my arm.

Oh my God, my left elbow is shattered and what's left of my arm is just hanging together by torn skin as blood is gushing out all over me.

I reach over with my right hand and I pick up my left arm and it felt like I was trying to pick up some Jell-O that has fallen apart on the ground.

I gently laid my left arm on my chest. I squeezed my left arm just below my left shoulder trying to stop the blood from gushing out.

I can't find the artery because my left arm is all wet with blood and its slippery. I kept on trying to stop the bleeding as my left arm is gushing more blood all over my face and chest.

The enemy gun fire is all around me.

As the machine gun bullets were flying all towards me reality was becoming increasingly clear each second.

It was all coming back to me now.

I am in Vietnam.

I am a Black Beret soldier.

I am in the Great Trojan Vietnam Soul War.

I have been shot.

I am wounded.

I am laying on the ground in the center of an enemy bunker complex that is firing machine gun bullets at me. I am methinking, I am going to be Swiss cheese for sure with all this gun fire all around me.

I am going to die.

Where is my CAR-15 rifle? I am bewildered. I am in shock.

I look around and see my AR15 rifle laying on the ground to my left.

I have to get to it. I can hardly move.

I struggle to reach my rifle laying on by back holding my left arm with my right arm. I am shuffling my body around using my feet to drag my rifle closer to me.

Bullets are flying all around me.

With every move I made I thought for sure it was my last move.

I kept going until I could reach my rifle with my left leg. How am I going to pick up my rifle if I am holding and squeezing my left arm with my right hand trying not to bleed to death? Somehow some way I dragged my rifle close enough to pick it up. Oh my God.

Suddenly I hear John behind me yelling what's happening?

I yell back to him I am hit, I am hit! John yells back, me too!

For some reason I start to laugh. Shock. I don't know why it all of a sudden appeared funny to me, but it was.

I could hear some of the other team members getting closer yelling, what's happening? John told them we have been hit.

As the other Teams were getting closer to Johns position the enemy bullets were being directed towards them.

I decided that this was the time to let go of my left arm and pick up my rifle and return fire upon the enemy in the bunker complex to cover for the other men in our squad who were getting closer to our position as quickly as they could.

As I was shooting at the bunker laying on my back blood was gushing out all over me and I was loosing much blood. I was getting weak and I felt like I was going to pass out. I was really exhausted.

A Rocket Propelled Grenade (RPG) was fired by the enemy and hit a tree that fell down behind me about 10 yards away. At this point some of the men in our squad were behind us returning fire upon the enemy.

Our medic made his way to behind the fallen tree.

He yelled to me that he was there and if I could make it to the tree he could pull me over the tree and help me. Somehow I mustered up the strength. I believed that if I could somehow low crawl backwards to the tree holding my left arm on my chest I would make it.

Those 10 yards were the longest 10 yards of my life.

Every move I made was accompanied by enemy bullets all around me. It was a true miracle that I only got shot once. Thank you Jesus.

As I get real close to the tree, The Hulk jumps over the fallen tree and me and is screaming as he rushes towards the enemy bunker complex firing his M-60 machine gun hosing down the enemy.

We call him The Hulk because he is so big and strong that a normal rifle is to small to fit in his hands. He even had weights shipped to Vietnam so he could work out. He is the Real Life Action Hero, The Hulk.

I was blown away by what he did. As he is rushing into the bunker complex, the Huey helicopter gun ships and Cobra helicopters are firing upon the enemy base camp and Air Force jets are making air strikes.

I am thinking, oh shit we are all going to die for sure.

I finally got to the tree and our medic reaches over the tree and pulls me over to his side. I have so much blood all over my face and chest that he thought I got shot in the chest besides my left arm.

The medic checks out my chest and then cuts off my left arm sleeve that is soaking in blood and puts on a tourniquet.

He takes out the biggest morphine syringe I have ever seen and sticks it into my right leg.

I Am so weak at this point I want to pass out.

Within minuets I am in yah yah land on my way to Heaven with a stop off in Nirvana.

John was close by. He got shot in his hand. He was lucky.

We later believed the bullet went through me and hit him in the palm of his hand. By now an air evacuation helicopter is flying up above the contact area.

But because there was such intense gun fire going on all over the place it would not land fearing it would get shot down.

We where in big trouble. I was still loosing blood and I was fucked up.

I guess that somebody in Heaven made a command decision.

The pilot, my Commander of the Command & Control (C&C) helicopter decided he would bring his helicopter down in the middle of the whole dam mess and pick me and John up.

I can still see this crazy pilot and crew flying their Huey Helicopter gun ship.

The pilot turns the helicopter on its side and begins a downward spiral descent with machine guns blasting all the way down and lands in the middle of the battle.

John and I are thrown into the helicopter with machine guns blasting and rockets exploding all around us.

The Air Force jets were racing down dropping bombs all around us and off we went into an upward spiral incline with guns blasting.

We were dropped off at some old abandoned air strip a few miles away.

The C&C Command ship needed to get back to the action for air support to the men below. We were told that another helicopter is coming to pick us up real soon.

I was loosing more blood. John was also high on morphine and we were getting very wobbly.

As I looked down the deserted old air strip I could see some North Vietnamese soldiers walking towards us in the distance.

We didn't even have a rifle to protect us.

We were wounded and very high on morphine and we did not know what to do. I just felt very weak and I wanted to pass out, but I was afraid to until I was some place safe.

Just as the enemy was getting to close for comfort out of the clear blue sky comes the Medivac helicopter to pick us up.

We made it.

On the C & C helicopter was my past commanding officer from military intelligence S-2. He tried to stop me from joining the Black Beret's because he new the Great Trojan Vietnam Soul War was all bull shit and full of lies. He was older and wiser.

He warned me that I was going to get shot or die and not to jeopardize my life and stay in intelligence at HHT but I wouldn't listen.

I wanted to find out the Truth for myself.

I did.

The Truth Hurts.

John and I were flown to a small army medic station in the jungle.

Once we got there I passed out. I don't remember anything after I passed out. The next thing I knew I woke up in an Army hospital in an Army Hospital.

The head surgeon was standing in front of my bed as I suddenly woke up. I looked over to left my side. My left arm was in a cast in traction and had turned totally red from my blood. The bloody cast smelled terrible.

The surgeon told me I was a very lucky man.

He told me I was wounded with a very large machine gun round or an AK-47 bullet.

He told me the bullet went through my left elbow and totally shattered the elbow into about 50 pieces.

The bullet also broke my left arm above and below the joint from the impact.

The surgeon told me he would normally have amputated my arm because it was severely damaged. He decided to leave it on and let the doctors on the mainland decide what to do. He said he removed the damaged parts and cleaned the elbow up. He lined up the bones the best he could and put my arm into the cast.

He said that he didn't know why he didn't amputate my arm other than I was lucky. He had that Angelic look about him. He also told me that I should take it easy when I get out or the Army.

He told me that my damaged 20 year old body was now more like an 80 year old body.

He neglected to mention to me then that I also had Malaria, Hepatitis, and Pseudomonas from the gun shot wound. Also the bullet was poisoned. I guess he didn't want to shock me anymore than was necessary. I was already blown away.

I asked him what's going to happen to me? He told me that I would be transferred to an Army hospital in Osaka, Japan. Then probably to an Army hospital in Alaska and eventually I would be transferred to some army hospital some place in the United States. I asked where would that be and he didn't know.

He said the Army usually tries to place the wounded close to their home state.

The surgeon said good luck young man. Then he quietly left my bed side. I never saw him again. God Bless him.

I found myself in a very impotent and vulnerable condition.

I was so high on morphine and in a great deal of pain that I really didn't know where I was.

I was constantly going in and out of my body.

As I looked around the hospital ward I found myself in a profound esoteric labyrinth.

I was unconscious most of the time. Dream Consciousness for Healing my wounded body.

The next day I saw John a few beds away eating an ice cream cone.

I never got any ice cream.

I was out of it. That day Lt. Doug Rich our commanding officer of our Black Beret unit and a few of the men showed up to say hello and see how I and John were doing.

I could tell by the expression on their faces that they knew I was physically all fucked up and on morphine and that I was in pain.

They told me how lucky I was to be alive. Yeah.

Doug told me the 11th Armored Cavalry would sent what personal items I have at base camp to my family. I told Doug thank you for everything.

John was cracking jokes as usual and I could hardly talk.

I was in a constant morphine stupor and in pain. I said a few words that I don't remember and went back to a morphine sleep.

I never saw John or Doug or the others for over 20 years.

That was the last time I ever saw anybody from Black Horse in Vietnam.

They are all good men. All the men in my Black Beret unit which was no more than 4 six man teams were all remarkable heroes who never wanted to be a hero.

They were just doing their job, living in hell.

I know for me I had the distinct honor to have served with the Best of our Country's Spiritual Warrior Kings.

The bravery of 11th Armored Cavalry Regiment soldiers and the Air Cavalry Troop Black Berets, Pilots, Crew Chiefs and Door gunners is where the film crews of ABC, CBS, NBC, and Hollywood came for its material to make movies from the heroic missions that these men conducted. Yes, I was lucky to be alive. Wow.

One minute I was in Hell, the next minute I was in Heaven.

The next minute I was back in Hades.

Yes, this is a profound experience for me.

I was going back and forth, in and out of my body, revisiting Heaven and Earth.

I was constantly dreaming.

I was constantly learning and doing things in my dream state.

I was constantly integrating moment by moment as my body was traumatized.

Yes, I was now really living my Karma from the past and my new karma moment by moment.

My Karma hurt really BAD.

I wasn't doing very well in the hospital.

I had lost a considerable amount of blood.

I also had malaria and I was burning up with a fever of over 104 degrees.

I also had hepatitis and pseudomonas helping to boil my body.

I was not what you would call a happy puppy.

I was supposed to go into surgery but my fever was too high. The hospital didn't have enough of those hot-cold electric blankets to cool me down or heat me up going through the malaria rushes.

The good nurse's put crushed ice all over my naked body to cool my fever down. I could not believe what was happening to me.

Denial.

I was freezing to death and then I would be burning up. There was never enough staff in the hospital.

It's amazing that our government can spend billions on war armaments, agent orange and peanuts on health care for soldiers and veterans even to today.

I know they really don't care about GI's.

Even most of our citizens do not care about our combat veterans and this is true today.

The government just uses us and then throw us away.

I was truly in a living hell.

My pain was so great that I felt like I was being tortured by the some evil devil.

My left arm felt like someone was making a pretzel twisting my arm through a loop and then pulling it tight.

It really hurt really bad. I was in constant pain. I don't recall eating for months. I had a drip IV in my arm for weeks at a time.

Some times it would back up with blood because it ran dry.

I would yell for help but nobody came.

There wasn't any nurses available to watch and care all the wounded.

I was only getting IV liquids for water. I was wasting away.

Yes, I was being spiritually tested to the maximum by life.

At night I would sometimes wake up and I would look around.

The ward would have a few lights on but it would mostly be dark.

Most of the wounded were either asleep from the drugs or crying out laud for somebody to help them.

Some would be begging God for mercy and help.

Some just wanted to die.

It was very depressing for me and I am sure for all the other patients.

I could tell by the look on the nurses faces it was depressing for them too.

The nurses looked like Beautiful Angels, who were over worked yet always had a comforting smile.

I rarely remember seeing any doctors. They were over worked too. The medics were also over worked.

It is very difficult to be in a hospital with every patient who is wounded and in pain and crying or cursing out laud. I didn't know what to do.

What could I do anyways? What would you have done? I could do nothing other than accept what I was going through.

Acceptance. I was always praying to God silently.

At night when I was awake and very weak and tired these Evil Spirits would fly into the room and they would circle my bed.

They were wearing these Black Cloaks like the Evil Emperor wore in the Star Wars movie.

They scared the hell out of me.

I would get goose bumps all over my body.

Then every hair on my body would stand straight out.

I have this distinct feeling that this visit is not a good visit.

They would try to touch me.

They tried to take my soul with them.

They knew I was very weak.

They were 6 vampire vultures circling all around a wounded animal which I was.

They had my undivided attention.

They have the distinct presence of evil and they are the devils angels.

I was stunned.

My mind was going a Zillion bits a nanosecond figuring out how to get these evil ones away from me.

They kept calling me to come with them.

I told them NO a million times!

Get away from me!

I was burning my brain up thinking of what to do.

I was praying to Jesus Christ for help.

These black evil spirits were going around and around my bed trying to get me to come with them.

Then in a moment of silence I received a message from Jesus Christ to Command them all to leave the room in His name.

I miraculously did as Jesus told me to do.

I yelled out loud, In the name of Jesus Christ, I command you to leave this room1

They didn't like this command and they quivered and left immediately.

Then as I commanded them the evil spirits flew out of the room.

Oh Yeah!

I was really relieved. I thanked Jesus and God for his Power and Commandment.

In Heaven God did say to me he would Guide and Protect me in all the days of my life. I thank God for blessing me. God and Jesus saved my life again.

I did not close my eyes until the sun rose in the morning. I Thank God for the Sunrise. Very beautiful.

God is The Sun and The Light.

Now I was ready to go to sleep.

I was exhausted.

CHAPTER 14
On The Black Ship To Hell

As we start to get a feeling of what it was like for me and the others living helplessly in a war zone hospital in Saigon you can easily realize it was hell every day and every night. I can say that nobody really ever slept peacefully.

They only sleep anybody got was through morphine and Mary Jane. I thank God for Poppies, the birds and the bees and all of Gods good herbs and medicines.

After some time in Saigon I was going to be transferred to an Army hospital in Osaka, Japan on a C140 medical evacuation air plane. I was in a terrible condition like most of the other wounded men. I needed 2 pints of blood just to make it on the flight.

I remember that the plane is on the runway waiting for me tonight while I lay naked on a steel gurney receiving cold blood because the medical staff didn't have time to warm up the blood to the proper temperature.

I laid on the cold gurney shaking because of the cold transfusion. I was covered with a bed sheet in the breezy cold night in an empty hanger area next to the airport runway.

I felt like a frankenstein monster being given a transfusion of who knows who's blood I was being feed. I can guess by my adverse reaction and shaking it was probably some wino's blood full of Thunderbird from skid row or some junkies blood from NY full of cut heroin as I shook with conscious rejection.

After the transfusion I was rushed out to the waiting C-140 medical ambulance airplane. As I was carried on a stretcher up into the air plane by the rear ramp.

I could hear soldiers moaning, groaning and crying from their pain.

I felt like I was being loaded into a flying black coffin going to another of Hades torture chamber.

There were times that I thought I would rather have been better dead than to have to suffer for so long.

Pain can seem to last for one hell of a long time. Some times pain feels like it lasts forever and in a dark void of doom for a thousand years.

This is my point about Heaven and Hell and anyplace in between. Depending on which side of the fence we are on it can be wonderful or horrible or some place in between.

As I was loaded into the plane I could see that most of the stretchers were stacked vertically on the right and left sides of the air plane. There is a row in the middle of the air plane.

Most of the stretchers were stacked 3 stretchers high. Somebody on the bottom, middle and somebody on the top.

I was placed in the middle of the plane in the middle of the stack. There was also an areas of the plane reserved for very critical patients.

As I looked around the plane it was amazing all the IV bottles and tubes hanging all over the interior of the airplane.

Almost like a crazy Christmas Tree decorated with war misery bulbs and strange silver tinsel. All the soldiers were given morphine or sleeping pills for the flight just to knock everybody including the medical staff out of their pain on the air flight to Hades is difficult and fearsome.

I really did not want to look any more at all this horror and pain, yet choice do I have a choice when I am in Hades but to See and Witness and Personally Experience the Hades for myself.

I woke up in a US Army hospital ward in Osaka, Japan. I never got to see any of those beautiful Japanese women I heard all about.

I hope I do one day. In fact, I rarely saw a nurse, medic or doctor my entire time in Japan on a daily basis. This was a horrible ward.

I found my self in bed with my left arm in traction with this stinking bloody red cast around my arm and it smelled horrible like a dead body.

I was wondering, Is my skin rotting away from being in this cast so long and the wound not being cleaned daily and the bandages changed daily?

How can my wound heal without any oxygen getting to it?

Oh God have mercy upon my soul!

As I was waking up from the morphine stupor I was in, I heard this Screaming going on behind me. I methinketh to myself, What is this Screaming all about?

I looked over my shoulder and there was a doctor doing a skin graft on a soldier in our ward behind my bed.

He was taking off layers of good skin from one part of this soldiers body and putting the skin in places where this soldiers body was burned from explosives. I finally found a medic and asked why are they doing a skin graft on our ward?

He said the doctor didn't have an Operating Room available to him to do the Surgery in or any other sterile place.

Oh my God.

Then I asked him why the soldier wasn't medicated because this soldier was Really Screaming Very Loudly and he was strapped down in the bed and he was in great fucking pain.

The medic said that this soldier was on such a high dose of morphine that nothing else would work.

I always wondered why they didn't give him an anesthesia and put the guy to sleep. Then do the skin graft. I then methinkethed, this is Hades and there is great pain and suffering in Hades and it is true Hell Hurts.

Then if this isn't enough to wake me up in life, the soldier opposite and across from me and right in front of me daily was unbelievably Toast horrible.

I was blown away and in shock.

This soldiers life looked like he went through a meat grinder and what was left was him as burnt Toast.

A body full of Pain and Horror with no face but Hades face.

I just cry when I think about him.

The man with no face and no name.

This man of ours had no face that we would want to live with in our life. His face was Hades Pain and Suffering and it was torturing this man with no name. Hades was frightful for me to look at and Hades scared me. I have compassion for him.

Hades head had no hair whatsoever.

Hades had no eye brows or eye lashes.

Hades had no eye sockets for his eyes.

Hades had two slits made for him into his Crystal Skull face so he could peer out at this world.

I don't even know if Hades could See The Light very well, if at all.

This Hades man had no nose. For a nose Hades had two holes made for him to breath through. Oh my God.

This Hades man had no mouth.

For His mouth Hades had an opening made for him for a straw to fit through this little hole so he could suck up a little water or juice once and a while.

I don't believe Hades had any teeth.

Hades head is all burnt up like a lighting bolt struck him from Zeus upon his wooers head and his brains crackled after all the blood poured out.

This soldier Hades had no right arm.

This soldier Hades had no right leg.

This soldier Hades had no left leg.

This Hades man had one right arm.

Hades entire body is severely burnt.

Hades is strapped in one of these rotating steel beds so the birds of death can come anytime and peck away on Hades's body in any position Hades is in.

Oh my God have mercy upon his soul.

This man Hades with no name would be clutching his left leg just below the hip with what remained of his left leg muscles draping over his hand.

His leg would have no bandages wrapped around it and it looked to me like he was holding a very large bloody foul roast beef for hours waiting for a doctor, a nurse or anybody to come help him and put his bandages on.

This soldier Hades was my beautiful Osaka, Japanese Women Sirens that I saw in the movies and heard all about in my life about Japanese woman and that I have to looked at Him 24 hours a day.

I Cried many times for this Hades soldier and for myself.

Please God help him!

Please God Help Me!

Please get Me Out of Here.

Please Forgive Me!

What kind of life is Hades man is going to live?

Why didn't they let Hades die?

God is a Great Mystery.

God Zeus the Giver of All Will give good or not so good, as Zeus wills it His Will.

I can remember the Benefits Counselor from the US Army telling this Hades soldier that the Army will pay for HIS prosthetic devices so Hades can have two legs and an arm.

The visiting Benefits counselor told him the Veterans Administration will by him a car and fit the car with special equipment so Hades can drive it. The benefits counselor told him the US Army and The VA will pay for his Education so Hades can Educate himself about Life and on and on and I Cried, Oh My God.

This soldier Hades could not even respond to His Army counselor.

At best we might be able to Tell and See what Hades understood by nodding his Burnt Head. (BH)

Oh My God please Release me out of Hades.

This was an Insane Ward of Hell.

All the Army hospital wards are insanely in Pain and Crazy.

I don't know how long I was in this Hades Ward for it was too long.

This is the Hades Ward I was in.

One day I was able to call home to my mother in Indianapolis to say to her that I have been wounded and I almost died, yet I am alive by a miracle.

When we talked she cried and told me she had a dream that something terrible had happened to me.

I asked her to call the Good Senator Vance Hartke and ask him to ask the Army that I immediately need to be transferred to another Army hospital anywhere in the USA.

Please get me out of here mother god. I do not know if she called the good Senator or not.

Well, it was not long in Osaka Hades, who knows a week, a month, a thousand years, I don't know because I was always high on morphine, and I was in pain, and I was being tortured as I prayed to God my Father and Mother.

Suddenly I was on another stretcher within the Black Ship and we sailed off to Alaska and then to Ireland Army hospital in Fort Knox, Kentucky.

Ireland Army Hospital.

My personal experience at Ireland Army Hospital and with Americas Ithaca Army medical procedures is what I and other wounded soldiers would call fallacious ungracious unlawful ill mannered illogical medical butchery of Americas soldiers.

Today, If God gave me the power of Gods Justice I would have these orthopedic Ithaca America Army surgeons arrested as war criminals and put into Hades.

I would also arrest for Conspiracy and Treason the leaders of Ithacas America Army, Department of Defense, The State Department, Congress, Senate and The President.

I would have them all arrested as war criminals and put into Hades for allowing this crime against humanity and these medical butchery procedures to be practiced on our sons, the good citizens of these United States of Ithaca.

The orthopedic surgeons operating on Ithacas soldiers at Ireland Army hospital at Fort Knox, Kentucky were similar to Hitler's surgeons experimenting on the Jews in WWII.

For me this is one of the most challenging and disturbing moments of my life. I just as well could have been in Auschwitz!

The doctors were insane. The Ithaca Army is insane. The Ithaca government has gone insane.

All their leaders are insane.

From the moment I arrived at this Dark Hades Hole of a hospital it was hell. Most of the staff was insane. I don't know why they were insane they just were crazy.

I knew of only one GOOD Beautiful tall slender Army nurse with brown hair and a beautiful smile.

She is really an Angel working in this insane environment obviously for my well being and protection.

God sent her to watch over me.

I know that there were a few other good people working in this hospital but the rest had definitely gone to hell. There was hardly any Compassion for Ithacas good warriors.

Most of the wounded soldiers had gone insane from the mistreatment they received at this hell hole of Hades.

I know why.

It was from the medical butchering procedures and the treatment they received which would scare the hell out of you.

It was the most inhumane hospital anybody could have the evil luck of being sent to by some evil god to recuperate from the Great Trojan Vietnam Soul War.

There was constant badgering of the wounded patients to do slavery work doing the tasks that the hospital staff was supposed to perform.

Most soldiers were criticized for being in Ithacas USA infantry and even for being wounded in the great war and everyone was tortured and all were miss treated and so was I.

No wonder veteran soldiers Do Not Trust their Ithacas government. All the wounded have PTSD from their own Ithacas USA treatment by the Washington, DC wooers request.

Even though I couldn't lift my head off my pillow for months I was ordered to push a juice cart around and clean the bathroom which I did not do nor could do being half dead.

I couldn't even get up in my bed or even lift my head up off my pillow for months. I was lucky to be alive?Anon methinketh.

I was emaciated from my gun shot wound, malaria, hepatitis and pseudomonas. I was completely yellow and extremely underweight.

I was constantly harassed for being a Black Beret living in the Trojan Black Horse by the Army's weird drugged out gay medics working on the ward. It was if all the medics were on some hell broth driving them crazy.

All I could do was Pray to God for help. Oh God release me from Hades. Oh God please forgive Me!

The other soldiers had this silent distraught disbelief in their eyes from the fear that maybe they will be the next medical experiment of butchery just as the Jews in Auschwitz!

This Hades hospital was much worse than the movie One flew out of the Wooers nest.

Soldiers were being drugged to the point of paranoia and schizophrenia and suicide from the depressive malevolent Army medical treatment and procedures.

I do not blame them one Iota for getting high on buds.

Anon now these wooers of Ithaca will pay for their good deeds and their seeds too. In Hades they will all go to doom.

For Odysseus The I Am, The Waster of Wooer Cities will Smitted them in Washington, DC!

I cannot count how many good men lost their heart, their minds, their body and limbs to these military butchers at Americas Ithacas Ireland Army Hospital.

There were a few smart soldiers that would spit out the drugs after the medics or nurses left their bed side.

I did the same thing.

I spit out their villainous vinyl poison.

They, our own people, the Washington, DC the Wooers of Ithaca, were trying to kill the others and even me, Odysseus I am, and take over my Kingdom OUR The USA and my wife Penelope while I am and my fellow warriors were at the Great Trojan Soul War.

I know this is hard to believe yet True.

Find a veteran combat survivor if you can and ask them how and what happened to them if they have any memory remaining in their brain from all the vinyl they consumed Methinking it would help wash the painful memory away of the Wooers Treason and Conspiracy of Americas Ithaca, and their mistreatment and torture when they returned home.

Ask any combat veteran soldier who was Coerced while on Morphine to sign documents giving the butchers Authority to Butcher off their Repairable Arms and Legs as they tried to do to me.

The Orthopedic surgeon who was assigned to me was threatening me and coercing me to amputate my left arm.

The butcher was Medical Doctor, a Captain in Ithacas Nazi US Army Ireland Hospital Medical Staff.

He was not aware he is talking to me Odysseus I Am, The waster of cities and wooers.

Giving me orders to sign medical documents to butcher off my left arm against my will. Oh Yeah dude.

You can imagine the Evil Anger and Justice in my eyes and heart and soul and body and even in Zeus's eyes for this little Washington, DC wooer Nazi Captain doctor.

The butcher of Americas good warriors and his black fate that I now smitten him with my silver sword into Hades and then into doom for him and his compadres.

This is The USA Ithacas military medical doctor who was absolutely insane as Ithaca is insane from all the Washington, DC wooers deeds to Americas best.

I would not want to know how Many Repairable arms and legs he and the other military butchers have butchered off our good soldiers bodies.

These butchers of Ithaca will eat those arms and legs for food in Hades first before they go into doom.

I am sure that it would be difficult for you to distinguish these butchers from the butcher of Auschwitz!

The difference is there uniforms of hate. Their uniforms look like The NWO President, The Vice President, The Senate, The Congress and The Supreme Court of The USA today.

After 4 months of very slow recovery I was able enough to get up out of my bed and go to the bathroom in my wheel chair.

I had very large boil on my sacrum the size of a base ball from being in bed for five months and sores all over my body from not being washed for months.

In the beginning of the sixth month I was able to go to the bathroom more frequently with my wheel chair that I lived in the last two months.

In the bathroom at night, late at night, at 2 in the morning, I would find soldiers crying in the bathroom.

I can still see these soldiers coming into the bathroom in their wheelchairs or with their crutches very late at night.

They would be looking into the mirrors for hours at a time for there missing arms and legs or other body parts crying with tears running down their faces.

Screaming to themselves and to God in the mirror, Look what the fucking wooers have done to me!

All I can Methinketh is Oh My God, and cry with them.

I would often go into the bathroom late at night and be with my fellow wounded soldiers crying with them in their pain.

It seems that the most painful moments of a soldiers life is late at night from 12 am to 4 am.

You just couldn't sleep anymore with the pain, anger, fear of butchery and frustration of this kind of soldiers hellish life in Ithacas wooers hospital of Hades.

Can you understand and feel the pain of these warriors life?

It may have been your own son or relative.

Jimmy, is that you?

Oh my God, even today my heart hurts with their pain, sorrow and despair.

My God, all of this pain and war is for nothing other than wooers Money, Greed, Control, Power.

The Wooers Slaughter Control of our young warrior men going to a useless war to die or be wounded so their elite wooers sons have no competition in life.

They do not want to be challenged on the planet Earth by the good souls. The wooers are a very evil group in Washington, DC.

They include their friends of Europe. The Evil European political wooers and their NWO agendas that have nothing to do with Goodness or God or our True USA.

We have been taken over by the wooers.

Anon one of the Holy Soul Sons of the Crying Ireland Army Hospital mirror's is from Harlem. Larry my Son Johns'son, and he Rides his horse to Harlem to Restore & Replenish his soul with the Boy's & Girls of Harlem.

Larry returns to Ireland Hospital from his vacation. He is Riding his Horse with a PTSD Heroin pain in his arm. Larry John'son has Saddle Bags of drugs on his horse. He offers me some of his heroin pain in his arm.

I said no thank you Larry Johns'son. I have my own pain to suffer. Larry then said, how about some coke? Larry I live in this bed where will I go all pumped up? No thanks.

How about a Frisco Speed Ball? Whats that? Heroin and coke together. I'll shoot you up. Larry I have never tried heroin or coke and I hate needles. I have had so many IV's in my arm I want nothing to do with needles. Larry has not given up on me.

He knows I need to see The Light of what is going on this amputee ward.

Larry told me that the Army doctors were going to load me up on morphine so I would be very doped up.

The doctors know that if you are all fucked up on morphine you will sign the medical release papers.

Larry warned me about the butcher.

Larry is trying to help me see his point of view that they Army is really trying to cut off my arm against my will as they have amputated many others on this ward.

They did butcher Larry.

He is the first brother I met in the bathroom at 2 a.m. crying in the mirror. Larry is the one who cried out, Look what they did to me!

Larry asked me again, how about some of this Blue Cheer.

What is Blue Cheer?

Larry said he did not know. He said I think they call it LSD.

Whats that?

Larry said he dint know.

Did you try it Larry?

No, I am afraid to try it.

Why?

The Boy's in Harlem Rave you will see God.

I need God Big Time and Right Now.

I have a major problem to solve.

I Methinketh to myself.

Why not try some Blue Cheer?

It may be better than crying in Ireland Army Hospital mirror's of no return at 2 a.m.

Somehow I may be able to free myself with Gods help.

Later this evening I tried this Blue Cheer.

Since I have never tried Blue Cheer I did not know what to expect. I waited patiently for about an hour and nothing had happened.

While I was waiting for some reaction I said a Prayer to God.

The Lords Prayer.

Suddenly Magic happened.

I got very high. I saw The Light come into my room through the wall.

The Light told me that tomorrow I will escape to free myself. Then the Light then went away. During the night I raved about God too.

God Bless you Boy's in Harlem and my Larry Johnson.

I told God Zeus, I was not going to let them butcher me, Odysseus I Am, the Waster of Wooer Cities.

No matter whatever I had to do to get out of Ithacas Ireland Army hospital in Auschwitz wooers Ithaca.

They will pay for what they did to my fellow veterans.

Just wait until my return at the Wooers Banquet in the Great Hall of Odysseus.

Where I will slay all the wooers as they raise their winged gold cups of wine to their lips of a death of a thousand deaths in Hades and their compadres will follow them to death.

Odysseus I am of many devices, who has been Locked Down and Confined to the Ward of Death by the butcher of Ithaca.

When I awoke in the early morning the door to my room was left ajar mysteriously.

My Room was locked down because the Army did not want me to be able to call anybody for help.

They were going to cut off my arm wether I like it or not.

The Butcher told me I was government property and they will do with me whatever they want.

The butcher said, do I know what GI stands for?

Government Issue.

The butcher said I was his property since he is in charge of this amputee ward. I told him he is nuts.

I am a VIP. I am a Black Beret. I am a combat war veteran.

I told the butcher of Ireland hospital he is in big trouble with me. He freaked out on me and had me locked down.

All I wanted was a second and third medical opinion concerning my medical condition. There was a well know orthopedic doctor on contract with the US Army from Louisville, Kentucky named Harold Kleinert.

Medical people claim Dr. Harold Kleinert is god from our shoulder to our finger tips. The butcher refused to let me see him.

The butcher said I did not need a second opinion. His opinion is all that matters. Wrong dude.

This morning I have with me my spiritual Mentors for encouragement.

The Goddess Athena has appeared and she will change my appearance into The Custodian.

I open my door.

Nobody is around. Great. I go into the custodians closet early in the morning. I put on the Custodians work clothes.

I open the ward door. I walk out and off the ward. I very gracefully walk out of the hospital as one of their custodians taking a smoke break. I have escaped off the ward. Oh Yeah.

I found a Pay Phone booth right out side the hospital. With Hermes help I made a collect call to Senator Vance Hartke and Senator Birch Bayh from Indiana. I asked them to come to Ireland Hospital ASAP immediately.

This is an emergency!

I asked them to STOP the amputation and Free me from this hospital. To also set me free from my service contract since I am seriously wounded and of no good to them.

Hermes delivers Odysseus' message and the Good Senator Hartke Appears at Ireland Army Hospital and Orders the Army to STOP the surgery and to release me.

The Army decides to retire me and I am set free. My Friends show up and I go home to Indianapolis, Indiana.

As mysterious as life is, miracles happen soon after my departure of Ireland hospital.

I discover I have a cousin in Chicago, Illinois who is a neurosurgeon. My mother said I should call him. I had never met him. I was tired of doctors but I needed real help. I could not move any fingers nor move my left arm up or down. I had no feeling in my left arm. I decided to call him.

He told me about a gifted doctor in Louisville, Kentucky and I should go see him. I told my cousin I have NO MONEY.

He said I did not need money. To just call this doctor and he will make an appointment for me to see me without having to pay anything. My cousin told me to tell this doctor I am his cousin.

My neurosurgeon cousin had worked with this doctor for a few years. Harold Kleinert has trained hundreds of doctors world wide. So I decided to call him up. Who is the doctor?

Doctor Harold Kleinert.

The one the USA Army butcher refused me to see at Ireland Army hospital.

So I went to Kentucky to see Harold. Beautiful office. Better than a Banks office. Harold is rich and he does not need money. Harold asked me what hospital I was in Kentucky?

I told him Ireland Army Hospital. Harold was amazed. He asked me why he did not get to see me since he has a contract with the Army?

I told Harold that the butcher did not want me to see him because the butcher claimed there was no other doctors available.

Harold got pissed off. He thought that was a travesty.

He decided to operate on me. Harold set up an appointment at the Louisville Veterans Hospital for my surgery. Harold decided to bill the government for my surgery. It worked.

Harold brought his entire medical team to the VA hospital and performed the surgery. Over ten hours of surgery.

They took out the nerves of my right leg and sewed them together and connected them into my left art. He cleaned up the many fragments in my elbow.

Well, months later I started to get some feeling in my hand. Later on my fingers started to move. It took me one year to hold a cup. And two years to button a shirt button. Everything got better as time passed.

Thank you Harold Kleinert and your medical team. Thank you God.

And thank you Larry for the LSD Blue Cheer. The Blue Cheer brought God and The Light into my life. The God gave me the courage to escape. Other wise I would not have a left arm.

With out Larry and The LSD, I probably would have killed myself.

Anon, Odysseus now prepares for the banquet of the Washington, DC wooers death and for The Word from Zeus and Athena for the time is near.

Odysseus I am must now Rest and Renew myself.

I need to Refresh my mind, body, heart and soul in Heaven and Spake with God and Gods God's and Goddesses.

This is how they treat our veterans in Ithaka USA back then.

I tried to find Larry when I got out.

I found out that Larry had over dosed on heroin and died in Harlem.

He obviously was one of my saviors.

CHAPTER 15
A Magic Majestical Ball of Love

My Basketball, Golf, Tennis, Sports, Meditation.

We may want to try this YOGA prayer and meditation for enlightenment.

I was meditating today using my basketball.

I walk around the basketball court bouncing the ball from one hand to the other while breathing in and out The Light in a balanced and focused prayer meditation.

This is like swimming through life with a basketball.

We can do this with any rubber ball, even with the big rubber balls we find in a sport equipment store.

This meditation balances the right and left brain hemispheres of our mind body.

Because when anybody walks and moves their arms back and forth it moves the spinal fluid up and down our spinal column from the sacrum up to our brain in our minds-body.

Moving our feet and arms, right, left, right, left, etc., coordinates the right and left brain hemispheres.

This prayer meditation yoga idea is, that we work every motion in Harmony with all the other motions, creating togetherness, into one flowing movement. Like a butterfly flying through the air.

First there is Walking.

We start out with our right foot then our left foot.

Right, left, right, left and on and on without missing a beat, breathing The Light in and out regularly.

Second there is Bouncing the ball.

Then we bounce the ball on the court starting with our right hand to our left hand and on and on without missing a beat, breathing The Light in and out regularly.

Right, left, right, left and on and on.

Third is Breathing.

Then we do our Spiritual Light breathing exercise, breathing The Light in and out regularly. We breath love Light in and love Light out. Love Light in and love out and on and on without missing a beat.

Fourth is Meditation.

Then we add a silent word prayer meditation as we walking around the court, breathing The Light in and out regularly.

Fifth is Coordination.

In time, we begin coordinating all four actions into one Harmonious flowing prayer yoga meditation all around the basketball court, breathing The Light In and out regularly.

We are doing this for one hour approximately depending on our daily schedule.

It just depends on our Divine Guidance.

Sixth is Extra Curricular Activity.

If we are working on a problem, and we need a solution from Divine Guidance, we patiently wait for an answer as we are doing this basketball yoga.

Suddenly, we have received an answer from within ourselves, to our problem. We will know The Truth of the answer by how the basketball shot went through the hoop.

We shoot the basketball at the hoop and See if the basketball goes gracefully swishing through the center of the hoop.

To See if it is an answer from our ego mind or if it is an answer from Divine Guidance.

If we are relaxed and if the energy is flowing effortlessly through us we will know the true answer by where the basketball goes and what it does.

I have noticed that if we missed the shot, I could have been tense within our minds-body with our own expectations. Wanting to hear and see what I wanted to hear and see.

Instead of what God wants us to HEAR and SEE from within us. It is because the answer is not yet complete from Divine Guidance, and Divine Guidance wants us to try the shot again for clarification and refinement of the solution and the answer.

To see if we are relaxed and in a very Zen relaxed Posture and Attitude from within our self.

We begin by walking around the basketball court. We are guided to stop and shoot the basketball from any location that we have heard from within us to stop and Shoot and See the basketball go through the hoop.

When I first started this meditation I would get close to the hoop because all of my problems needed to have a simple and accomplishable goal to be successful.

I started with the easy shoots close up. Even those can be difficult to make in the beginning.

The more relaxed and focused I Am with regular breathing the more successful I Am at making my shots. The answers majestically spiritually will come through the hoop. We might want to try this magical yoga with a Good Basketball.

It is very interesting which spiritual answer comes with which shoot that goes through the hoop. I have found this Ball Yoga to be Very Inspiring.

In fact we can do this Yoga doing Any Sport like Baseball, Soccer, Boxing, Football, Tennis, Swimming, Rowing, Healing Massage and even in Kissing and Making Love.

We know we may laugh yet Every Kiss With Love we Give and Every Gentle Stroke Of Love we Give will give us a Divine Answer of how well we are doing in OUR Life!

GOLF.

This GOLF prayer yoga Light meditation calisthenics can also be played with a Golf Ball, playing golf on a golf course in any country.

It is the same process as the basketball yoga. If we are working on a problem, and we need a solution from Divine Guidance, we patiently wait for an answer as we are playing this GOLF yoga.

Suddenly, we have received an answer from within our self to our problem. We will know from how the shot went.

We start by Teeing off on the first hole. We consciously and effortlessly strike the Golf Ball on the Sweet Spot, in the center of the driver. We listen if the Golf Ball goes Crack and if it goes gracefully swishing through the air, exactly were we wanted it to go.

To see if it is an answer from our ego mind or if it is an answer from Divine Guidance, and if we are relaxed and if the energy is flowing effortlessly through us. We will know the answer by where the golf ball lands and the sound it made at impact.

I have noticed that if I missed the shot, I could have been tense within my minds-body with my own expectations. Wanting to hear and see, what I wanted to hear and see. Instead of what God wants us to HEAR and SEE from within us.

If we missed the sweet spot, it is because the answer is not yet complete from Divine Guidance. Divine Guidance wants us to try the shot again for clarification and refinement of the solution and the answer.

Anon to see if we are relaxed in a very Zen relaxed Posture and Positive Attitude from within. If we missed the shot we may have been tense and wanting to control the answer to be the one we want to hear and see, instead of what God wants us to HEAR and SEE from within us.

In time and with Patience and persistence all good things will happen in a very Zen effortless flowing manner.

Sometimes I didn't stop and consciously breath The Light in and out. Grounding my energy and relaxing.

Knowing I am having fun focusing my minds-body on seeing the ball do exactly what I wanted it do which is to go effortlessly through the air and to the sweet spot I have in my minds-body third eye.

I could be impatient and tense and unfocused taking the shot out of balance which meant I was not listening 100% to my inner voice.

In the beginning when I started to play Golf, I would walk around the course by my self with a few irons and woods.

I Am guided to stop and shoot the ball from any location that I have heard inside of me to stop a, and hit the Golf ball, and see the golf ball go where I wanted it to go. Or where I thought I wanted it to go.

When we started this Golf yoga meditation, we would make it easy and relaxed for us just playing by ourselves. Wanting to just have fun and not worry were the golf ball goes. Working on our breathing and conscious relaxed strokes. Because all our problems needed to have a simple and accomplishable goal to be successful.

We started with the easy shoots as on a putting green at a Putt Putt Golf course for kids. Then we would go to a driving range.

Even those simple shots can be very difficult to make in the beginning. The more relaxed and focused we are the more success we are having making the putt and driving the golf ball and the answers majestically comes through the stroke.

We might want to try it the easy way first if we have never played Golf which is a life time sport. It is very interesting which answer comes with which shot and how and where it goes.

In the beginning being Golf can be Very Frustrating.

We have found this Zen Golf Yoga Prayer Meditation Sport to be Very Inspiring on the Magical Green Meadows of Life. Even if all we do in Golf is walk around the course in our bare feet and breath in and out the fresh air on the biggest green lawn of life we have ever been on. We will feel very relaxed and calm and a healing answer to our problem will come to us just by walking around in this beautiful green meadow.

Seventh is Heaven.

By Doing all of the above and having fun playing with our Majestical Magical Ball of Love we will CO-create for our self a healthier, more successful, more abundant, more wiser, more knowledgeable, more receptive, more compassionate, more loving, more forgiving abundantly enjoyable life.

In all sports that have a ball, stay focused by paying attention to the ball. Keep your eye on the target.

Later on after some practice with the Magic Spiritual Ball, we walk around looking straight ahead in life with a good positive attitude, a good posture, good breathing in and out. All while we are relaxing, we are praying in spiritual meditation.

It is important to only listen to our inner soul self. Do not to listen to anything nor pay attention to anybody else while doing this practice consciously.

If we do, we will see that we will miss a beat, the shot, the target.

If we are distracted it is better to stop and start all over when we are focused. Clear our mind, taking a deep breath and beginning anew.

It takes practice. We stay focused on our prayer and meditation. We are open to receiving Divine Guidance by bouncing the ball around.

It is another way to have fun and play a game. By watching and paying attention to our breathing. By how we are walking with good posture.

By listening to our personal spiritual word meditation and prayer. By looking at our Positive Visualization.

By shooting the basketball through the hoop or putting the golf ball into the cup or serving the Tennis ball correctly we learn all about our self having fun.

We alternate different Words to Meditate, Pray and Visualize upon as we are in Spiritual Light and Love. We are in Compassion. We are in Forgiveness. We are in Health. We are in Wealth. We are in Divine Guidance. We are in Peace. We are in Harmony. We are in Success. We are a Winner.

We are in God. We are as Good as our personal prayer meditation.

We also have found that it is a good way to solve many problems by doing something different.

We never know what Compassionate Opportunities Will come our way while playing ball.

As I was doing my meditation that looks like I am playing basketball and it is playing with a ball, I was visited unexpectedly by three people.

There are two Basketball courts and a Tennis court at Greenwell Memorial Park in Captain Cook, Hawaii. Two women and a child about two years old walked unto the court and stopped at the tennis net and watched me as I played with this new bright orange basketball.

I smiled and said hello.

The women remarked to the young child, See the ball.

Look, he is playing basketball.

Look, he made a basket.

As I was playing with my magic spiritual basketball and shooting at the hoop, I missed a shot and this bright orange basketball rolled towards them. I ran after the basketball so that it would not hit the little girl.

The little girl was very excited by the ball rolling towards her.

The women commented to the child, See the ball as it rolled towards her. The little girl's eyes lit up and she smiled. She was very young to say anything or do anything but smile and I continued to play.

The child was just starting to walk on her own. I felt her to be a special child and that she recently had surgery. I could tell just by the way the child walked as the two women held her hands.

After a short while the two women and the child returned to a picnic table where three other adults were sitting and talking.

As I was playing my meditation prayer yoga basketball, I realized that the child was a special child and the group of adults were hospital staff members having a meeting with the parent at Greenwell Park, instead of the hospital.

Why not breath fresh Spiritual Light air when we can.

As I continued to walk and breath in and out The Light and bounce the basketball around my inner voice was talking to me about Compassion and Love.

God was explaining to me that Love, Compassion, Healing and Forgiveness is already in my hands as the magical Orange basketball that I was bouncing around.

All of a sudden this basketball became a really bright magical majestical basketball of Spiritual Love.

God has already given all of us Spiritual Love, Compassion, Healing and Forgiveness in life.

God has placed them into our hands to share with others. Most of us need to recollect this information. This majestical Ball of Love is now bouncing into Your court.

Catch the ball!

This Majestical Ball of Spiritual Love is now in your hands.

What will you do with it my friend?

As I continued around the basketball court, I realized that the child walked upon the basketball court because what she really wanted to do is touch this bright orange magical ball, that I was bouncing around the court.

She was only about two years old. She could not express herself other than going in the direction she wanted to go in while these two women held her hands.

My inner voice said to me that this magical ball of Love is in my court and in my hands now.

My inner voice asked me if I would I like to have the Opportunity to Share Compassion with this Special Child and help make her day a Happier.

My inner voice asked me if I would I like to walk over to the picnic table where everyone is gathered around the child, while she played with the Old McDonald barn set with little animals, and let the child touch this bright orange magical basketball, if she wanted to.

I thought to myself that I should have been more attentive when she first arrived on the basketball court with the two women.

I thought they just wanted to watch me play and they did.

I didn't want to interrupt them because I thought they were just walking around with the child and it was OK to watch me play my basketball meditation.

As I was playing and shooting at the hoop the ball suddenly rolled towards them. I ran after the ball so that it would not hit the child.

The women commented to the child, See the ball as it rolled towards her.

I am only illustrating this story to point out the subtle interplay amongst us all and how attentive we have to be to be receptive to our inner spiritual thoughts, feelings and intuitions in the moment.

I also had second thoughts of doubt and fear at this time. I thought to myself that I didn't want to embarrass anybody nor myself if the child did not want to touch the ball. I just had a feeling about it.

The situation reminded me the time my daughter was given a piece of candy from Indian Guru Baba Hari Dass at Mount Madonna Center, Santa Cruz, California who is a Silent Monk.

He gently unwrapped the candy for her and handed it to her. She immediately started to cry. He quickly put the wrapper aback on the candy and handed it to her. She was now happy. He doesn't speak, so he wrote on his chalk board, I am sorry She wanted to unwrap the candy herself.

I decided that I would like to take this Opportunity of Compassion, even if I was going to be embarrassed, and take this magic ball of Spiritual LOVE and my soul self over to the child and ask the little girl, If she would like to touch the Magic Orange Ball.

I got my courage up and walked over to the picnic table and I recognized Mary Lou who works at the hospital and I said hello.

The little girl was playing with her old McDonald farm set.

I looked at the little girl and said to her:

You wanted to touch this magical ball, didn't you?

I held this bright orange basketball out for her to touch.

She gracefully looked over to me and she reached her little right arm out with a big smile on her face, touched the ball.

It was magical to see her Big Smile. One of the women nurses commented, Yes, it is a Magical Ball of Love.

I returned to the basketball court and continued on with my meditation. I was happy that I took the opportunity to share my magic spiritual ball of love through compassion. Thank you God.

Love, Compassion, Healing and Forgiveness are now in your court.

Is there someone that you can share your Compassion with?

Is there someone that you need to Forgive or Talk to?

Is there someone who will come into your life, even if they are momentarily passing by in your busy life, Who you can have Compassion with For Understanding life.

Compassion is something WE receive from God freely and we can also give it freely.

Compassion is Love.

Compassion is Life.

Compassion is Light.

There is nothing to give in Compassion.

We can only SHARE Compassion.

To have and share Compassion in life is Spiritually Important.

Life is Very Short.

Compassion can also be a simple act of giving someone directions on how to get to the grocery store who is not from your own area or town.

Later in the afternoon I returned to Yano Memorial Hall, across the street from the famous Manago Hotel.

John the Park manager was watering the front lawn. It has been very dry year in Kona, Hawaii.

After John adjusted the sprinklers, he left to do other things.

It is windy this afternoon and the VOG is coming over the mountain into Kona. I noticed some trash laying on the ground so I decided to pick it up and put into the garbage can.

As I approached the walk way I heard a Bird Calling out.

I looked down on the ground and there was a tiny little baby finch who had fallen out of his nest.

I reached down to comfort him in Compassion. He let me pet him on his sweet little head.

He was afraid.

I told him everything will be OK.

I thought about moving him off the walk way and closer to the tree that he had fallen out of.

There by the tree was his mother who was frantic that her baby had fallen out of her nest.

I picked up her little baby and moved him closer to her up in the tree and went back my room.

I named him Herbert.

I went back a few days later to check up on Herbert and he and his mother were back in their nest together and Herbert even flew around for a little while showing me he could now fly.

Opportunities for sharing Compassion are really all around us if we would just stay open minded and Conscious of what is going on all around us and in front of us.

Compassion is something we can share with anybody in Earth, human's, animals, dolphins and plants.

We are all in a Spiritual Body and we are all a Somebody. There are times in our life when WE do need to receive Compassion.

We never know what is going to happen in our life.

Some little Angel Bird might come right down from Heaven and land by you when you are down and out and depressed and share some of his or her compassion with you.

There is a song by Bob Marley called Three Little Birds that you might want to listen to one day when you need some Inspiration.

Compassion is something that is SHARED and Will let US know, Everything's Going To Be All Right.

CHAPTER 16
CO-Creating Good with Gods Love

A Very simple YES Co-Creating Process of Methinkeths for our good soul self talk creating the I Am that I am in us and in Good and Goodness. Positive Thoughts Daily Reinforced helps us heal our mind, body, heart and soul.

YES, some good things to Recollect!

Yes, God is Good when we are in Harmony with God.

Yes, Good is God when we are in Harmony with God.

Yes, All Good is in Harmony with God. Yes, God Created everything Good for Us.

Yes, God, Everything we are CO-Creating is for our Own Good. Yes, God Is Spiritual Light Love.

Yes, our Love is Gods Spiritual Love. Yes our Spiritual Love is Gods Love when we are in Harmony with God.

Yes, Spiritual Love is God Energy in Motion.

Yes, Gods Love is Wonderful & Miraculous.

Yes, God lives in Us and We live in God when we are in Harmony with God.

Yes, God is in us and we are in God consciousness when we in Harmony with God.

Yes, God Loves us because we are Gods Child. Yes Father & Mother God Gives us All of our good for our own good and for Gods Good when we are in Harmony with God and even when we are not in Harmony with God.

Yes, God Everything Good we are creating is Good and in Harmony with YOU.

Yes, We are in ABUNDANCE when we are in Harmony with God.

Yes, We are in GOODNESS when we are in Harmony with God.

Yes, We are in HEALTH when we are in Harmony with God.

Yes, We are in WEALTH when we are in Harmony with God.

Yes, We are in RICH when we are in Harmony with God.

Yes, We are in LOVE when we are in Harmony with God.

Yes, We are in BEAUTY when we are in Harmony with God.

Yes, We are in HARMONY when we are in Harmony with God.

Yes, We are in MUSIC when we are in Harmony with God.

Yes, We are in FUN when we are in Harmony with God.

Yes, We are in DANCE when we are in Harmony with God.

Yes, We are in SONG when we are in Harmony with God.

Yes, WE are a Beautiful Spiritual Woman when we are in Harmony with God.

Yes, We are a Handsome Spiritual Man when we are in Harmony with God.

Yes, We are a Good Soul in Great Spirit when we are in Harmony with God.

Yes, We are Strong in Spiritual Mind when we are in Harmony with God.

Yes, We are a Good Free Soul when we are in Harmony with God.

Yes, We are Free from Fear and Doubt when we are in Harmony with God.

Yes, We are a Believer in Father Gods Spiritual Love when we are in Harmony with God.

Yes, We are a Believer in Mother Gods Spiritual Love when we are in Harmony with God.

Yes, We are what Good we Believe In and Have Good Faith In when we are in Harmony with God.

Yes, We are a Good Child of God when we are in Harmony with God.

Yes, God has already Created, All of OUR Goodness in OUR Life, in Abundance, in Health, in Wealth, in Love, in Happiness, in Heaven and on Earth and in Harmony with Us.

Are WE in Harmony with God and all of our GOODNESS in methinketh?

Yes, God is Forever Increasing OUR Abundance when we are in Harmony with God. Yes, God is working for US Now and forever with All of OUR Goodness when we are in Harmony with God.

Yes, We are Fortunate to Receive Gods Spiritual Love working for Us when we are in Harmony with God.

Yes, God is Guarding and Protecting US with Gods Guardian Angels and All of OUR Goodness when we are in Harmony with God.

Yes, WE are Happy, Healthy, Wealthy, Abundant and Wise with All of Gods Good Spiritual Wisdom, Knowledge and Love when we are in Harmony with God.

Yes, WE are Gods Faith and Belief and Spiritual Love when we are in Harmony with God.

Yes, We are Gods Child when we are in Harmony with God.

Yes, We are Gods True Expression of Spiritual Love when we are in Harmony with God.

Yes, We are Gods Spirit in Heaven and on Earth when we are in Harmony with God.

Yes, We are Gods Spiritual Love Child when we are in Harmony with God.

Yes, Gods Love is Health for us when we are in Harmony with God.

Yes, Gods Love is Harmonious for us when we are in Harmony with God.

Yes, Gods LIFE is Peaceful for us when we are in Harmony with God.

Yes, Gods Wealth is Good for us when we are in Harmony with God.

Yes, Gods Justice is good for us when we are in Harmony with God.

Yes, Gods Truth is good for us when we are in Harmony with God.

Yes, Gods is Spiritual Love Light when we are in Harmony with God.

Yes, God is in every Atom. Yes, every Atom is in God. Yes, God Is in Every-thing and in Everybody. Yes, God Is All GOOD.

Yes, God is the I Am All that I Am in LIFE and within us and in our life when we are in Harmony with God, I am Amen.

Divine Spiritual Guidance and Inspiration.

Things to methinketh about that are also healing.

All Spiritual Divine Guidance and Inspiration comes from God.

We will at some time in our life have to ask God for Divine Guidance and Inspiration.

We will at some time in our life Self Realize that our friends and family and everything that we know about in our life will not be able to help us through some difficult problem other than GOD.

As all great teachers and saints have gone to Nature, to The Mountain Top, for Prayer in Divine Guidance and Inspiration from God.

As an example is George Washington, Abraham, Moses, Jesus, Mary, Krishna, Buddha, Miyamoto Musashi, Chief Joseph, Chief Black Elk, Chief Don Jose Matsuwa, Chief Joseph Eagle Elk, Abraham Lincoln, Mahatma Gandhi, Martin Luther King, Jr., John F. & Robert Kennedy, Mother Teresa, James Prattas, Albert Hofman and Many others.

There are many good men and good women like ourselves who do ask God for Spiritual Divine Guidance daily. Moment by moment, even breath by breath as we are in Prayer.

Going to the Mountain Top means that we need to reach for our higher spiritual ground. When we ask God for Spiritual Guidance we are also asking God for help in our life.

We really do not have to go to a mountain to pray and receive Divine Guidance.

We could go to a safe place in our own neighborhood and home town as our own living room, our closet, our bathroom, our bedroom, our garden.

To the Ocean, to the River, to the Pond, to a Garden Park, to a Ball Park, to a Movie Theater, to a Charity Deed in Service, to an Amusement Park, to something Fun for ourselves or even on a walk down the busy street of Columbus and 86th Street in Manhattan walking towards Central Park in Peace and Breathing in and out Peace, Love and Light in Harmony.

Usually we do find ourselves going to some place in Nature. Far and away from the maddening crowds of life to Find Solitude.

Some of us will go to another city or to another country just to get away from everyone that we know.

We want to get a clearer perspective on our life.

We want to clear our mind from any influences or cares that we may have in life.

It's not that we can get away from life. It is that we will find another way to over come our difficulties and go on with our life more effortlessly.

Usually we go to the mountain top to Over Come our Fear and Doubt by talking with God and Mother Nature in Peace.

When We go to Pray for Divine Guidance and Inspiration, Gods Love Answer Comes in many ways that are visible and invisible.

Guidance will come directly from God by a Spiritual or Physical manifestation.

Divine guidance can be God Himself or Herself, or an Angel from Heaven in disguise as a person at work. While walking on the street, or in school, or at Church or in the Temple or in a beautiful garden. Or even a clear intuitive telepathic message that we feel in our soul, in our heart, in our body or in our mind.

Divine Guidance can be a little bird, or three little birds on a fence that comes to us. Or any one of the other many friendly animals that live in Nature.

It could be as simple as seeing a beautiful Rainbow in the Sky or walking into a Beautiful Meadow full of Monarch Butterflies.

Spiritual Guidance can also come to us from a friendly stranger who just happens to come by us as an Angel from God in disguise.

Spiritual Guidance can come while we are at work or taking care of our children.

Spiritual Guidance can even come while we are playing golf, basketball, tennis, football or rowing. Guidance is available 24 hours a day.

Even at night we can Look Up into the Sky and See Gods Stars as Spiritual Guidance of Inspiration.

We may even see a Shooting Star or two while we are asking for Spiritual Guidance.

We may receive a phone call from someone we have not heard from for a long time sharing an Inspirational story with us.

Spiritual Guidance can come when we are exhausted from worrying and praying and we Finally are Giving Up and Letting Go.

Then suddenly spiritual divine guidance arrives within us. Spiritual Divine Guidance is Gods Wonderful gift to us.

God does know how we are doing here on Earth and that Life can be very difficult for us.

Sometimes life appears impossible for us to handle anymore and we feel all alone.

God does know that sometimes life can be hell on Earth and we do need Spiritual Divine Guidance and Inspiration.

I am Thankful to God for His Spiritual Divine Inspiration. His Infinite Good Ways to give me more Faith, Hope and Strength to over come my difficulties. Amen.

CHAPTER 17
God Is A Beautiful Day CO-Creating

Things to Methinketh about in CO-Creating our life that appear very simple and are C0-Creating Wealth for us now very simply said Being Positively Reinforced daily.

Impersonal Personal Meditations.

I Am Happy, I Am Happy, I Am Happy!

I Thank you God because Life is Beautiful.

I Thank you God because Life is Good.

I Thank you God because I am Happy.

I Thank you God because I am thankful for my life.

I Thank you God because I Am Hearing and I am Seeing the Birds Sing Songs of Love for You & Me. I Am Seeing & Feeling the Monarch Butterflies dancing upon Wild Flowers of life in Your Name God in Your Beautiful Abode.

I Thank you God because I am feeling a gentle spiritual breeze and the Air is Refreshing me.

I Thank you God because the Sun is Shinning All Ways.

I Thank you God because Your Air is Refreshing me Filled with Spiritual Manna, Prana and Health.

I Thank you God because All the Stars in Heaven Shine so Brilliantly Showing me Your Spiritual Way. I Thank you God because I Am in Peace with Your Love in Spiritual Peace. I Thank you God because I Am Healthy with Your Spiritual Love in Health.

I Thank you God because Your Spiritual Mountains are Beautiful and are Inspiring me.

I Thank you God because All Your Animal friends upon the Earth are Healthy and Happy and are my friends too.

I Thank you God because the All of Your Spiritual Rivers Run Freely and Clear and are Happy and Healthy and so am I.

I Thank you God because Your Spiritual Ocean of Love is Clear and Beautiful, Happy and Healthy and I am a Lotus blossom floating in your Ocean of Unconditional Love.

I Thank you God because All Your Animal friends of the Ocean are Healthy and Happy and they are my friends too.

I Thank you God because All of My Family is Beautiful, Healthy, Wealthy, and Happy and I am too. I Thank you God for Surrounding me with All of My Beautiful, Healthy, Wealthy and Happy Spiritual Friends from Around the World. I Thank you God because I Am in Harmony with You.

   I Thank you God because You are in My Life and I Am in Your Life.

   I Thank you God because I Am with You God and You are with Me.

   I Thank you God because We are One God.

   I Thank you God because Your Life is Compassionate for Me and Everybody else.

   I Thank you God because Life is Forgiving.

   I Thank you God because Life is Healthy.

   I Thank you God because Life is Wealthy.

   I Thank you God because Life is Rich.

   I Thank you God because Your Spiritual Life is All Good for Me and Everybody.

   I Thank you God because Your Life is Fun for Me and Everybody.

   I Thank you God because Your Life is Enjoyment for Me and Everybody. I Thank you God because I Am Enjoying All in My Good Life Today. I Thank you God because I Am Abundant in All of My Good in My Life Today. I Thank you God because I Am Seeing You God in Everyone, in Everybody and in Everything. I Thank you God for My Healthy Vision. I Thank you God Be Cause I Am in Your Spiritual Love.

   I Thank you God because Good is Good in our Eyes. I Thank you God because I Am Hearing All the Birds and Angels upon the Earth and in Heaven Sing Your Songs of Spiritual Love. I Thank You God for I Am My Healthy in my Mind, Body and Soul. I Thank you God because I Am One in Spirit with You and All in the world.

   I Thank you God because Everybody and Everything is In Harmony with You. I Thank you God because I Am in Peace with My Mind, My Heart, My Body and My Soul.

   I Thank you God because your Universal Spiritual Peace is Within Everyone, within Everybody and within Everything in Heaven and in Earth that you choose.

   I Thank you God because All of My Needs are Taken Care of by You. I Thank You God for Taking Care of Everybody's Needs.

   I Thank you God because I Am in You and You are in Me.

   I Thank you God because Your Spiritual Love is Flowing Through Me and Through Everyone, Everybody and Everything as you Will. I Thank You God.

I Thank you God because I Am Wealthy in All Your Ways because You are Wealthy. I Thank you God because I Am All the Good in Life because You Love Me. I Thank you God because I Am Enjoying Everything Good in My Life Today. I Thank you God because I Am Rich with Your Love. I Thank you God because Your Good Wealth Flows to Me Easily and Effortlessly as the Manna Rain Falling from Heaven upon the Earth.

I Thank you God because Your Good Manna and Prana Flows Into and Through Me Easily and Effortlessly as I am breathing in and out your spiritual air from Heaven on Earth. I Thank you God because I Am Sharing My Good in Heaven and on Earth As You Willed it. I Thank you God because I Am Guarded and Protected by You and Your Angels. I Thank you God because I Am Spiritually Divinely Guided by You.

I Thank you God because I Am Spiritually Divinely Inspired By You.

I Thank you God because I Am Happy with You and Myself.

I Thank you God because You Are Happy with Me.

I Thank you God because I Am Honored doing Good Deeds for You.

I Thank you God because You are Sharing your Divine Spiritual Love with Everyone on Earth through this Good Book Love Is The Door Way In.

I Thank you God because Your Healing Love Flows through Me Easily and Effortlessly to Everyone In Heaven and on Earth as the Sun is Shining in Your Universe As You Will It.

I Thank you God because Your Good Words have become My Good Words.

I Thank you God because You are All of My Spiritual Wisdom and All of My Spiritual Knowledge of You and LIFE.

I Thank you God because You are My Breath and My Life and My Mind and My Body and My Heart and My Spirit.

I Thank you God because You are My Good Soul and I Am Yours.

I Thank you God because You are My Spiritual Love and THE Light in My life.

I Thank you God because I Am Now in All of My Goodness in Abundance and my Abundance is Growing Daily.

I Thank You God because I Am Enjoying All of My Goodness in My Life Today.

I Thank You God because I Am in Health.

I Thank You God because I Am in Love.

I Thank You God because I Am in Harmony.

I Thank You God because I Am in Beauty.

I Thank You God because I Am in Peace.

I Thank You God because I Am in Wealth.

I Thank You God because I am in Richness.

I Thank You God because I Am in Abundance.

I Thank You God because I Am in Wisdom.

I Thank You God because I Am in Knowledge.

I Thank You God because I Am in Good.

I Thank You God because I Am in Goodness.

I Thank You God because I am in Good Deeds.

I Thank You God because I Am in Compassion.

I Thank You God because I Am in The LIGHT.

I Thank You God because I Am in Spiritual Forgiveness.

I Thank You God because I Am in Spiritual Healing.

I Thank you God because You are Enjoying All Your Good in Your life Through Me.

I Thank you God because I Am Blessed by You Forever.

I Thank you God because I Am Living Eternally with You in Your Spiritual Kingdom of Heaven and on Earth by Your Will.

I Thank you God because I Am That I Am.

I Thank you God because I Am Spiritual Love.

I Thank you God because I am The Light.

I Thank you God because You are I Am That I Am.

I Thank you I Am. Amen.

CHAPTER 18
CO-Creating Spiritual Healing Love

Things to Methinketh about that are very Spiritual and Wealthy for us Being Reinforced Daily for our Spiritual Healing Today.

We All need Spiritual Love in our lives.

We all need to Give Love to Receive Love.

With Spiritual Love in our life we have Health in Spirit, Wealth in Spirit, Happiness in Spirit and Peace of Mind.

The most Important Person in our Life to give Spiritual Love to is YOU first!

If we do not have Love for ourself we cannot give Love to anyone else.

Love is like money.

We cannot give money to someone unless we have money. If we do not have LOVE we cannot give LOVE.

We all need Love as We all need our breath.

Our Health needs Love for a healthy Spiritual Love Circulation.

Where is the first place WE feel a lack of Love?

In OUR HEART!

LOVE is VERY important in our Spiritual Health!

No True Spiritual LOVE in a persons life creates unbalance in that persons life and poor health is the result of no True Spiritual LOVE.

Spiritual Love is a True Spiritual Essence that flows through the Universe as the Suns Love Light Beams and Radiates into our entire structure of our body giving us all life.

If a person closes their Heart to LOVE they become ridged mentally, physically and Spiritually.

This is why God said, Go with the Flow and Breath In and Out Spiritual Love Light in and out until it is our time to move on.

Spiritual Love is the True Spiritual Essence that flows through all of our cells as a Spiritual Nutrient called LIFE.

If a person closes their heart to love, this spiritual essence cannot enter into our cells and rejuvenate them moment by moment without our permission.

We can lead a Horse to water but we cannot make the Horse drink the water and so the same with spiritual love. We have to want to receive spiritual love to give spiritual love.

Spiritual Love is the True Spiritual Essence that flows through all of the parts in our body in relation to our Structure, Order and Relationship in our body that keeps everything in our body in a Harmonious Order called HEALTHY.

If a person closes their heart the Harmonious Order of their minds-body and their life is out of Harmony.

As in a Polar Shift, our life is heading for a collision being out of harmony. Simple.

The quality of our Spiritual Love is determined by our spiritual good thoughts.

Are our Thoughts and our Attitude, Good & Positive?

How is our Health?

How is our LIFE going?

Good or not so good?

Compare the quality of our thoughts and our attitude about life in general.

What about our spiritual life particularly to our health, abundance, enjoyment, work, family, LOVE, relationships, government, religion, education and we will know where we TRULY are. In our life, and in our Health, and in our Thoughts, in our family, and in our business, and in our workplace, and of course in our LIFE on scale of LIFE between 1 to 10.

This personal honest assessment is as looking in the spiritual mirror of our life.

Mirrors do not tell lies. What we see is what we really are.

Our health today reflects our inner self thoughts and self esteem through out our Minds-Body, Heart and Soul.

Health is what we Methinketh it is!

I Am that Methinketh that I am Methinking, I Am.

Sounds funny does it not?

Yet some times it is not funny at all if we are not thinking Good POSITIVE thoughts!

Negative thoughts with Anger and Hate can kill us.

Good thoughts to methinketh about.

We may want to think about these very simple thoughts that are of Spiritual Abundance and Health to us very simply said.

I Am in Good Spirit.

I Am in Good Spiritual Love.

I Am in Respect of God Father and God Mother.

I Am in High Self Esteem of my own Spiritual Soul, My True Self.

I Am living in Balance in Nature.

I Am living in Harmony with God.

I Am living in Peace with My Self, Others and God.

I Am Content with All of my goodness today.

I Am breathing fresh clean positive thoughts into my minds-body and soul in a continuous healthy rhythm.

I Am eating healthy nutritious good food.

I Am chewing my good food well.

I Am drinking plenty of good clean water.

I Am free of all obstructions in my Soul, Heart, Mind and Body.

I Am free of fear and doubt.

If I can be, I Am Athletic.

I Am Saying my Good Prayers to God daily.

I Am Meditating and Visualizing on All of My Goodness Daily.

When I Am tired I will rest and take a nap and dream of My Goodness.

I Am reading good books on many different subjects.

I Am Listen to my Inner Voice God.

I Am Listen to my Good Intuition.

I Am Listening to Divine Guidance within me.

I Am listening to Divine Inspiration within me.

I Am Thinking Good I Am.

I Am Thinking Healthy and I Am.

I See My Self Healthy and Abundant in Goodness in my mind and I am that I am.

I Am taking my good vitamins and good herbal supplements when my body needs them for my cellular support and good maintenance of my health.

I Am in the Sun Light regularly absorbing Gods Goodness from Gods Sun Light. I am protecting my self from UV radiation.

I Am Walking in Peaceful walks.

I Am in the Country Breathing Fresh Clean Country Air.

I am on The Mountain Top Breathing Fresh Clean Spiritual Air.

I Am walking on the Beautiful Beach Breathing Fresh Clean Ocean air.

I Am in Spiritual Peace wherever I am.

I Am Hearing and Seeing the beautiful birds singing beautiful songs.

I Am seeing The Good in my life.

I Am Seeing God in my LIFE.

I Am Thankful to God for all of my goodness.

I Am Enjoying my life.

I Am receiving my good in many ways.

I am now in receipt of all of my good and I am thankful to God.

I Love you God.

God Loves me.

I Am Healthy.

When we look at our health, our body, our heart, our mind and our soul we are also looking at our Whole Self.

We and our soul live in our Structure our Temple which is our body.

Our Physical Order which is all of our body parts inside and out and our Spiritual Mental Relationship to our self that We See in the mirror is how well and Healthy all the spiritual parts will work Together as One Mind Body Soul namely us.

We are Naturally in Harmony when we are in Harmony with God.

We may look at our health and body as an automobile.

Are we in need of a servicing?

Can we focus on a particular part of our life that needs repair?

There Is a simple Way we can repair our body.

Clean out our mind of all anger, hate, fear and doubt and forgive everybody that has hurt us.

Forgive yourself for hurting others. Forgive yourself.

Then as we Willfully and CONSCIOUSLY look around to clean up our apartment or house or Palace or Church or Temple or Tee Pee or Halau or Government, White House, Senate, Congress, or Agency, or Department, or Country. Our Home from the Ceiling to the Floor.

Do you SEE if there is Any kind of psychic lackadaisical physical metal spiritual opinionated dirt that is not in HARMONY in any place in your living area, or work area? Methinketh.

Anon YOU, not the maid, not the monks, not the servants, not your mother, father, brother or sister, YOU Clean IT UP.

Get YOUR life in ORDER today.

Make an appointment with your Destiny to clean up your life and your living environment today and YOU will be Spiritually HAPPY!

Anon we consciously clean things out. Methinking Cleanliness is next to Godliness, just as we were in a Monastery, Church or Temple or on Earth which we are and that is our spiritual body outwardly and inwardly.

Anon, we do not need the dirt, dust or the junk that is clogging up our physical and spiritual life house.

Clean all those things up.

Sell or give the junk you call Treasures to Charity.

Start living in Spiritual Harmony with your mind, body, heart and soul and with God.

A good cleaning out our Minds-body and Brain is very similar to us cleaning out our spiritual house thoroughly.

Cleaning our automobile or our bicycle or motorcycle or airplane or horse stall or dog kennel or bird cage or The White House.

YOU will be amazed at how Correlated and Interrelated All these THINGS are to your Life's Health, Wellbeing and Success.

If you see your house is a mess you can pretty much guess your Minds Body Heart and Soul is a mess.
Get to work you lazy god kids!
Chop this Wood and Carry this Cosmic Spiritual Light Water.
We are Lazy Zen, Christian, Jewish, Buddhist, Hindu, Islamic, Moslem, Taoist, Funky, People Country, Government Grateful Dead Heads.
We better ship UP or we will be shipped OUT!
They could make little green chips out of you!

CHAPTER 19
Here Comes the Sun CO-Creating Good

More things to think about that are very simple and Sunny for me and you.
I Send My Sun.
I Send My Son.
He is The Light.
I love you my Sun.
I want to thank you for your Love Light My SUN.
I want to thank you for Shining Brightly upon our Earth and throughout our Life and Creation.
I want to thank you for Casting out The Darkness in this world so we all can see our Life and The Truth.
I want to thank you for your Love Light showing everybody The Way here on Earth and in our Universe.
Oh my Sun, I have Seen how Dark and Cold the Earth can be without you my Sun.
I love you my Sun for Sharing your life with me.
You truly Radiate The Way of Spiritual Love Light.
God Bless our Good Mother & Father God for Their Love. For They have Blessed us all with a Sun so Noble as You.
You are our Sun King and Universe The Light.
You are my God in so many ways.
Without you my Sun there would be Nothing on Earth or in our Universe.
God Bless You my Sun.

CHAPTER 20
I Am CO-Creating Good

Many Messiahs, Saints, Mystics, Artist, Poets, Writers have referred to God as the I Am within us all.

God said: I am that I am God.

How can we realize and experience God the I Am within us today?

By asking God in Prayer to Speak to you within your heart, within your mind with your body and within your soul.

By being in Silent Prayer and Meditation we can Listen within ourselves to Gods Inner Voice Conversing with us. We will notice the difference between our ego talking to us and God talking to us by the quality of the spiritual conversation.

Gods voice is always saying Good, Positive, Uplifting Words for our well being that everything is in fact OK Ola Kala!

God is always saying that LOVE is Letting Go of Fear and Doubt about our life. Everything will work itself out for our goodness because God mother and father love us and know us. Gods Omnipresence knows what we are going through in our life.

Life Tests everybody either man, woman or animal to see Who has faith in God. Who Loves God and Respects God and Gods Justice.

God will say to us and show us The Way of having Patience in all good things that are His Will of goodness for us.

There is a Time And a Place for all good things to become manifested in our life.

Patience is a Virtue.

Many of Gods Good Words of Spiritual Wisdom & Knowledge will come to us as we Let Go of our Frustrations, Pain's and Anger of not being able to do what we want to do when we want to do what ever we want to do.

It Will Come!

Have patience and give God and ourselves the Faith and Belief that all of our good will come to us as we move forward in Positive Action.

Some times Doing Nothing is Doing Something Good.

Patience.

Some times LOVE is letting go of What we Want and Need. Love Will Miraculously come to us after we have let our Desires go to God and they go in FAITH.

We will receive better than what we thought of my friend.

We cannot beg God to do something for us because we feel we need it NOW.

Everything we need in the Moment of our life is provided to us if we will just get out of the way of our true soul self. Our goodness will manifest.

True Spiritual Love is letting go of fear and doubt about our success in life.

Our Thoughts of Fear and Doubt are an illusion in our life that we have manifested by our not good thinking.

Our thoughts of fear and doubt will cause us to NOT act upon our good dreams of success.

I am that I am.

I am here within you to serve you my brother and sister.

Please listen to me, I Love You.

Please call upon me when you need Guidance and Inspiration and help.

I am everything good in your life my brother and sister, I am God and I am Good.

I am your Spiritual Enlightenment.

I am within You and you are within me when you realize this truth. How can you not receive your good?

Look at a Coconut Tree.

It will produce coconuts in a healthy environment.

You will also produce your good also in a healthy environment.

God Wills It Good.

Only by being in denial of the truth will we not receive our good. All good is God. Good manifests by us being in Harmony with God.

God is being in Harmony with our wishes because God is Omnipresent, Omniscient and Omnipotent in LIFE. In us and in everything good.

Good will come to us in our good time as God Wills, IT.

I am that I am.

You are living in my Temple in my Image in my Holy Life.

I am within every cell of your minds body, heart and soul.

I am Spiritual Love in your life.

I am Beauty.

I am Health.

I am Peace.

I am Harmony.

I am Wealth.

I am Abundance.

I am Wisdom.

I am Knowledge.
I am Music.
I am Dance.
I am Food.
I am Water.
I am Air.
I am Funny.
I am Fun.
I am Protection.
I am Guidance.
I am Inspiration.
I am Faith.
I am Belief.
I am Rich in All Goodness.

When you my dear relative are in Harmony with me God, all good things will be yours if you work for your the good.

I am not for the weak and lazy.

I am not just wishful unfocused thinking.

I am not wishful unfocused prayers.

I am not wishful unfocused meditation, visualization or goals.

I am Good God.

I am All Ways Working for you 24 hours a day, 7 days a week forever.

God wants to See if we are really Committed to our True Soul Purpose in life. Are we doing Gods Good Deeds and Will in our own personal life way, or if you are just greedy like so many?

We may even give ourselves Greed just to corrupt ourselves and teach us a good lesson in Gods Justice & Laws.

God will not be mocked!

Fear God and not man or government or anything for God is Real Justice and God is Good.

I am the Sun & the Moon and All the Stars above, below and all around you Beyond 360 degrees.

I am the Earth and everything in and on and above and below it.

I am the Stars of Heaven Spiritually Guiding & Inspiring your way.

I am in Compassion for you.

I am in Forgiveness for you.

I am in Healing for you.

I am in Abundance for you.

I am in Spiritual Love for you.

You are my Christ.

I am All that I am.

I am in YOU!

CHAPTER 21
The I Am in Meditation

A personal self realization experience of the God I am within us for our Healing.

You will need an Imaginary Chalk board and Eraser.

Please take your chalk board out and one piece of chalk and draw a large circle in the middle of the chalk board.

Place your name in the middle of the circle and draw a circle around yourself as a Hub within the large circle.

Please draw spokes in your wheel similar to a wagon wheel from your Center Hub to the Outer circle.

Draw 12 Spokes.

You are now in the middle of the Hub of your life circle with 12 sections Radiating out of your life.

The spokes spaces are each apart of your life to today. Each piece by piece spoke adds up to your whole life to date.

Please divide your life experiences up by the 12 spokes of your life in Order.

An example would be, beginning with your birth as a baby, a child, a teenager, a young adult, an adult, an older person, and your near death experiences if you have any.

Include your important good and bad and not so good life experience's that have influenced your life that are important to you in your life in timeline.

From conception, to birth, to your family relationships, to your environment's that you have lived in and throughout your life. Your schools and education, your neighborhood and community, your friends and relatives, your military or government service, your community service, your religion of life, your good service deeds to others, your work and your carrier, your disabilities, your self esteem issues and your failures & success's till today.

Realize that everything in your life wheel is an evolutionary process of your souls experience from conception to today.

Your life's karma.

Please place all of your life experiences within the different spokes in the circle on the chalk board by a time line. Start at number 1 spoke and end at number 12.

Please take your time.

Please make sure that you divide your experiences up evenly by your life's many facets like a diamond has facets that Radiate the Light. Your life is very similar to a diamond, because you have many facets.

The life of piece of Black Coal, like a Soul, through the Pressures and Challenges and the Trials and Tribulations of time eventually becomes a Diamond in the Ruff, just like all of us.

Now the diamond needs Cutting & Polishing to show its Virtue and Brilliance of Radiating Light. As your Life in Life.

You may be only a teenager or a 100 year old person. It does not matter. So please do this accordingly to your personal life experience.

Now take a good look at what you have experienced from your conception to today.

Who you are today because of your experiences? What have you become of as a person by your experiences?

A healthy happy soul because of all this Majestical Spiritual Journey you have been on?

Please Remember to breath Spiritual Love Light In and Out as you look at your life.

I am sure that there are many moments that you would not like to remember or experience again because you have learned the truth.

There are also many Good experiences that you may want to explore on how to enjoy them better and more wisely getting more out of them because they are fun and good.

The Acceptance of your life is Important to you because this is really what has made you in this Life called YOU.

Please do Not Judge Yourself nor anybody else.

Look at all this experience in an Impersonal Way as looking at a movie in a movie theater.

Please forgive yourself and others if you need to do this act of Compassion through your Understanding of YOU.

Just look at your life as it is up to this today with No Opinion.

Remember to Breath Light In and Out and Blow Out of your life all the Past Painful Experiences.

Spiritual LOVE is letting go of FEAR and DOUBT.

Now I am asking you to look at each spoke of your wheel and accept each spoke of your wheel as how your life was then with all of your experiences good and bad and were you are today. Ola Kala.

This is how you have learned about LIFE and your environment and GOD.

All of your experiences have brought you here today.

I would like you to realize that you really have been on a Majestical Magical Mystery Soul Journey called Your life through the Will of God and through the Choices you made each step of The Way.

Look Peacefully at all these choices you made and thank your self for your experiences in Understanding Spiritual Knowledge and Wisdom about you and your life and God.

Now that you have accepted of the Spokes of Your Life, I am asking you to Take your Spiritual Eraser Out and Erase Each Spoke of your Wheel one by one after you have Reviewed and Accepted them.

Re+Member & Re+Collection.

PLEASE start with the most painful experiences and work your way to the most enjoyable experience you have enjoyed in your life.

Remember to Breath in and out Spiritual LOVE Light.

Blow fear and doubt out of your life forever as you are Spiritually Healing and Erasing and Removing your history, your Karma of the Past, step by step.

When you have finished with all of your spokes of your life I would like you to Breath In and Out The Light and Realize these experiences are the past and they are all gone from you with Gods help.

YOU are FREE!

They are only a memory of the past.

Now erase your hub in the wheel of yourself.

Please take a deep breath in and let it out.

There is no more old oh O you.

You have been Spiritually Reborn.

You are New!

Begin a New Life Today.

Nothingness is Everything too.

Now there is nothing drawn or written on your karmic chalk board of life.

All that there is left for you now is an invisible spiritual presence of nothing but good.

You do not have a Body or a Mind or Heart or a Soul. You are now of a spiritual essence of God I Am in Spirit. We are FREEDOM.

We Floating in Harmony, in Peace, in Spiritual Love and in Spiritual Light in God.

We are In Spirit in Gods Great Creation within all the Universes with all the other Radiant Stars Being One God.

We are looking at all the Stars Floating effortlessly in the beautiful Sky up above on a Clear Night. We are within all the stars.

We are a Radiant Star among all the other radiant stars of our universe.

We are Freely and Easily Being One with all the other Stars and Constellations. We are Breathing Spiritual Love Light in and out of our being.

We are Breathing Spiritual Love In and Out by Gods Will.

We are Evolving into Oneness and nothingness in an Ocean of Unconditional LOVE.

Now please breath spiritual love in and out and on and on in your Love Forever.

Realize and say to yourself.

I Am that I am.

I am me.

Please enjoy your Me.

I am a Spiritual Soul Journey.

CHAPTER 22
I Am the Instruments of God

You are a Unique Individual thank God. We are All Unique!

Look around and you will see that All of Creation is Unique.

Everything is a Beautiful Mystery called God. Life really is not a mystery it just appears that way to the uninitiated. To some souls Life appears as an Illusion.

Life is so simple it appears very complex and complicated. Life is simple.

The greatest truths are simple.

All universal laws are simple. Life is a cosmic joke and a riddle when you scramble your brains trying it figure it all out.

Life is nothing to figure out. Life is to be experienced and those experiences in our life IS Good.

God is very simple.

Life is very simple.

Humans out of Harmony make life complicated.

The physical plane is very simple. Everything is a word and God Spoke the Word and it Manifested.

Just like you Speak Words and they manifest in your life.

Gods words are Good and God said All is Good because God created them.

You feel the same way with what you speak do you not?

What words do you Spake and Think daily? What are you creating as a result of your Thoughts and Word said by you? Is it good for you?

Life is God and God is Good because God Thinks Good Thoughts.

Life is also YOU a child of God with the ability to think.

You think thoughts, but are they good thoughts?

What Good have you my friend created for you, your family, your community, your government, your country, your religion, your leadership in your life?

Some times life is funny and wonderful because we think this is funny and the happy ways and Days.

Other times it is depressing and tragedy because of negative tragic and depressing thoughts or experiences.

Most of us on Earth do not remember or even know how we arrived here. Where we came from and were we are going.

Most of us do not know our true soul purpose nor our true destiny.

Most of us do not know we have a choice in our life.

Most of us do not listen to our intuition, our mind, our heart or our body or God or Nature.

Most of us listened to others, and we heard many unusual fairy tales that were negative instead or the Real Fairy Tales that are positive when we were grown up.

Television is full of negative stories that many of us believe are true.

Because we have been Misdirected in life We ask God for Help to Restore our Soul. To help us get back into Spiritual Harmony and Balance with God in our life.

We can listen to that small still voice of God within ourselves.

Most of us allow fear and doubt to rule our lives.

Most of us on Earth, 99.9% do not have a True Soul Purpose other than to be a slave of economics instead of a ruler of economics having fun creating good times.

We think that because our parents got together one day and made love in the back seat of their automobile and conceived us unknowingly and became pregnant and later on we were born that we are our parents creation their children. That is a reasonable assumption.

Yet if we Research a little further in our life we will see that there are others that we are related to. We do not know them all as our grandparents. There are our great grandparents.

Then there are our great great great great great great-grandparents who of course we do not know All about them.

Where are your roots now? Who's Roots?

Who did you say You are you related to?

Adam and Eve, HIM & HER?

Life is simple when we see life as a Perfect Structure, Order, and Relationship throughout our life and our Life's cosmic universe.

All life is in Harmony and Balance. Even in what most humans call Chaos.

There is Spiritual Structure, Order, and Relationship.

Most of us upon the earth cannot trace our history 500 years back nor 10,000 years back in time. The Queen of England nor any King, Queen, President, Minister, Chairperson, pauper nor anybody on earth can find their biological roots because God has Cleansed the Earth several times.

RND & DNA will not work.

Some educated Scientist want us to believe that you evolved from some cosmic particle millions of years ago from a Big Bang.

Maybe it was a Big Orgasm in the Jungle.

Other scientist want us to believe we evolved as a relative of a whatever animals through cave man times as in our humble beginning after the polar shift!

Of course we lived in caves because the Earth was cleansed of most humans because we lost our way, The Way from being in Harmony with God.

We became egotistical and arrogant and out of balance back then very much as we are today.

Especially in Washington, DC.

Most of humanity back then and even today started thinking and began to believe that Man is Superior to God and Nature and that there is no God. That one must be a fool to believe in God, and humanity followed its vain inharmonious ways until we destroyed our selves out of vanity. Just as we are today.

Mirror Mirror on the wall who is the most beautiful vain wooer of them all?

Of course those that were allowed to survive had to find shelter in caves and began scratching out a life again with nothing but themselves and their minds-bodies.

Slowly we rediscovered our true selves and found our hearts and our souls with the help of our humble plant sacrament friends from Mother Earth. Here we are now once again in the same situation as an evolved human race from where we began.

All life was created in the beginning by God our Father and Mother. We are their expression.

We are their children. We have been given free will. We have been given free choice. We are unique. Our Parents as Any Good parent has given us All our good for our good and to Do good as we will it through our thoughts and actions.

All that God has ever asked us to do is to enjoy our life and live in peace and in balance and in Harmony with our fellow brothers and sisters, our animal friends and with Nature. To be thankful to God for all our Good.

How simple!

Imagine how far we have come from having to start over so many times. It is not hard to understand how so many scientist have had to reach so far away into the universal sky and their little imagination or so primitive a thought as to believe we are so beastly and so far from the truth.

This is a simple thought.

Be here now.

Ponder this Methinketh.

You and I are really one of Gods many infinite manifestations of Gods Mind. We are made with Spiritual Love and we are Gods children. So are the animals and plants and minerals in Gods creations. The some total of All Life is called God by many people all over the world. It is possible that God does not have a name. He may be the man with no name.

We humans decided to call Him something.

I Am You are, We are All Gods Children and at the same time We are unique individual souls.

Many on Earth believe that Our Children are related to their families by their birth into their individual families.

Relation by blood. Most also believe Children are related to us as we are related to them by birth and on this idea goes.

God crated Man in His image and God is related to Us. We are related to God. By Spirit and blood. This is simple. Everybody is related to each other as a Human Race family and we are all related to God. We are One big family called God.

Even All the Animals and plants and minerals and everything in All Gods creation is related to God and to ourselves.

All of Gods Creation has Structure, Order, and Relationship.

If we stop looking at our egotistical little selves and we step back and look at ALL of life as a Creation. As looking at a beautiful painting, or a beautiful garden, or beautiful woman, or beautiful automobile, the Invisible will become Visible.

WE will SEE the Whole Beautiful Creation in a Microcosm of the Macrocosm.

Our Life has Structure, Order and Relationship to God. This is simple. God is everything including you. WE are Related in Gods Order and within His Structure called Spiritual LIFE.

Our real true spiritual self is naturally One with God. God is naturally One with us. We ALL are One with All Life. Most humans do not understand God.

All citizens of our planet Earth are in fact Instruments of God.

We are all Instruments of God whether we Believe IT or not.

God Created man in His Image.

We are The Children of God. Our Farther who Art in Heaven and on the Earth and Our Mother who Art in Heaven and on the Earth are our Eternal Parents.

Spirit and Matter.

Him & Her.

God.

Two Heavenly Spiritual Lights that Create ALL Life.

All Thought.

We are a wise soul and we are one with them. They are one Great Spirit within us.

Our Father in Heaven is our Spirit Soul. Our Mother in Earth is our Spirit Soul Body.

We are Spirit Embodied on Earth.

We are Blessed by God.

WE are blessed or cursed by our own unique individual egotistical and societal group thoughts.

We become as a person, family, group, community, village, city, state, country, continent, and planet by what we think.

What we think becomes our CO-Creation and our contribution to Life and to God.

Our thoughts become ourselves and our life. We also become our personal vehicle of our own blessing. Or, our own Personal hell or Group hell or National hell or Planetary hell of self destruction.

God gave us all Free Will to choose Good Will because God loves us All.

We can bless our selves if we chose to. What will be our choice as a Country called the USA?

What about your Country?

God Blessed America.

In God We Trust.
What will be our choice of thoughts as an individual?
We May Well Think: I Am in love, I Am in Peace, I Am in Harmony with God and in Nature.
I Am living in Balance,
I Am Happy.
I Am thankful God.
I Am listening to Divine Guidance.
I Am listening to Divine Inspiration.
I Am Healthy.
I am Abundant Wealth in all my goodness.
I Am.
I Am that I Am.
I Am The Instrument of God.

CHAPTER 23
Visiting with God and me I am

I would like to tell you a Thinking Story that is simply good.
 We are what we are Methinking.
 We may not know that we consciously believe what we are thinking even if it is not true to us.
 Lets look at our thinking.
 How do we see ourselves?
 How do we think about ourselves?
 What words do we use to describe our self?
 The words we do use that are what words and thoughts we have in our mind are in our minds Third Eye, and in our heart, our body and our soul.
 The good words we use create our self image of our self is the Spiritual Force and Spiritual Energy helping us create our good or not so good.
 I am what I am thinking I am.
 I am healthy. I am beautiful. I am optimistic about my future.
 I am me.
 Welcome Jimmy!
 I am happy that you have come to visit with me.
 I am very happy to see you.
 Please come in.
 I have been thinking of you lately.
 Please come into my living room and have a seat over here on the Turquoise Green Velvet Couch.
 You must be tired and thirsty after your long spiritual soul journey on Earth to see me.
 Can I offer you a glass of cool refreshing spring water and a sandwich?
 You look wonderful.
 Thank you Father.
 How have you been?
 Very Good Dad.
 Please tell me all about what you have been doing with your life.
 How was your Odyssey?

Great!
We won.
All right.
What do you want to do now that you have decided on some new soul journey?
Well, Dad, I want to Have more Fun and good times enjoying my life.
Jimmy, I am very impressed with your good dreams and inspirations and you true soul purpose.
Jimmy, I am confident that All your good will come to you very quickly.
You Can do it!
Have Fun.
I Love You.
Go now and enjoy creating your good life.
God Bless you Jimmy.

CHAPTER 24
Spiritual Love

What is Spiritual LOVE? What is a Soul Mate? What does All this Love mean to Us?
Spiritual Love is God Mother Spiritual Energy and God Father Spiritual Energy Together. Flowing throughout All Life.

The Great Majestical Spiritual Light Magnets of Life. They Are of Yin and Yang. Good Positive and Good Negative Spiritual Universal Electricity. Spiritual Love Coming Together, as the Greatest Passionate Universal Lovers of All LIFE Creating All Life having a ball.

When Handsome Father God and Beauty Mother God are Coming Together Passionately and are Spiritually ONE in Oneness, as when we are in LOVE with our LOVER coming together, in Spirit, Mind and Body we are Creating LOVE Energy just as They are Creating Their Spiritual Love That Creates all life with their Creative Love Energy.

Their LOVE Created the Big O.

We also have the ability to have a Big O within us because we are their Christ Child. Love Energy CO-Creates Love Energy.

Oh My God.

O.

The Big Universal Orgasm.

A Super Nova wow.

A World of Wonder that Radiates this Energy every where in the universe.

Gods LOVE is their Christ Child. Us.

This Christ Energy is their Love Child and is their Spiritual LOVE and their Spiritual LIGHTS Magnetic Energy that Lights Up and Attracts and Creates All Life from Within.

Their Christ Children is a Christ Son and a Christ Daughter because they are Gods Children and so are WE.

Christ is Spiritual Light Energy.

Christ Consciousness.

We are Christ when we are One with God.

We have the spiritual soul energy to CO-create our good on Earth.

Anon because God Father and God Mother Passionately LOVE each other they Conceived from their LOVE a Sun and a Daughter in their IMAGE a Virgin Spiritual birth of goodness.

God Is Happy. God Blessed their Good Children, US with All of Gods Goodness. Because God Loves their Children US, the Sun and Moon and the Earth, the Spirit and Matter, their Majestical Love, US.

Everything IS GOOD because THEY are the Real His Royal Highness and Her Royal Highness GOD Mother and Father.

THEY ARE THE GOOD Creators of us and all life in all universes known and unknown to humankind.

Puppet Sovereigns as in Europe, Arabia, USA etc, are forgeries claiming they have the power which they do not. VAIN Wooers they are.

Spiritual LOVE is Gods Spiritual Energy of Love Eternally Radiating as Spiritual LOVE Light Waves. Just as the Sun is Radiating Spiritual Love LIGHT upon and through All the Earth and All Universes Creating Life and showing us the way.

Gods Spiritual Love is Sun Light Radiating as Gods Love Light is Radiating as the Sun Spiritually Radiates Magnetic Electrical Energy to everybody and everything God Created in Gods Heaven and on Earth with Unconditionally LOVE.

All that God Created which is everything, including YOU and Me for Being in One Love with All Life CO-Creating Life with God through this Spiritual Light Energy Radiation.

Gods Spiritual Love is the Invisible Medium, the Spirit, The Energy, this Spiritual LOVE Electricity that God uses to Create LIGHT in Gods Good Universe and that LIGHT is Gods LOVE and Gods LOVE is GOOD.

It is Amazing.

There are really no words in any language that explains God.

It has to be experienced as our Life.

Gods Spiritually Created Good Thoughts of Goodness and Love and Gods Compassion for ALL that God Created Unconditionally Creates Gods Light of LOVE in Spirit and in Matter in All of Gods Good Universe. This Good Spiritual LOVE LIGHT is the Giver and Creator of ALL LIFE.

It is Gods Spiritual Methinketh's that Manifest Life.

Gods Spiritual Love is the Giver of all Good in Heaven and on Earth and that is what God said is Spiritual Love which is Gods Omnipresence within Everybody, and in Everything Spiritual and in Matter.

It is Universal Love Energy.

Because God is the LIGHT that cast out the Darkness in our Life and in all Life that GIVES Life to All. God Thinks Spiritual Life Force Energy into Every Atom and Cell as even you and me and Adam and Eve. In All Life Soul's and in Mind's and in Matter's. This Love LIGHT is what is Gods Spiritual LOVE Manifested.

Anon, Without Gods Spiritual LOVE, Nothing would exist because it would have no life. No Spirit.

Anon because a life without Gods Love LIGHT is darkness and death and a Void and a Doom, a Nothingness and that is nothing good.

Anon the Void, the Darkness is Cold and Lifeless because it has no LIFE, no LIGHT, no LOVE, no Spirit. The darkness cannot breath, and the darkness cannot see, and the darkness cannot feel, and so the darkness is a Dark Void, a Black Hole in the Universe that God uses to create some-thing good from no-thing.

A Reprocessing Center in The Universe.

If God and Gods Sun stopped Radiating Spiritual Love Light Waves upon the Earth Unconditionally for All, and if the Sun stopped and did not even exist, All Life on the planet Earth and all other planets throughout Gods Eternal Universe would perish in the doom of darkness.

Not one good thing would exist, live and grow.

Nothingness.

WE, a child of God, could Not Breath air and we would Gasp and we would choke to death, because it takes Gods Spiritual Love Sun Light Mana to Create Clean Healthy Air for US to Breath In our LIFE.

We, a child of God, Would Thirst to Death. Because their would be No Water, because it takes Gods Electrical Love Sun Light to Create Good Clean Healthy Water.

Anon, WE, a child of God, would Starve to Death because there would be no food. Because it takes Gods Love Sun Light to Create good Clean Healthy Food.

Because it is Gods Sun Light of Spiritual Love, and not our inflated ego that draws the Seeds of Life to Germinate and Rise Upward out of the Earth Growing towards Gods Lovely Sun Light in Reverence to Omnipotent God Mother and God Father The Givers of LIFE, The God and Goddess, The Love and Light of ALL Life.

Anon my dear ones, because even plants and animals know that without God their Mother and Father making Love, their is no plants and their would be no animals in the Earth because all would perish.

There would be no Dolphins or Whales or fish in the Sea because the Ocean needs Gods Love Light for her growth and for the micro organisms and the plankton. All the fish would perish because even the fish know God.

Anon even Salmon fish need to eat and drink and breath like we do.

How would the Universal Ocean of Unconditional Love exist and be Created without Gods Magnetic Electrical Love Sun Light Causing the Air and the Water and the Elements to Come Together to Create the many Earth's with Gods Love Water?

The Rivers and Ponds and Oceans and Snow and Earth would be No-Way. Even the elements could not find their way to each other or attract each other without spiritual love as you would not be able to find each other or our soul mate in the cold darkness of the VOID.

Thank God we can have a really big Orgasm!

If everything this very moment changed by Gods Will for any-body on Earth who does not believe in God and Gods Love and Gods Light and Gods Justice would now live in doom.

Life is a Miracle.

Anon because nothing would be left alive and if we were alive for a moment in a Black Panic we would have to eat anybody else who does not believe in God, and eat each other for food.

Yikes!

Anon in this Majestical Spiritual Light Movement by God's Will, God Raised UP All the Good Souls into Heaven with Gods Angels Who believe in HIM & HER and saved them from Doom while He left the Rest to Die who did not believe in Him.

Thank You God.

Anon and you would have to Suck out the Blood of your own family and friends if they are still alive for water if you are thirsty wooer from Washington, DC. Oh my God.

Anon you would have to Open their Chest Cavity and Hope to Breath some Foul Air for maybe a moment, and after short moment you would perish having Devoured nothing good including yourself and so would everybody else left on Earth by Gods Will in a Dark Void.

God.

Anon because you could not See and Breath and in a Black Panic you would also Freeze to Death in Fear of Gods Justice because their would be no Spiritual Sun Light to SEE your Way to Run and hide your face from God. Nor Warmth for the planet Earth and The Ice Caps would Melt and Flood the planet and whatever is left of you would perish again by Gods Will.

Help us God.

Anon because without God and Gods Love there is No Spiritual Light and there is no life and there is nothing but a cold darkness of a Void that is lifeless just like a dead body whose soul has left and it is stiff and cold and lifeless and so are you without God.

Gods Spiritual Love Light is Gods Good Spiritual Creative Thoughts of what is called Spiritual LOVE.

Anon And if you NOW understand what I am saying to you that nothing exists without Gods Spiritual Love because God is Compassion and God is Forgiveness and God is Love for US All.

Thank You God.

Because God Self Realized that without a Soul, which is Spiritual Love Light we would be dead and we could not CO-Created anything good.

Because God loves us, Gods Creation, Gods Christ, in Gods Image, God breathed into us a Spiritual Soul Life, a real soul, because God is GOOD.

God wants us to CO-create with Him & Her.

Anon and because God Loves us God created his Son our sun to show us The Way because otherwise we would be lost in the darkness of the night of eternity. This Goodness that God Created my friend is what the Gods and Goddesses in Heaven call Gods True Love Gift.

Anon and Gods Love is Great Love.

Gods Love is The Light.

The Light Shows us all the way home.

Anon and Gods Love is in everybody and everything. Everything God Created is GOOD.

Anon because If there was anything other than GOOD which is not good, it would not exit.

Without Gods air, Gods water and Gods food and Gods shelter which all come from within the Spiritual Earth the Great Goddess Mother Earth Gaia and Through Spiritual Water there would be no Life on Earth.

Anon anon because Gods Spirit Soul Loves Her, His Beautiful Queen Penelope, His Good Spouse, Their Great Passionate Spiritual Love Orgasm Creates All Goodness in LIFE. Happy.

Anon even our good mind body and soul and all of the abundance we can have is created from Her bosom because God Mother and God Father Give the BEST for us because They are Us.

They have Spiritual Love and Compassion and Forgiveness for Us and even for themselves because without Us they would be all alone so they God Created Us their children to populate the Earth and to CO-Create our good to enjoy the goodness and to live our life in Harmony and in Peace and in Health and in Abundance of all goodness and to learn about God and how majestically miraculous God is and how our entire life is a Miracle.

Happier.

Anon every single moment is a Miracle of spiritual love because if God Mother and God Father stopped passionately loving each other there would be No Love Light, No Christ Child, No Big Orgasm of Electrical Magnetic Energy Called Mana. Because it is their spiritual love that LIGHTS the FIRE within their Heart that CREATES souls that Lights UP this World with Gods love and light and gives all Goodness, Creativity and Mans Inventions.

The Big O.

Anon and that is why we cannot buy love.

Anon we can only give love and receive love freely.

Anon Spiritual Love it is NOT a material thing nor a Modonna Material Girl or Material Man.

True LOVE is a Spiritual Love of two good souls in Spiritual Love light as the Great Love of God father and God mother coming together in their gigantic cosmic orgasm that is so Powerful it Radiates Love Light waves throughout the eternal universe as Spiritual Love because they love each other and attract each other as Magnets do.

Anon this LOVE is good because they are Soul Mates.

They are Spiritual Mates and they are Friends because they are Great Spirit in Heaven and on Earth and the Great Majestical Magnets of LOVE LIGHT that Create ALL the Electrical Mana Energy that Creates ALL Life and they have Come Together sending good shock waves throughout the Universe.

The Great Yin and Yang.

Man and Woman, Spirit and Matter.

Spiritually Positive and Spiritually Negative Energy and all good, in Harmony having Fun.

Just like us.

CHAPTER 25
Spiritual Love is an Aspect of God

Just as God, who is a spiritual male and a female energy, a man and a woman, so is WE humans made in the image of God. Some of us are a male and some of us are female.

Just as there is positive good and negative good of electrical magnetic energy.

Spirit and Matter, Yin and Yang.

Anon so being a human being with a soul in our body we are a child of God.

We are either a man or a woman soul. Some humans can be even a combination of both as a hermaphrodite but in this text we are only going to discourse what is love for a woman and a man human soul being in love. Hermaphrodites have self love. They have both male and female energy.

Because every man and a woman in LOVE are like cosmic magnets. We are opposite good of each other and complimentary good to each other when we are together in Soul Mate Oneness.

Which is being spiritually complete and whole as ONE Being. Because we can combine our spiritual energies together into a totally balanced energy.

As in Nature, as HIM & HER in Harmony, CO-Creating our own spiritual love, and our own good.

Everything in Nature is positive good and negative good energy.

Day and Night.

The Sun and the Moon.

As spiritual cells, as atoms, as Adam and Eve which have a positive and negative good properties to themselves, as to God they are Wholly One.

When this Spiritual Electrical Magnetic Light Energy that is positive good and negative good attracts each other and Comes Passionately Together we have True Spiritual LOVE.

A Man cannot procreate by himself in Spiritual LOVE because he is only one half of the energy field which is good.

A Women cannot procreate by herself in Spiritual LOVE because she is only one half of the energy field which is also good. We need somebody to love.

Men and Women are Totally Equal in Energy and in Spirit and in Gifts and in Talents because God created both man and woman Spiritually Equally.

In actuality to be Together Whole as a human being means to be in Harmony with God, the male and female spiritual soul energy within ourselves being one.

Yes, a man does not need a woman to live day in and day out for his survival. Nor does a woman need a man for her day in and day out survival to live.

Because each of them, man and woman are Whole and Complete Within Themselves and very Capable to take care of themselves without someone LOVING them because God Loves Us.

Some souls cannot find their soul mate because they died in a war.

Many women from the WWII, Korea or Vietnam war era cant find true love for this reason.

Same for the younger women or men of the Desert Storm or Afghanistan War Era and ETC.

The only difference is the Quality of LOVE a person alone lives in.

A person alone can Live in Spiritual love with God and Nature.

Many Monks, Nuns, Gurus, Priests and Spiritually Minded People do this all over the world and this is good for them because this is their good choice to live this way in Spiritually with God.

What is LOVE?

An exciting LIFE experience.

Our Love. Gods LOVE.

What is this Soul Mate Love that We Cherish beyond all things of value?

Gods LOVE. Our Love.

What is more Important than all the gold and diamonds of this Earth?

Gods Love. Our Love.

All Spiritual Soul Lovers need each other to experience Soul Mate Consciousness.

Example.

If the world is destroyed and all that is left is us a Good woman and a Good man on the Island in the middle of the pacific, God blessed our souls from destruction. We would probably be lonely.

Such is this life in this situation.

Lets say that we are each on the opposite side off the island and we do not know each other is alive nor do we know if anyone else is alive but ourselves.

Obviously life can be boring or depressing without someone to share our life with.

Obviously this life that each is living, is a little depressing and is the end of our life when we pass away, we think.

At this moment there is no hope to continue on in our life, not even as a human race. This is the end we see.

As each of us sits under the Coconut Tree of life we are wondering and thinking it would be good if someone else is alive.

Especially it would be GOOD if that someone else could be a Friend, a Mate, possibly a Lover.

We feel we got to crack our coconuts together.

Some other good soul as ourselves, that we can really relate to and to spiritually communicate with and Come Together with.

Becoming One In Spirit, Mind and Body, in Harmony playing LIFE.

Yes, there may be a monkey alive or a mongoose or dog or a cat or bird or horse or pig or a gecko and they become a good friend, but they are not the same as us, a human spiritual soul.

The animal has a different kind of soul than a man and a woman has and yet it is a good soul.

The man and the woman can have spiritual love with their animal friend. Meaning come together in mental physical oneness with their animal friend and nothing other than hold them and pet them and talk with them.

Even though this friendship is good, it is not good enough to full fill our life's passions being stranded here on Earth in the middle of nowhere.

Nor can we procreate and create more human life. Nor is it satisfying to us being a human spiritual soul.

If there is HOPE in our mind, we want and we are looking for our FRIEND our LOVER to pass the time with until the end my friend.

A Soul Mate. Our Spiritual CO-Created Compliment.

Which is another human soul to share our life with, and talk with about our and their life's joys and concerns.

To Laugh with, and to eat with. To love with, and enjoy with. To drink with, and breath with, and run and play with.

To spiritually love with, or have an orgasm with.

Even a shoulder to cry on. To snuggle together with. To share all the good that two good soul's go through in life on Earth.

By thinking about someone good that we can share our good life with, we are Magnetically Electrically Spiritually Methinking about someone good who likes similar good things as we do to share our life with while we are STILL ALIVE.

Anon and we are thinking about someone good who likes to do the same kind of good things we like to do.

We are thinking about someone good who is also a little different or even very different from us yet really good, and is also truly honest and good and kind and loves loving us.

A Dream Comes true.

Anon because we also want good excitement in our Good life and because we know what good we can do in this situation, we want someone good who can also do good things in our life here in the middle of no place.

Who also understands us and knows us and what we can do. Even better than that, they can do some things we cannot do and this is Complimentary for our life.

Anon that someone, that very special someone, that Spiritual Soul Mate we are Looking for, Will do that Healing Miracle that they do which is called I LOVE YOU.

And that LOVE which is Majestically Spiritually Miraculous will add to our pot of soup of our life and help make our life and their life more majestically wonderfully GOOD.

Just like a potato and water soup without any seasoning or other vegetables in it, gets old and boring very fast.

If that is all we have in our Lot and that is our life, it is humble and boring, and soon it will be the end of the potato soup and life.

This is why we think about some other Passionate Spiritually Loving Soul Mate of life who can compliment us and help us make our life worth really living for Passionately in Goodness.

It Will Be Fun, Exciting and CO-Creative.

As two love birds we are children Having Fun in The Sand Box of Life Seeing how each other Builds Sand Castles and how we can build a Good Spiritual Sand Castle Together in Harmony.

CHAPTER 26
My Dear Love

Myrrh and Frankincense.
My Dear Love, You made my heart so very happy to see you so beautiful, yet sad because you hardened your heart towards me during The Great Soul War.

I do understand and I do not blame you one little bit.

My dear Queen did not know what to do, so you wove a web by day, and UN-wove the web by night.

You did not know, nor did you believe anymore, but secretly within your soul, that I King James would return, and reclaim my Kingdom, and slay all the evil wooers, those wooers who were devouring my Kingdom and wooing my Wife and Other Innocent Souls in The United States of America.

I know My Dear is Very Wise and you have a Great Spiritual Faith in me and in God. Even though you have waited patiently for me to return, you did not know what to do, and you were bewildered and so very disenchanted, because no one had heard news of me from the Great Soul Battle that I was fighting in with all the other brave hearts.

You did not know if I would even return, to you alive, or dead, and in one piece or less. In peace of mind, or none at all, from a land so far away, The Great Soul Star War from Within Our Universe.

My dear love you didn't want to be alone any more and you cried and suffered weeping many a night. All of your friends and noble suitors told you, you must go on with your life, and let the kaddish be.

So you my Queen devised a plan within yourself, and set a time limit, for all this goodness to happen, that somehow, and by some way, and by the Grace of God, and the God's and Goddesses, I King James, Odysseus I am would return or you my Queen would marry another.

So the Good Love Story goes on.

I King James, know that no matter how great my fame, and how great my fortune is in my life, all this is nothing, without the Love of my Queen or my good health. Nor is my life worth living, without Freedom in my Good Kingdom the United States of America, which is also Gods Good Kingdom.

This is my souls odyssey my dear Love, and I am finished with the Soul War by my Great Victory in this soul battle.

My Spiritually Smiting of the evil emperor of the Evil Wooers, King Evelyn George Antinous Hussein O, and his cohorts.

I am finishing writing this good soul history book for myself, and for you, my Dear Love, and for you my friends and you God.

I King James knows I Am just a Soul from The Sun, The Son of King John, the seeds of Zeus. Yet I Am Gods Soul, doing His humble Service, with his Lord Jesus, and God Father and God Mother, as all good Warrior Kings and Queens and Princes and Princesses do for God, in the Name of God, in Service to God and Country.

Yes, this is my True Soul Purpose, as a Great Sun Warrior King, from Sparta, Greece, and from many a life's past, that I have reincarnated again onto the Earth. This time to our Ithaka our USA in 1948. I have gone off to fight another Victory in the Great Soul War, only to find my Ithaca, my United States of America, and my Good Earth taken over by the Evil Vain Wooers, while I was away at the Great Soul War.

By a miracle of Athena, I have returned in disguise, with Zeus's Lighting Bolt's and Gods God's and Goddess and All the Evil Wooers will now receive their Good from Me and Zeus.

I am being directed by God, to write this Good Book to heal myself, God and his Good Children, and to slay all the Evil Vain Wooers out of Gods Good Kingdom through a Good Spiritual Soul Journey. With the help of my Good Mentors and with a Good Spiritual Love Story about my soul life, which I am in belief others can identify with, as even in their own soul life.

My Dearest Love, I always said when I was in the Great Vietnam Soul War, if I can do anything to help make our USA and this place on Earth be a better world for myself, others, our children, God and Goodness, I Will by the Grace and Will of God do it.

I know that you and myself, God and Good is all TRUE and Justice too.

I know that everything will work out for the Good and God, and for His and Her children's goodness, and for yours and my good also, my Dear Love.

For you my dear Queen are also Child of God and of Goodness.

For me, King James that I am, I just want the best for myself and you, for our United States of America, Our Good Kingdom, and for everybody else who is our Gods Good Children and Their Countries.

As a Spiritual Warrior King from the Sun, and of Zeus I am.

I have had to do many things, and to learn many things. To suffer many things, and to give up many good things to write this Good Soul Book for Myself a Soul History, and for You.

This is also my Gods Good Work Book in CO-Creating Good, and is also the CO-Creative Process for CO-Creators, Gods Good Children, and this has taken me 45 years and many life times to arrive into Be Here Now.

My Dearest Love, please forgive me. For it is not that I do not love you, it is that I Do Love You.

It is that I also have a Sacred Agreement with myself, and God, to Fight and Win the Great Star War Soul Battle of Good over Evil.

To Spiritually Slay all the Evil Vain Wooers with the Help of God and the God's and Goddesses and with Zeus's Spiritual Lighting Bolt's from Heaven upon their Evil Wooers heads. To write my good odyssey book, Gods Good Soul Book, Love Is The Door Way Into our mind, body, heart, soul and into Heaven.

My Dear Queen, my Love my Holy Woman and of the Holy Grail.

I know that it has been very difficult for you and for myself. I do understand the pains of Life and Spiritual Love and Sacrifice.

I also am in a Great Pain, mentally, and physically, and soul wise. I am very lonely on this Great Soul Battle Field of Good over evil among the Soul Stars in our Universe. My task is very difficult as God well knows.

I have Succeeded by Gods Spiritual Strength and Justice flowing through me. I am The Light Force Commander on the battle field on Earth.

I am here in this hideous gruesome soul battle on Earth with a few good men in this Great Battle for Spiritual Freedom in America and it is challenging me to say the least.

I am here with the other good Great Kings and Princes of God working with God and Gods God's and Goddesses, and with Gods Angels, and few souls on Earth would understand this Great Soul Battle of the Star Wars in our universe for SPIRITUAL FREEDOM.

I am here myself upon this Great bloody Battle field my dearest.

I Am the Sun Soul Sovereign Himself Victoriously and in Soul Purpose leading valiantly the Auspicious Way of Gods Spiritual Warriors of Justice and Freedom on Earth.

There are many Evil Wooers moaning and groaning and writhing in their bloody pain of their doom from Zeus's Smiting Lighting bolt's upon their feeble minded heads and weak degenerated bodies.

My Dearest Queen, few could recognize me today.

Even you my Dear One.

King James that I am with the Evil Wooers blood splattered all about my face and chest and hands and feet.

My Shining Armor battle worn thin and stained. Ugly, Shredded and Damaged from the Ravages of this Great painful savage war of sorrow for FREEDOM IN AMERICA.

At Last, The Great Soul battle has now ended and we have won the war my dear.

I am removing my torn armor. I see my clothing is bloody and ripped apart from the battle and I am bleeding and in pain.

Slowly in pain I remove all of my damaged armor off me.

I lay naked on this bloody cursed battle field healing my bleeding wounds among the dead with our sacred herbs my dear.

I lay here upon this writing battle field of Hades and look all around me and all I see are so many that are no more in vain or pain.

I am Scavenging among the dead for clean cloth bandages for my bleeding wounds are many.

All that I can find are these tattered rags off the dead bodies, which I will have to use and make do.

I am worn out and wounded and exhausted and I need your wonderful healing love. Your touch my listening willing soul mate spouse, you a Great Queen and Goddess.

As I walk this soul path of pain and suffering, most only see this beggar man I am my raged attire.

I stumble and walk in pain the cobbled stoned streets of Washington, DC's agony upon my way back home to you my dear Queen Love and to my Good Kingdom.

I am a humble me in disguise.

King James I am. The Lion Hearted One. The Brave Hearted One. The Good One by the Grace and Will of God.

My dearest Love, I do know you understand the importance of Spiritual Freedom in America and Victory for God and Country. Even though this pain of mine is a great pain, ola kala.

I King James go forward through our Cities in America as a Great Spiritual Warrior King Wills it Good with Gods Strength Freeing our people out of mental and physical slavery.

I am now in tattered beggars clothes of the dead in disguise. I am directed to tell this story Love Is The Door Way In by God.

Magically I am turned into Baucis and Philemon traveling the world Seeing For God what Humankind is doing on Earth.

I Judge not. God is MY WITNESS.

I King James have Succeed in Victory of this Great Soul Battle in the Name of God and Good and for All Countries throughout The Whole World.

My Dear, this love story is not only about me and you. Its about our Spiritual Soul Journey, and God Father and God Mothers Great Spiritual Soul Journey. I Am, and you are.

We all are Gods good children, and its about this Good Earths Spiritual Journey that we all live on, and our Animal Friends, and Nature. This is our Good Kingdom of Goodness. God does want Good for me and you and everyone good, for God is Goodness and Justice too.

My Dear Love, in Truth, I am just a no-thing, a no-man is my real name in times of old long ago.

No-man they call me in truth, my father and mother and all my good friends, but a humble servant of God I am and so are you.

Yes, at times I may appear as I am a Spirited Black Horse Trampling upon The Evil Wooers Heads our enemy in the middle of the dark night of war in our Victorious battle with blood splattered all about me and on my Black Horse.

At other times I am all scared up and I am ugly. I know that nobody can love me. I am an elephant man, and I have bloody sheet over my head, and I am crying aloud in my writhing mortal pain, and all that I can do, I am. All that I am doing is with nothing that I have of my own, but my Spiritual Love and Spiritual Strengths from God. I am doing my best that I can, and so are you my dear love.

I do know that you must go on living your life my Dear Queen.

You will receive Your Goodness by the Grace of God in many Miraculous Ways no matter what you decide to do. For all the good you have done for me I King James and Gods Angels we give to you in return.

I do know that I must Complete my difficult task in Victory, before I am free to live and enjoy happily on in my good life.

My Dear, I also am Tempted by life, and by the Sirens, and by the Evil wooers.

When I am looking them in their eyes. I do not See my Good Queens Eyes of Radiant Beauty. I do not see my Good Queens Golden Heart of Spiritual Love.

When I shake their hand, I do not feel my Good Queens warm Loving hand of Healing Love. Nor do I see My Great Queen, my Love, that I see in my minds soul painting, my Goddess that I have within my souls wall, within my Great Lion King Hearts Soul.

My Dear Love, If it is Gods will for you and I to go on in Love, so be it, with Gods Good blessings of Spiritual Love and Goodness and Abundance, and Harmony. I know God has Graced you and me with all of His Good for God is Good.

I am also of the good belief, that what is to be, will be. As any Great Spiritual Warrior King knows who goes to battle for God and Country, I Must Do Gods Will, as Responsibility requires of me.

For one magical day I am going to pass on, and return into Heaven, for it is Gods True Purpose, and I Choose To Do His Good Will.

My dear love, I cannot ask you, nor anybody, to do anything, other than what is right and good for you. All Good is from God, and I am doing my good for myself, you, Country and God.

So my dear love, I thank you for smiling your Sweet Spiritual Love upon me. Your Rosie fingered one. Gracing me, this Sunny Day, and do as God wills it good. I King James have returned.

My Good Spiritual Love Book I do carry to all the world my Dear Queen from my Great Soul Odyssey.

My great trials and my difficult tribulations of my soul from the Great Vietnam Soul War, and back again to you.

To my United States of America that God Has Blessed. To my Good Blessed Kingdom Reclaimed. Fo all that I have passed through to return home again for Freedom In God We Trust.

Yes, I am no longer in my beggars clothes of past. I have ripped them off of me. I am now in our God Blessed Kingdom, in My Shining Brilliant Golden Purple Dalmatic Spiritual Armor of Zeus.

I have finished all this business of slaying all the evil wooers of Gods Good Kingdom in The United States of America and all around this good planet Earth.

Now my Dear Queen we are together again, in Peace, and in a Great Passion of Loving, and Making Love and Having Fun, and in Harmony, with each other in Nature.

With our Animal Friends in our Majestic Forest and Woods enjoying our Good Abundant Life together, in All of Our Blessed Goodness.

I know this is my Great Soul Story, Love Is The Door Way In, and King James I am. Because of my Spiritual Life and Love is from God, as Gods Love Is the Door Way into our Mind and our Body, and our Heart, and our Soul, and into Heaven, WE HAVE FREEDOM!

Anon the Royal Couple Greatly Came Together once again, Creating The Big O, Oh My God, Passionately in Love.

The Good Earth Quavered in love, and in the Blessed Rites of Loving each other in their Good Holy Loving Chamber, and they are taking their fill of Sweet nectar of Love and they have delighted in the Holy Tales of Goodness on Earth.

Anon the Beautiful Queen spoke of all that she had endured in the halls at the sight of the ruinous throng of Evil Wooers in Americas Ithaca, who for her sake slew many buffalo, swine and goodly sheep and goats and many casks of wine was drank.

Anon in turn The Good King James of the seed of Zeus the Son of The Sun King recounted all the grief's he had wrought upon men and all of his own travails and sorrows.

The Queen was delighted with the love story, and a Sweet Sleep fell upon her beautiful eyelids as the good love tale is ended in a beautiful dream.

Made in United States
North Haven, CT
22 May 2025